Competition Law in Kenya

Competition Law in Kenya

Second Edition

Brenda Pamela Mey

This book was originally published as a monograph in the International Encyclopaedia of Laws/Competition Law.

Founding Editor: Roger Blanpain†
General Editor: Frank Hendrickx
Volume Editors: Francesco Denozza & Alberto Toffoletto

Wolters Kluwer

Published by:
Kluwer Law International B.V.
PO Box 316
2400 AH Alphen aan den Rijn
The Netherlands
E-mail: lrs-sales@wolterskluwer.com
Website: www.wolterskluwer.com/en/solutions/kluwerlawinternational

Sold and distributed by:
Wolters Kluwer Legal & Regulatory U.S.
920 Links Avenue
Landisville, PA 17538
United States of America
E-mail: customer.service@wolterskluwer.com

Printed on acid-free paper

ISBN 978-94-035-6210-0

e-Book: ISBN 978-94-035-6220-9
web-PDF: ISBN 978-94-035-6230-8

The Author

Dr jur. Brenda Pamela Mey is an attorney-at-law and an admitted advocate of the High Court of Kenya. Dr Mey holds a PhD in Law from Ludwig-Maximilians-University in Munich, Germany, an LLM in German Laws from the Johannes-Gutenberg University of Mainz (Germany), a Postgraduate Diploma in Legal Advocacy from the Kenya School of Laws and an LLB from the University of Nairobi, Kenya. Dr Mey has experience in intellectual property (the law of patents), competition, data protection, IT and contract laws.

Dr Mey works at Infineon Technologies AG Am Campeon 1-15, 85579 Neubiberg, Germany.

The Author

Table of Contents

List of Abbreviations

AKR	Association of Kenya Reinsurers
ARM	Athi River Mining Company Ltd
AU	African Union
AVC	Average Variable Costs
BAT	British American Tobacco
BCI	Blue Circle Industries Plc
BTA	Basic Telecommunications Services
CAK	CAK of Kenya
CBK	Central Bank of Kenya
CCCC	COMESA Competition and Consumer Commission
CCK	Communications Commission of Kenya
CMA	Cereal Millers Association
CMC	Carboxymethylcellulose
COFEK	Consumer Federation of Kenya
COMESA	Common Market for Eastern and Southern Africa
EAC	East African Community
EACA	East African Court of Appeal
EACCA	East African Community Competition Act, 2006
EAPCC	East African Portland Cement Company Ltd
EPRA	Energy and Petroleum Regulatory Authority
ERB	Electricity Regulatory Board
ERC	Energy Regulatory Commission
FFD	Failing Firm Defence
GATS	General Agreement on Tariffs in Services
GATT	General Agreement on Tariffs and Trade
GCM	Guidelines on Conglomerate Mergers
GDP	Gross Domestic Product

List of Abbreviations

HHI	Herfindahl-Hirschman Index
ICN	International Competition Network
IPA	Industrial Property Act
IRA	Insurance Regulatory Authority
JKIA	Jomo Kenyatta International Airport
KAA	Kenya Airports Authority
KBC	Kenya Broadcasting Corporation
KCB	Kenya Commercial Bank
KEFRA	Kenya Franchise Association
KIPI	Kenya Industrial Property Institute
KPLC	Kenya Power and Lighting Company
KPTA	Kenya Posts and Telecommunications Act
KPTC	Kenya Posts and Telecommunication Corporation
KTDA	Kenya Tea Development Agency
KTDC	Kenya Tourist Development Corporation
KWS	Kenya Wildlife Service
LAPSSET	Lamu Port-South Sudan-Ethiopia Transport
MFN	Most Favoured Nation
MICT	Ministry of Information, Communication and Technology
MOA	Matatu Owners Associations
MoU	memorandum of understanding
NCPD	National Council of Population Development
NSE	Nairobi Stock Exchange
NSSF	National Social Security Fund
OECD	Organisation for Economic Co-operation and Development
PIT	Public Interest Test
PPD	Public Procurement and Disposal Act
R&D	Research and Development
RJ	Retired Justice
RPM	Resale Price Maintenance
RTPMPCA	The Restrictive Trade Practices, Monopolies and Price Control Act
SADC	Southern African Development Community
SAP	Structural Adjustment Programs
SCA	State Corporations Act
SCAC	State Corporations Advisory Committee

SIEC	Significant Impediment of Effective Competition
SLC	Substantial Lessening of Competition
SoEs	State-Owned Enterprise(s)
SSNIP	Significant Non-transitory Increase in Price
TRIPS	The Trade Related Aspects of Intellectual Property Rights
TTC	Toyota Tshusho Corporation
UNCTAD	The United Nations on Trade and Development
UNEP	United Nations Environment Programme
WCMA	Wildlife Conservation and Management Act
WTO	World Trade Organization

List of Abbreviations

General Introduction

§1. Kenya: General Background

I. Geography, Population and Language

1. Kenya, often referred to as the 'cradle of mankind', covers an area of 582,646 sq. km (225,000 sq. miles), has a population of 52.4 million people as of mid-2024, and a literacy rate of 82.4% for women and 82.8% for men. About 97% of Kenya's population, mainly concentrated in the major counties, namely, Nairobi, Mombasa, Kisumu, Eldoret, Thika and Nakuru, are of African descent. Kenya's population was hardly affected by COVID-19 deaths.[1]

2. The rest of the population consists mainly of Arab, Hindustani and British immigrants. There are over forty tribes in Kenya. These tribes fall into three ethnic groups: Nilotic, Cushitic and Bantu-speaking tribes. Among the major tribes in Kenya are the Luo, Luhya, Kalenjin, Gusii, Kikuyu and Kamba. In addition, Kenya has since the 1970s been hosting a huge refugee population from Rwanda, Burundi, Ethiopia, Eritrea, Somalia and Sudan. The number of refugees has risen considerably since the 1990s, peaking after the 2011 famine in Somalia.[2]

3. Kenya is located across the equator on the eastern coast of the African continent and is named after Mount Kenya, the second-highest mountain in Africa and the highest in the country. Africa's highest mountain, Mount Kilimanjaro, is located in northeastern Tanzania near the northern border with Kenya. Kenya is bordered to the north by Ethiopia, to the west by South Sudan, to the northeast by Somalia, to

1. Makoloo, O.M. and Ghai, Y., 2005 'Kenya: Minorities, Indigenous Peoples and Ethnic Diversity', pp. 10–11 and 15; 'Kenya National Bureau of Stastistics, "2023 Statistical Abstract" – https://www.knbs.or.ke/reports/2023-statistical-abstract/; National Council of Population Development 'The State of Kenya Population-2020, p. 3,available at: https://kenya.unfpa.org/sites/default/files/pub-pdf/state_of_kenya_population_report_2020.pdf'; World Population Review, 'Literacy Rate by Country -2024', available at: https://worldpopulationreview.com/country-rankings/literacy-rate-by-country.
2. Elliott, H, 2012, pp. 1–6, 'Refugee resettlement: the view from Kenya- Findings from Field Research in Nairobi and Kakuma Refugee Camp', KNOW RESET-RR2012/01, Robert Schuman Centre for Advanced Studies, San Domenico di Fiesole (FI): European University Institute; Makoloo, O.M. and Ghai, Y., 2005 'Kenya: Minorities, Indigenous Peoples and Ethnic Diversity', pp. 10–11 and 15;The World Bank Group, 'Desk Review on Livelihoods and Self-Reliance for Refugees and Host Communities in Kenya', pp. 11–12, available at: https://documents1.worldbank.org/curated/en/685581553241680189/pdf/135485-WP-P169281-PUBLIC-Livelihoods.pdf [accessed November 2024].

the west by Uganda, to the south by Tanzania and to its southeast by the Indian Ocean coastline. Kenya and its East African neighbours, Uganda and Tanzania, share the world's largest tropical lake and the second largest freshwater lake, Lake Victoria. Kenya was a route of migration by people from all over Africa and the Middle East, and was at various times in history, colonised by the Portuguese, the Arabs and the British. The Portuguese arrived in Kenya in the fifteenth century and ruled for two centuries until expelled by the Arabs in 1729. The British colonial domination of Kenya, which lasted seventy years, ended the Arab presence and rule in the country in the eighteenth century. The British rule ended in 1963 when Kenya attained independence. Around the tenth century, Kiswahili, a language of Arabic origins, evolved as Kenya's lingua franca. Kiswahili facilitated communication and trade between the people of Kenya and colonial masters. Today, Kiswahili has grown in popularity and is a subject of study in many prestigious academic institutions in Africa, Asia, America and Europe. According to section 7.1 of the Constitution of Kenya, Kiswahili is the national language. English and Kiswahili are, according to section 7.2 of the Constitution, the official languages of Kenya. English is, however, the medium of instruction in Kenya's institutions of learning.[3]

II. Climate and Religion

4. The key religions in Kenya include Christianity, Islam, Hinduism, Baha'i and an array of indigenous African religions. Christianity, which the Portuguese brought to the country, remains the faith most ascribed to in Kenya. Under section 8 of the Constitution of Kenya, Kenya is religion-neutral and protects freedom of religion in section 32 of the same constitution. In terms of climate, Kenya has a tropical climate that is largely influenced by its location near the equator and therefore generally pleasant throughout the year. The northern and eastern parts of the country are flat, bush-covered plains and enjoy a hot, dry climate. Nairobi, which is located at a high altitude, has a mild temperate climate, was established in 1899 and is the capital city of Kenya. The word 'Nairobi' stems from the Maasai phrase *Enkare Nyirobi*, which means 'cool water'. Nairobi is today home to numerous Kenyan businesses and over one hundred major international companies and organisations,

3. Swahili is derived from the word *sahils-awahils,* the Arabic word for edge or coast. Among other familiar words, *safari* is Swahili, meaning simply *travel.* A wildlife safari through Kenya gives anybody visiting Kenya an unforgettable opportunity to explore Kenya's spectacular savannah plains and its rolling grasslands, and to see at a close range Kenya's unparalleled plant varieties and animals in their natural habitat, not to mention the country's great climate; KLR, 2010, 'Constitution of Kenya ', , available at: https://new.kenyalaw.org/legislation/ [accessed January 2026]; For more information *see* Moshi, L., 2006, pp. 169–175, 'The Globalized World Languages: The Case of Kiswahili', Selected Proceedings of the 36th Annual Conference on African Linguistics: Shifting the Center of Africanism in Language Politics and Economic Globalization, Cascadilla Proceedings Project, Somerville, MA; The History of Kenya by 'Mwenda Ntarangwi & Kenneth Ingham', November 2024 available at: https://www.britannica.com/topic/history-of-Kenya.

including the United Nations Environment Programme (UNEP). Nairobi is home to several universities, including the University of Nairobi, the oldest and largest university in the country.[4]

5. The central parts of the country enjoy a similar climate. The coastal areas are characterised by a hot and humid climate. The season of extreme heavy rainfall in Kenya is from March through May, and to a lesser extent, from October through December. January, February and March are the hottest months in Kenya, while July and August are the coldest. In sum, Kenya's climate may be cool, hot or humid depending on the region. Indeed, the cool climate in the highland regions of Kenya is what contributed to the success of British farmers in Kenya's Great Rift Valley, which is reputed to have extremely spectacular landscapes.

6. The greatest wildlife show on earth and one of the seven wonders of the world, namely, the annual migration of wildebeest, takes place between June and September. The Maasai, a Nilotic ethnic group of people residing in Kenya and Tanzania, are one of the most well-known African ethnic groups due to their unique customs and distinctive dressing.[5]

III. Government and Politics

7. From 1963, Kenya was a de facto one-party state until 10 December 1991, when a constitutional amendment repealing section 2A of the old Constitution ushered into the country competitive multi-party politics and ended years of the Kenya African National Union's (KANU) monopoly of political power. Kenya is a presidential representative democratic republic that maintains a strict division between the legislative, judicial and executive branches of the government.

8. According to section 93.1 of the Constitution of Kenya, Kenya has a bicameral Parliament made up of the National Assembly and the Senate. Section 176 of the Constitution of Kenya, as read with section 6.1 of the First Schedule of the Constitution of Kenya, makes it clear that Kenya is divided into forty-seven semi-autonomous counties consisting of a county assembly and a county executive headed by Governors. This division is based on the delineation of administrative districts as created under the Provinces and Districts Act of 1992. Section 3.c, of the County Government Act, 2012 states that the act's objective is to give effect to section 176.2 of the Constitution of Kenya by enabling the county government to

4. Broberg, C., 2002, pp. 8–21, 'Kenya in Pictures (Visual Geography (Twenty-First Century))', Lerner Publications, Rev Exp edition; Colonial Reports Annual, 1929, 'Colony and Protectorate of Kenya: Report for 1929', pp. 2–16, No. 1510, available at: http://libsysdigi.library.illinois.edu [accessed June 2013].
5. Njenga, N.G., 2010, pp. 5–23, 'A Synopsis of the History of Kenya Before Colonisation', available at: https://www.studocu.com/row/document/umma-university/bachelor-of-education-arts/a-synopsis-of-kenyas-pre-colonial-history-insights-and-analysis/129567646 [accessed January 2025]; Waithaka, J., 2012, pp. 21–29, 'The Kenya Wildlife Service in the 21st Century: Protecting Globally Significant Areas and Resources'. The George Wright Forum, 29(1), 21–29.

decentralise its functions and services, to provide room for citizens to actively participate in county development. The First Schedule of the Constitution of Kenya lists the names of the counties. According to Chapter 11 of the Constitution as read with Part 2 of the Fourth Schedule of the Constitution and the County Government Act 2012, the counties, which are complete with elective posts of senators, governors and county representatives, are units of devolved government and so to say, the second level of governance after the national government.[6]

§2. Kenya's Economic System

9. Since independence, Kenya's economic growth has been driven by a sound and stable macroeconomic environment characterised by, among other factors, free-market economic policies, increased investor confidence, fiscal and foreign policies based on national interests and cooperation with East African Community (EAC) partners. As a result, and owing to its geographical location, Kenya has been able to create a market-based economy, with a liberalised external trade system. This has in turn led to improvements and growth in most sectors of the economy. Kenya has as a result succeeded in placing itself as prosperous regional economy and to date remains the most industrially developed country in East Africa. Kenya's Nairobi Stock Exchange (NSE), registered under the Societies Act, is the largest in sub-Saharan Africa. It operates under the umbrella of the Capital Markets Authority of Kenya. The NSE provides a trading platform for listed securities and regulates trading activities of member companies, thereby playing an essential role in the growth of the Kenyan economy by encouraging short and long-term savings and investment.

10. The Port of Mombasa, which is linked to world's largest ports in Europe, North and South America, Asia, Australia, the Middle East and the rest of Africa, serves as a distribution hub for the EAC's market, providing connection to EAC hinterland countries of Uganda, Tanzania, Burundi, Rwanda, Democratic Republic of Congo and South Sudan.[7]

---

6. Owino, K., 2006, p. 244, 'Kenya', in Mehta, P., 2006, 'Competition Regimes in the World: A Civil Society Report', CUTS International; Ogot, B., 1995, pp. 239–245, 'Transition from Single-Party to Multiparty Political System 1989–1983', in Ogot, B. and Ochieng, W., 1995, 'Decolonization & Independence in Kenya, 1940–1993', East African Education Publishers, Nairobi, Kenya and Ohio University Press, USA; Oloo, A., 2010, 'Elections, Representations and the New Constitution', Constitution Working Paper No. 7, Society for International Development (SID); Patel, P., 2001, pp. 155–160, 'Multi-Party Politics in Kenya', Revista Ciencia Política, XXI (1). Sections 4 and 93.1 of the Constitution of Kenya. *See also* Chs 8, 9 and 10 of the Constitution; Sihanya, B., 2010, 'The Presidency and Public Authority in Kenya's New Constitutional Order', Constitution Working Paper No. 2, Society for International Development (SID). Section 3.c of the County Government Act, KLR, 2012, 'The County Government Act, No. 17 of 2012', available at: https://new.kenyalaw.org/legislation/ [accessed January 2026.
7. Aidan, E. and Gitau, J.M., 2007, p. 183, 'Economic Policy and Performance in East Africa: A Survey of Tanzania, Kenya, Uganda and Rwanda', in East African Scenarios Project Research Compendium, a publication of the Society for International Development (SID); Ole Turana, J., 2013, 'Kenya's Economy May Expand at Fastest Rate in Six Years in 2013', Bloomberg, May; Wanyama,

11. Following the promulgation of the new Constitution in 2010, the government implemented judicial, electoral and land structural reforms and fiscal and monetary policies meant to drive economic growth. Kenya recently reached lower-middle income status, after its Gross Domestic Product (GDP) per capita exceeded the threshold set by the World Bank. As a result, it has succeeded in building a diversified and dynamic economy.[8]

12. Another factor that has boosted economic growth is the deepening of the regional integration initiatives, in particular, the transformation of EAC countries into a fully-fledged Customs Union and Common Market to promote regional investment and trade. The launching of the Common Market has resulted in a single and enlarged common trading and investment market that has boosted regional trade and commerce. Article 6 of the EAC Common Market Protocol, which came into force on 1 July 2010, allows the free movement of goods, services, people and capital in a market that now serves a 130-million people strong EAC. The EAC is also on course to become a Monetary Union. The future looks rosy for the EAC, following the expression by South Sudan to join the EAC states.[9]

13. Besides membership in the EAC, Kenya is also a member of the Southern African Development Community (SADC) and the Common Market for Eastern and Southern Africa (COMESA). The signing of the COMESA-EAC-SADC Tripartite Free Trade Area (TFTA) has set the stage for the establishment of a single market for the twenty-nine African tripartite in the Eastern and Southern African regions. The tripartite cooperation of these three trade zones is built on three pillars: market integration, infrastructure development and industrial development. The zones' Member States together represent 53% of the African Union's membership, more than 60% of Africa's GDP (USD 1.88 trillion), and a combined population of 800 million. The elimination of import duties, trade remedies and rules of origin and preferential tariff treatment for goods originating in and traded among the COMESA-EAC-SADC countries will help create dynamic economic gains.[10]

L., 2013, pp. 5–9, 'The Economic Diplomacy of Kenya's Regional Interests', South African Foreign Policy and African Drivers Programme, Occasional Paper No. 137; Watkins, D.C., 1993, 'Kenya: Overseas Business Report', OBR9301, USDOC, International Trade Administration; Nairobi Securities Exchange, 'NSE', available at: https://www.nse.co.ke/about-nse/ [accessed November 2024].

8. The World Bank, 2012, pp. 1–7, 'Kenya Economic Update', Edition 7, December; World Bank, 2013, 'Kenya Overview', available at: http://www.worldbank.org/en/country/kenya/overview [accessed June 2013], USAID 'Economic Growth and Trade-Kenya, 2019', available at:https://de.scribd.com/document/744418970/Kenya-Economic-Growth-February-2020 [accessed January 2026];].
9. African Development Bank, 2011, pp. 7–8, 'African Economic Outlook 2012: Promoting Youth Employment-Kenya', available at: http://www.afdb.org [accessed June 2013]; IMF Survey Online, 2012, 'Truly Integrated Market Would Bring Benefits to East Africa', March 15; Miriri, D., 2013, 'UPDATE 2-Rebound in Key Sectors Seen Driving Kenya Economy in 2013', Reuters, 23 May; Odongo, M., 2011, 'Towards an East African Community Common Market: Challenges and Opportunities', The Institute of Economic Affairs, Kenya, Trade Notes, Issue 33, January.
10. United Nations Economic Commission for Africa, 2012, pp. 4 and 26–29, 'Progress Towards Sustainable Development in Africa: Summary Report'; Wanyama, L., 2013, pp. 10–11, 'The Economic Diplomacy of Kenya's Regional Interests', South African Foreign Policy and African Drivers Programme, Occasional Paper No. 137; Were, E. and Ligami, C., 2011, 'Nairobi, Africa's New HQ for

14. Kenya's economic growth is expected to receive a boost once the Lamu Port-South Sudan-Ethiopia Transport (LAPSSET corridor) is completed. This corridor will complement the Port of Mombasa by relieving it of its heavy transhipment experiences. The LAPSSET corridor is intended to boost economic growth in Kenya and the surrounding East African countries. The corridor will promote economic development, facilitate trade and investment in agriculture and manufacturing in these countries, and provide the landlocked ones with important access to international markets. The connection between the port of Lamu and South Sudan and Ethiopia is expected to improve regional connectivity by creating alternative trade and transport routes. This, in turn, will reduce dependence on existing corridors, diversify trade routes and facilitate the transport of goods and services and access to the markets of neighbouring countries. Moreover, the strategic location of the port on the East African coast of the Indian Ocean will not only create a range of economic opportunities for businesses and individuals along the corridor but also establish a link to the port of Douala on the West African Atlantic coast. This will facilitate trade by reducing distances through an efficient land transport system.[11]

15. Regarding the country's economy, according to recent press releases, the Kenyan economy slowed down in 2024, with estimated real GDP growth of 4.6% compared to 5.6% in 2023, mainly due to a slowdown in growth in most economic sectors. This notwithstanding, key indicators of economic activity still point to improved performance in the first quarter of 2025. The economy is expected to recover in 2025, with real GDP growth forecast at 5.4%. This growth is supported by the resilience seen in key sectors such as services, agriculture, and improved exports, etc.[12]

16. The solid performance of sectors such as agriculture, finance, transport and communication, construction and tourism, all of which still witnessed growth in varying magnitudes, also contributed to the uptrend in economic growth. Agriculture has dominated Kenya's economy since colonial days and remains the most dominant sector almost five decades after Kenya obtained its independence. The sector accounts for 27% of the country's GDP and 45% of government revenue. Other than contributing to more than 50% of export earnings, the agriculture sector employs over 60% of Kenya's labour force and produces the bulk of the country's agricultural exports that include, among others, tea, coffee, rice, pyrethrum, dairy

---

Multinational Firms', The East African, 24 July; Mwangi Gakunga, 'Tripartite Framework win Accolades at the AU Mid-Year Summit', available at: https://www.comesa.int/tripartite-framework-win-accolades-at-the-au-summit/ [accessed November 2024].

11. Lapsset Corridor Development Authority, Status Report, September 2017, available at: https://aid.nepad.org/m_assets/uploads/document/15054818871514304844.pdf [accessed May 2025]; Schrer Katja, 'Lamu Port in Kenia: Meilenstein oder Millionengrab?', available at: https://wirtschaftinafrika.de/lamu-port-in-kenia// [accessed May 2025].

12. Available at: https://www.centralbank.go.ke/uploads/mpc_press_release/2072351219_MPC%20Press%20Release%20-%20Meeting%20of%20April%208%202025.pdf [accessed May 2025].

and horticultural products. Kenya is Africa's leading tea producer and the fourth in the world behind India, China and Sri Lanka. Coffee ranks as Kenya's fifth leading foreign exchange earner.[13]

17. The horticulture sector, which includes flowers, fruits and vegetables, is Kenya's third-biggest foreign exchange earner, after tea and tourism. Kenya supplies a third of the cut flowers sold in Europe, and is renowned as the world's largest producer and exporter of pyrethrum, a flower that contains a substance used in pesticides. All in all, the overall economic growth in Kenya showed improvement despite the many challenges Kenya has been facing; thanks to the new constitution, whose provisions guarantee transparency and accountability, Kenya's strengthened governance record enhanced regional economic cooperation in recent years and increased investor and business confidence due to the peaceful 2013 General Elections.[14]

§3. The Legal System in Kenya

18. Although Kenya's first court system began in 1895, when the country was still part of the East African Protectorate, the actual genesis of Kenya's legal system can be traced to the East African Order in Council of 1897, later repeated in the 1902 Order and the Crown Regulations relating thereto. The Order in Council applied to Kenya by virtue of a reception clause, the substance of the English common law, the doctrines of equity and statutes of general application in force in England at that date, and prevailed over all local statutes. However, the statutes of general application applied to Kenya only in so far as the 'circumstances of Kenya and its inhabitants permitted, and subject to such qualifications as those circumstance rendered necessary' as stated by Denning L.J. observed in *Nyali Ltd v. Attorney General*:[15]

> … the common law cannot be applied in a foreign land without considerable qualification. Just as with an English oak, so with the English common law. You cannot transplant it to the African continent and expect it to retain the tough character, which it has in England. It will flourish indeed, but it needs careful tending … In these far-off lands the people must have a law, which

13. African Economic Outlook, 2012, 'Kenya', available at: http://www.afdb.org [accessed June 2013]; Kenya Bureau of Standards, 2012, 'Statistical Release: Gross Domestic Product Third Quarter 201 2', available at: http://www.knbs.or.ke/pdf/Third_Quarter_gdp_Release_2012.pdf [accessed June 2013]; Kenya High Commission UK, 2010, 'Economic Survey 2010', available at: http://www.kenyahighcommission.net/khccontent/economy.html [accessed June 2013]; Ombok, E., 2013, 'Kenya Second-Quarter Tea Output Seen Rising 22% on Improved Rain', Bloomberg, 18 April.
14. Omondi, G., 2013, 'Agriculture's Strong Growth Spurs Kenya Economy to 4.6pc', Business Daily, Kenya, May; Stein, P., 2010, pp. 14–18, 'The Economics of Burundi, Kenya, Rwanda, Tanzania and Uganda', A Report prepared for Swedfund International AB; Sihanya, B., 2010, 'The Presidency and Public Authority in Kenya's New Constitutional Order', Constitution Working Paper No. 2, Society for International Development (SID).
15. *Nyali v. Attorney General*, [1956] 1 QB 7.

they understand, and which they will respect. The common law cannot fulfil this role except with considerable qualifications.

19. The Order in Council established a dual court system: one for the European settlers and the other for the native Kenyans. The dual court system, which lasted five years, had at subordinate level, colonial courts, Native courts/tribunals and Muslim courts, and at superior level, her Majesty's Court at Zanzibar and the Privy Council. Under the Order in Council, her Majesty's Court at Zanzibar had a dual role that enabled it to exercise jurisdiction over the British subjects in Zanzibar and to serve as the first Court of Appeal for the East African Protectorate (after 1920, the Kenya Colony and the Kenya Protectorate). The Court of Appeal for the East African Protectorate was later renamed the East African Court of Appeal (EACA).[16]

20. All appeals from domestic courts lay with EACA, whose jurisdiction was defined by an Order in Council. Its Jurisdiction was subject to limitations put by the domestic laws of the East African countries. It was the highest court in Kenya. Appeals from the EACA lay directly to the Judicial Committee of the Privy Council in London. Under Article 4.2 of the Kenya Colony Order in Council 1902, colonial courts were to be guided in all civil and criminal cases to which the natives were parties, by native law and custom, provided such laws were 'not repugnant to justice and morality or inconsistent with any Order in Council or Ordinance in force'. This stipulation notwithstanding in pre-colonial courts in Kenya judicial independence was virtually non-existent.

21. The judges appointed under the Order in Council held office at the pleasure of the Crown and could be dismissed summarily by the Governor who enjoyed remarkable discretionary powers in the discharge of his judicial duties. Unlike their counterparts in England, the colonial judges did not hold their offices for life. Kenya thus became independent in 1963 with a judiciary that was far indifferent to the needs of the ethnic groups that it was meant to serve. Describing the judicial system in the colonial era, Vyas, cited in Trebilcock and Daniels below, affirms that:

> during the colonial era the judiciary was an integral part of the executive rather than an institution for administration of Justice. The colonial administration was mainly interested in the maintenance of law and order. It had no respect for the independence of the judiciary of the fundamental rights of the ruled. It was therefore, identified as an upholder of colonial rule. To an average citizen, the judiciary as an institution of control of executive power lacked credibility and enjoyed little respect.

22. There was, therefore, a need to change the Constitution to bring about separation of powers. Thus, at independence, Kenya received the Westminster Model

16. Maina, C.P. and Kijo-Bisimba, H., 2007, pp. 60–61, 'Law and Justice in Tanzania: Quarter Century of the Court of Appeal', a publication for Legal and Human Rights Centre, Mkuki na Nyota Publishers, Dar-es-Salaam, Tanzania.

Constitution, which replaced the colonial political order. The Westminster Model Constitution, which was amended several times and aimed at maintaining the independence of the three branches of government, established Kenya as a republic with an executive, legislative and judicial branches of the Government. This Constitution, which provided for a democratic system of government, lasted one year and was replaced in 1964 by the Independence Constitution. This latter marked the beginning of a truly independent and impartial judiciary.[17]

23. In its sections 171–179, the Independence Constitution[18] established a four-tier legal system consisting of the Supreme Court, headed by the Chief Justice, as the superior court of record and gave it absolute jurisdiction to determine civil and criminal matters and to determine whether the executive powers were exercised within the parameters laid out in the Constitution. It also established the Court of Appeal for Kenya and other subordinate courts such as the martial courts, and the Kadhi courts for people professing the Muslim religion. Section 3.1 of the reception clause, which was re-enacted as the Judicature Act Chapter 8[19] of the Laws of Kenya, laid down the laws to which, the High Court, the subordinate courts and the Magistrates' Courts Act would be subject and abolished the African courts and replaced them with district, resident magistrate and Kadhi courts.[20] The Judicature Act also streamlined the administration of Justice in Kenya by repealing all colonial statutes and spelling out the laws applicable to all the courts established under the Constitution. The Independence Constitution also established to Judicial Service Commission, whose duties included, *inter alia*, appointing, disciplining and removing judges, magistrates, Kadhis and other key members of the subordinate courts. The first African to occupy the office of Chief Justice was the late Honourable Kitili Maluki Mwendwa.[21]

24. Kenya's legal system is still modelled on English common law today. The Constitution remains the supreme law of the land. All laws that are repugnant to the Constitution are null and void. On 27 August 2010, Kenya promulgated a new Constitution that establishes the framework for restoration of constitutional and democratic governance in Kenya. The first elections, which were held on 4 March 2013

17. Cotran, E., 1970, pp. 111–114, 'Kenya', Annual Survey of African Law, in Rubin, N. and Cotran, E., 1970, Frank Cass and Company Limited, London; Cotran, E., 1983, pp. 42–47, 'The Development and Reform of the Law in Kenya', Journal of African Law, 27(1), Tudor, J., 1986, pp. 8–10, 'The Law of Kenya', Kenya Literature Bureau; 3rd edition, Nairobi, Kenya; Trebilcock, J.M. and Daniels, J.R., 2008, p. 88, 'Rule of Law Reform and Development: Charting the Fragile Path of Progress', Edward Elgar Publishing Ltd, UK, USA.
18. 1963 Kenya Constitution (Independence Constitution), available at: https://www.legislation.gov.uk/ukpga/1963/54 [accessed January 2026].
19. KLR, 1967, ss 3–9, 'Judicature Act', Ch. 8 of the Laws of Kenya, available at: https://kenyalaw.org/kl/fileadmin/pdfdownloads/Acts/JudicatureAct_Cap8.pdf [January 2026].
20. KLR, 1967, 'Kadhis' Courts Act', Ch. 11 of the Laws of Kenya, available at: https://new.kenyalaw.org/akn/ke/act/1967/14/eng@2022-12-31 [accessed Janauary 2026].
21. Muigai, G., 1992, pp. 93–113, 'The Judiciary in Kenya and the Search for a Philosophy of the Law: The Case of Constitutional Adjudication', in Kibwana, K., 1992, 'Law and Administration of Justice in Kenya, International Commission of Jurists (Kenya Section)', General Printers Ltd, Nairobi, Kenya.

and recorded the highest electoral turnout in Kenya's history, were conducted under the new Constitution. President Uhuru Muigai Kenyatta and his deputy, William Samoei Ruto, became the first president and the deputy president under the new Constitution, respectively.

25. In accordance with the new Constitution, Kenya's three main organs of the state are the executive, the Parliament and the judiciary. The administrative and decision-making powers are distributed and held separately among these three arms of the government. According to Chapters 8, 10 and 11 of the Constitution, the executive arm of the government comprises the national and devolved or county government. Section 6.2 of the Constitution stipulates that the central and devolved governments are distinct and interdependent. The national government is made up of the cabinet and the Parliament. Section 152 of the Constitution states that the cabinet shall consist of the President, Deputy President, the Attorney General and fourteen to twenty-two Cabinet Secretaries, formerly known as ministers.

26. According to sections 93–98 of the Constitution, Kenya's bicameral Parliament consists of two houses, namely, the National Assembly and the Senate, headed by a Speaker. The members of Kenya's two chambers of Parliament have the mandate to represent peoples' interests at both national and county levels. At the same time, Chapter 11 of the Constitution establishes forty-seven counties, each with its own government made up of a county assembly and a county executive. The county governments draw their powers from the central government and are headed by a governor and represented by a Senator in the Senate. The table below shows Kenya's three autonomous arms of the government, which according to Chapters 8, 9 and 10 of the Cosntitution of Kenya consists of there meian arms: the Executive, which is responsible for implementing and enforcing laws; the Legislature, which is charged with duty of law making and oversight, and the Judiciary whose role is to interpret the laws and ensure justice . The County Government Act of 2012 spells out the functions and powers of the county governments.

27. Sections 159 and 160 of the Constitution create an independent judiciary and in section 166 thereof, the judiciary has autonomy from the executive. Section 166 of the Constitution states that the President shall appoint the chief justice and judges of the superior courts, subject to the recommendations of the Judicial Service Commission and the approval of the National Assembly. By placing limitations on the president's powers to appoint and dismiss judges, the new Constitution promises to enhance the independence of the judiciary. Section 159 of the Constitution gives an array of courts and tribunals the power to exercise judicial authority in Kenya. The Judicial Service Act No. 1 of 2011, the Vetting of Magistrates and Judges Act No. 2 of 2011, and the Supreme Court Act No. 7 of 2011 are legislations enacted to give effect to the new Constitution and to streamline the judiciary.

28. The Chief Justice appointed in accordance with section 166 of the Constitution by the President on the recommendation of the Judicial Service Commission, and whose appointment is subject to the approval of the National Assembly, is the head of the judiciary. The Judicial Service Commission, whose goal is to enhance the independence of the judiciary, derives its mandate from sections 171 and 172 of the Constitution and is chaired by the Chief Justice. Section 161 of the Constitution states that the judiciary consists of the judges of the superior courts, magistrates, other judicial officers and includes the office of the Chief Justice, deputy Chief Justice and the Chief Registrar. Sections 163–165 and 169 of the new Constitution expand the independence and accountability of the judiciary by distributing power to a hierarchy of courts; namely, the Supreme Court, the Court of Appeal and the High Court, the subordinate Courts (which include the magistrates' courts, Kadhis' courts, Court Martial, Children's Courts and any other courts which may be created by statute). The Honourable Chief Justice Willy Mutunga is serving as the first Chief Justice under the new Constitution.

§4. The Historical Background of Kenya's Competition Law

29. When Kenya was declared a British protectorate, it had no legal system of its own, a situation that remained until the country obtained independence in 1963. The post-independence competition law was the Price Control Ordinance of 1956, which was renamed the Price Control Act of 1956 and extensively revised in 1972. The development of Kenya's competition law as will be seen in the next paragraphs evidences the fact that laws in Kenya borrow immensely from the UK legal system. After independence, Kenya began to industrialise and localise the economy and to meet the Kenyan and EAC requirements. In this regard, it introduced price, import and export licensing controls and adopted import substitution.[22]

30. To achieve this, Kenya promulgated, in addition to the Price Control Act, the Trade Licensing Act,[23] which, through denial of trading licences to foreign companies, permitted the takeover of foreign-owned companies and their transfer to indigenous Kenyans. At the same time, the government also enacted the Import, Export and Essential Supplies Act,[24] which legalised export and import controls on all goods, including essential consumer goods.

22. Gachino, G., 2009, p. 142, 'Industrial Policy, Institutions and Foreign Direct Investment: The Kenyan Context', African Journal of Marketing Management, 1(6), 140–160; Murungi, M., 2011, p. 108, 'Cyber Law in Kenya', Wolters Kluwer, Kluwer Law International, the Netherlands; Njehu, K.F., 2010, 'Competition Law in Kenya: A Snapshot', Centre for Competition, Investment & Economic Regulation, available at: http://www.cuts-international.org [accessed July 2013]; United Nations, 2005, pp. 85–97, 'Review of Recent Experiences in the Formulation and Implementation of Competition Law and Policy in Selected Developing Countries: Thailand, Lao, Kenya, Zambia, Zimbabwe', available at: http://archive.unctad.org/Templates/Page.asp?intItemID=4150&lang=1 [accessed July 2013]; At this time the EAC was made up of Kenya, Uganda and Tanzania. Following revival in 1999, the EAC block was enlarged to include Rwanda and Burundi. For more information *see* OECD, 2001, pp. 1–4, 'Global Forum on Competition: Contributions from Kenya', CCNM/GF/COMP/WD (2001)2; The World Bank, 2012b, p. 24, 'Kenya Economic Update: Walking on a Tightrope. Rebalancing Kenya's Economy with a Special Focus on Regional Integration', Edition No. 6, June.
23. Trade Licensing Act, Chapter 497 of the Laws of Kenya (repealed).
24. *See* the Preamble to the Imports, Exports and Essential Supplies Act, Ch. 502 of the Laws of Kenya, (repealed by Act No. 17 of 2006).

31. After the break-up of the EAC in 1977, Kenya's state-induced strategy of driving local economic growth through, among other things, the import substitution industrialisation began to experience setbacks. For instance, Kenya's exports to Uganda and Tanzania, which in the early 1970s constituted more than half of output, fell to less than one-tenth in 1980 as Tanzania and Uganda opened their markets to imports from Asian countries.

32. Amid the stiff competition for markets coupled with weak economic slowdown, Kenya quickly lost its competitive edge in the EAC region. To reverse the inevitable decline, to further protect the process of competition, and to allow the building of a dynamic and efficiently functioning economy, the Kenyan government decided to change from a regulated market economy to a free-market economy. It thus eased its policy of protecting domestic industries from foreign competition by allowing imports. In this regard, in the Sessional Paper No. 1, the government underscored that it would depend 'less on instruments of direct control and increasingly on competitive elements in the economy', and would enact a law that would prohibit restrictive practices and at the same time provide legal mechanism to address and prevent such practices.[25]

33. The passing into law in 1988 of the Restrictive Trade Practices, Monopolies and Price Control Act (hereinafter 'RTPMPCA')[26] was the culmination of these coordinated efforts. The RTPMPCA was viewed and served as a national competition law that could be applied uniformly to all extant businesses in Kenya. Its thrust was to encourage competition in the economy by prohibiting restrictive trade practices, controlling monopolies and concentration of economic power, and regulating prices of essential goods and services with a view to protecting consumers against anticompetitive forms of pricing. This law was initially intended to be a transitional measure to allow the government to move away from instruments of direct price control to a competitive market economy. However, by the late 1980s, the clamour for the de-controlling of prices of essential commodities forced the government to change its price control policy that by the end of 1994, all price controls had been eliminated.

34. On realising that, the RTPMPCA had outlived its usefulness and could neither serve as a comprehensive competition policy in Kenya nor be used to effectively protect the consumers against unfair trade practices and unscrupulous exploitation, the government of Kenya decided to replace RTPMPCA with a modern competition law. In 2009, the Parliament of Kenya legislated a replacement act;

---

25. Government of Kenya, 1986, pp. 24 and 100, 'Sessional Paper no. 1 of 1986 on Economic Management for Renewed Growth', Government Printer, Nairobi, Kenya; Mwangi, S.K, Mbaku, M.J. and Mwaniki, N., 2003, p. 154, 'Restarting and Sustaining Economic Growth and Development in Africa: The Case of Kenya (Contemporary Perspectives on Developing Societies)', Ashgate Pub Ltd, England, USA; Njehu, K.F., 2010, 'Competition Law in Kenya: A Snapshot', Centre for Competition, Investment & Economic Regulation, available at: http://www.cuts-international.org [accessed July 2013]; OECD, 2001, pp. 1–4, 'Global Forum on Competition: Contributions from Kenya', CCNM/GF/COMP/WD(2001)2.
26. KLR, 1988, RTPMCA is repealed.

namely, the Competition Act, 2010 (hereinafter 'Competition Act').[27] The enactment of the Act reflects the government's commitment to strengthen the national, legal and institutional framework for enforcing competition and developing policies that support well-functioning markets and competitive prices. Section 99 of the Act repeals the RTPMPCA. The overall goal of this law according to its Preamble and section 3 thereof is to promote and safeguard competition in the national economy, protect consumers from predatory and fraudulent commercial practices, prevent unjust concentrations of economic power and help streamline appeal procedures.

35. The Competition Actserves to maximise the efficient allocation of resources, increase welfare in society and secure prosperity through well-functioning fair markets. The Competition Act aims to promote innovation and bring national competition law, policy and practice in line with the best international practices. The goal of the Competition Act is also to help the country keep pace with the developments in the COMESA and other EAC Member States, whose newly enacted competition laws also contain provisions for the protection of consumer welfare.[28]

36. Section 21.1 of the Act prohibits all agreements between undertakings, decisions by associations of undertakings, decisions by undertakings or concerted practices by undertakings which have as their object or effect the prevention, distortion or lessening of competition in trade in any goods or services in Kenya or a part of Kenya. This provision is further boosted by section 69 of the Industrial Property Act, 2001 (IPA),[29] which prohibits anticompetitive clause in agreements for the transfer of technology involving intellectual property licensing contracts. The provision contains 133 restrictive practices which, if contained in a licensing contract, may cause the managing director of Kenya Industrial Property Institute (KIPI) to refuse to grant a licensing contract, for the reason that, taken as a whole, the contract may be harmful to Kenya's economic interests.

37. Further, section 7 of the Competition Act establishes the Competition Authority of Kenya (hereinafter 'CAK'). According to section 9 of the Act, the CAK has a very broad role of supervising competition law and promoting competition in the Kenyan economy and, in particular, enforcing the provisions of the Competition Act as well as investigating, controlling, evaluating and precluding

27. KLR, 2010 'Competition Act, 2010, No. 12 of 2010', available at: https://new.kenyalaw.org/akn/ke/act/2010/12/eng@2022-12-31 [accessed January 2026]. Amended by Legal Notice 23 of 2011, Statute Law (Miscellaneous Amendments) Act, 2015 (Act No. 25 of 2015), Competition (Amendment) Act, 2016 (Act No. 49 of 2016), Statute Law (Miscellaneous Amendments) Act, 2017 (Act No. 11 of 2017), Statute Law (Miscellaneous Amendments) Act, 2018 (Act No. 18 of 2018), Competition (Amendment) Act, 2019 (Act No. 27 of 2019), and 24th Annual Supplement (Legal Notice 221 of 2023).All these instruments are available at https://new.kenyalaw.org/legislation/ [accessed January 2026].
28. Shantayanan, D., Dollar, D. and Holmgren, T., 2001, pp. 497–498, 'Aid and Reform in Africa: Lessons from Ten Case Studies', World Bank Publications, Washington, D.C; UNCTAD,2005, pp. 1–2 and 31–37, 'Voluntary Peer Review Report on Competition Policy: Kenya', UNCTAD/DITC/CLP/2005/6.
29. KLR, 2001, 'Industrial Property Act', No. 3 of 2001, available at: https://new.kenyalaw.org/akn/ke/act/2001/3/eng@2022-12-31 [accessed Janauary 2026].

competition impediments and restraints that may lead to an unreasonable abuse of market power. Section 71 of the Act also establishes the Competition Tribunal to hear appeals from decisions of the CAK. Since its establishment, the CAK has made efforts to streamline competition law in Kenya. It has come up with Guidelines on vertical and horizontal mergers, market definition and exemptions on horizontal practices. The CAK currently under the Ministry of Finance and Planning has released multiple Strategic Plans over the years, the last one being for the years 2021/2022–2024/2025.[30] The previous Plans successfully achieved CAK's key goals of regulating market conduct, market structure, abuse of power and consumer protection. The current Plan is aligned with, *inter alia,* the Constitution of Kenya, Kenya Vision 2030 Blueprint, Data Protection Act of Kenya, 2019 and regional regulatory instruments, including those of COMESA and EAC Competition Authority. It covers the period of fiscal years (FY) 2021/22 to 2024/25 and is titled 'Expanding Enforcement Frontiers for Increased Consumer Welfare and Sustainable Economy. The Plan describes CAK's expansion strategies as follows: Increasing efficiency in production and distribution, promoting innovation, maximising the use of resources and ensuring consumers' right to access goods and services at competitive prices.'

38. The Strategic Plan aims like previous plans to help the CAK enhance its visibility, and implement the Competition Act, and section 46 of the Constitution of Kenya as read with section 7a–c of the Fourth Schedule of the Constitution of Kenya. These provisions not only mandate antitrust and consumer protection but also place the duty of protection of the consumers on the county and national governments. CAK's plans to eliminate bid rigging and collusive tendering make it a partner of the national government in fighting anti-corruption initiatives that are, so to speak, anticompetitive.

39. The Strategic Plan contains several objectives, including:

1. enforcing the Competition Act;
2. controlling mergers and acquisitions to prevent market concentration and potential monopolistic behaviour;
3. championing consumer welfare by safeguarding consumers from unfair and misleading market conduct and promoting the creation and strengthening of existing consumer protection institutions;
4. investigating and addressing instances where suppliers are exploited by businesses with significant purchasing power. This includes monitoring low prices, cost pressures and potentially unethical or illegal purchasing practices;
5. implementation of cooperation frameworks with local, regional and international agencies to complement CAK's mandate as spelt out in the Competition Act; and

30. CAK, 2025, p. 4, 'Strategic Plan 2021/2022–2024/20257', available at: https://www.cak.go.ke/sites/default/files/CAK_STRATEGIC_PLAN.pdf[accessed March 2025].

6. the actualisation of competition and consumer protection treaties, legislations, regulations and agreements.[31]

40. The CAK is mandated in accordance with the powers conferred on it by the Competition Act, with publishing consolidated guidelines on how the provisions under Part III of the Competition Act, which deals with restrictive trade practices, are applied. These guidelines are not a substitute for the provisions on anti-competitive practices in Part III of the Competition Act or other regulations issued under that Act. The guidelines must be read in conjunction with the Competition Act and all related regulations or applicable legal instruments of Kenya, including binding or persuasive precedents in competition law. The guidelines do not constitute legal advice, have no legal force and are not binding on the Competition Tribunal or any court in Kenya. These guidelines provide, among other things, guidance and clarity on anti-competitive agreements, including horizontal and vertical agreements, which are prohibited under sections 21 and 22 of the Competition Act. In particular, the guidelines set out the principles for assessing vertical practices, what such practices are, how they should be handled and how their potential anti-competitive effects can be addressed. The CAK is also responsible for defining the categories of restrictive vertical practices for which exemptions may be granted, establishing the procedure for granting exemptions and reviewing vertical practices to ensure that they do not restrict competition.[32]

41. Arguably, the Competition Act and the Price Control (Essential Goods) Act, 2011 (hereinafter 'Price Control Act'),[33] which in my opinion complement each other, both contribute to consumer protection and work effectively together to achieve different but related goals. While the Price Control Act focuses on setting upper limits for essential goods and medicines that are considered essential for the basic needs and well-being of the population and on ensuring that these goods are available to consumers at reasonable prices when needed, the Competition Act focuses on the long-term prevention of unfair market practices that could harm consumers. The responsibility for price control lies primarily with the Cabinet Secretary responsible for financial matters. Section 2.1 of the Price Control Act empowers the Cabinet Secretary to declare goods essential by notice and to set maximum prices in consultation with industry. A bill (The Price Control (Essential Goods) (Amendment) Bill, No. 41 of 2024) to amend the Price Control Act was recently tabled in the Kenyan Parliament. The bill aims to give the Cabinet Secretary the power to regulate the prices of essential commodities to ensure their availability at reasonable prices, particularly for Kenyans with low incomes. The bill will also update the list of essential goods subject to price control, stabilise their prices so as to save Kenyans, including those with low incomes, from unscrupulous market

31. *Ibid.*, pp. 4–9.
32. CAK, 2023, 'Consolidated Guidelines on Restrictive Trade Practices', available at: https://cak.go.ke/arch/sites/default/files/Consolidated%20Guidelines%20on%20Restrictive%20Trade%20Practices%20.pdf [accessed January 2026].
33. KLR; 2011, (Act No. 26 of 2011), revised by 24th Annual Supplement (Legal Notice 221 of 2023), available at: https://new.kenyalaw.org/akn/ke/act/2011/26/eng@2022-12-31 [accessed May 2025].

actors and exploitative pricing and monitor compliance with prescribed maximum and minimum prices of essential commodities to prevent price gouging. According to section 2.1a of the draft law, the essential goods for which the government must set prices include maize, maize flour, wheat flour, rice, cooking oil, sugar and prescription pharmaceutical medicines. Sections 3B & C of the bill propose that the Cabinet Secretary establish a price control unit to monitor compliance with price control measures, in particular the prescribed maximum and minimum prices for essential goods, identify and address significant fluctuations or abnormal price increases, and collect data for market analysis to assess general price trends and market dynamics. In addition to cooperating with other regulatory authorities to enforce existing competition law and prevent market manipulation, the price control unit will also be responsible for enforcing and implementing the price control directives of the Cabinet Secretary. The bill provides for enforcement mechanisms, including penalties (fines and imprisonment) for the sale or purchase of essential goods above the maximum price. In regulating prices for essential goods, the Cabinet Secretary must, according to section 4.2, take into account the least possible restrictions on competition, normal market conditions and the strengthening of the competitiveness of the domestic market. Once the law comes into force, it will be a criminal offence for anyone to sell or purchase essential goods above the price limit set by the government. According to section 3C, the price control unit along with the CAK will be empowered to impose fines on those who violate the price control regulations and any other related regulations.

Part I. The Structure of Antitrust Law and Its Enforcement

Chapter 1. Source of Antitrust Law in Kenya

§1. NATIONAL SOURCES

I. The Judicature Act

42. Section 3 of the Judicature Act lists several sources of law in Kenya; the very first one being the Constitution of Kenya.

II. The Constitution of Kenya

43. Section 2 of the Constitution of Kenya states that it is the supreme law of the land. The Constitution takes precedence over all other forms of law, written and unwritten. The Constitution prevails over any laws including customary law that are inconsistent with it. Such laws and any acts or omissions in contravention of the Constitution are void to the extent of their inconsistency. The Constitution also contains a number of provisions regarding consumer protection and fair trade competition. This includes section 40 as read with section 260 of the Constitution, which provides that natural and legal persons have the right to use and enjoy their property and are not to be arbitrarily deprived of their rightfully owned property except to the extent authorised by the Constitution or other written law.

44. Section 46 and the Fourth Schedule ((part two) of the Constitution) also vouchsafes for consumer protection, and provides that consumers have a right, among other things, to goods and services of acceptable quality, the protection of their economic interests, as well as compensation for loss or injury arising from defects in goods or services offered. Section 227 of the Constitution provides that in the procurement of public goods and services, State organs and public entities must ensure that they comply with the principles of fairness, honesty, integrity and ethical competition when executing contracts for goods and services. Section 22 of the Constitution endorses the right of every person whose constitutional right has been violated, denied, infringed or threatened to institute class action lawsuits without fear of legal costs.

III. The Competition Act

45. Competition is the rivalry between producers and manufacturers selling the same products and services in a market to the same customers. The rivalry resulting can manifest itself in various ways, e.g., through price competition, product improvements or increased marketing efforts, which ultimately affect consumer choice and outcomes. As producers of goods and services compete for more customers, this can lead to lower prices, better quality and a greater variety of goods and products. In practice, competition law is concerned with the promotion and sustenance of market competition for the benefit of society. Competition aims at contributing to competitiveness by bringing efficiency in markets and benefits in the form of innovation, revenue, profit and market-share growth. It corrects whatever market failures arise because of trade, and protects competitors and consumers from predatory business practices by ensuring that fair competition exists in the wide range of commercial activities transacted in any open market economy.

46. Competition laws and policies are essential for shaping markets and determining the degree to which products can compete on national and international markets. The transformation of the world economy through globalisation and liberalisation of markets has brought to limelight the need for fair trade and open competition in the market. This has created the need in many countries Kenya included, for effective national, regional and international laws to govern commerce, build competitive business environment, promote innovation and correct negative externalities that cause market failures and abuses and regulate the economy.[34]

47. The second source of law according to the Judicature Act is Acts of Kenyan Parliament, specific Acts of UK Parliament, subsidiary/ delegated legislations, i.e., rules, orders, regulations and guidelines made by competent authorities. A good number of Acts of Parliament, including the Competition Act, which is the primary source of competition law in Kenya, are enacted pursuant to specific provisions in the Constitution.

48. Kenya's very first competition law, the British Price Control Ordinance of 1956, applied to Kenya together with the English common law by virtue of the East African Order in Council of 1897. The latter applied to Kenya, through a reception clause, the substance of the English common law, the doctrines of equity and the statutes of general application in force in England as at that date, and later, the Kenya Judicature Act. The Price Control Ordinance of 1956 served as a prototypical model Price Control framework for subsequent competition laws until 1989, when it was replaced by the RTMPCA. As already said here before, the first formal

34. Taylor, M., 2006, pp. 8–15, 'International Competition Law: A New Dimension for the WTO', Cambridge University Press; Geiger, R., 2010, pp. 235–238, 'The Development of World Economy and Competition Law' in Zäch, R., Heinemann, A. and Kellerhals, A., 2010, 'The Development of Competition Law: Global Perspectives', Edward Elgar Publishers.

competition law was the Price Control Act of 1956. The latter was followed by the RTMPCA, which has since been repealed and replaced with the Competition Act.

49. Section 21 of the Competition Act prohibits voracious trade practices of monopolistic and restrictive nature whose purpose is to prevent, distort or reduce competition in trade, or that may directly or indirectly be used to determine price of goods. The Act also outlaws trade conduct, which may limit or control production, market outlets or access to such markets. Section 24 of the Competition Act not only precludes business practices that restrict or distort competition, but it also lists practices that amount to abuse of dominant position, and defines the penalty associated with such abuse. Section 55 of the Act restricts false and misleading representations about the standard, quality, value, history, previous use, existence, price or place of origin, etc., of goods or services. The statutory remedies against acts outlined in section 55 are set forth in section 63 of the Act, and include compensatory and punitive damages. The goal of section 55 of the Competition Act is to promote and protect the interests and welfare of consumers.

§2. International Sources

I. Regional Sources

50. Regional developments have also led to the successful adoption of unified competition policies and laws in the EAC Member States with respect to business transactions that have a community dimension. The Sixth EAC Development Strategy for the period 2021/22–2025/26 contains strategic goals that the members of the EAC must achieve during the period. This Strategy is the fourth one since the establishment of the EAC. It was concluded after the successful conclusion of the fifth Development Strategy and the onset of the EAC Common Market.[35] It is believed that the implementation of this Strategy would steer the EAC region to greater heights of regional and international competitiveness and bring about faster and robust socio-economic development. The Strategy is expected to also boost the welfare and prosperity of the people of East Africa, and help put in place competition laws and policies that will expand opportunities for doing business within the EAC and globally, and harmonise policies, legal and regulatory framework.

51. To implement the competition policy, it was proposed that a central common authority be established in line with the provisions of the EAC Treaty.[36] Section 75.1.i of the East African Treaty exhorts EAC Member States to come up with, among other Protocols, the competition Protocol. Indeed, since the revival of the

35. COMESA, 1993, 'Treaty Establishing a Common Market for Eastern and Southern Africa (COMESA)-COMESA Treaty', available at: https://www.wipo.int/wipolex/en/treaties/details/218 .pdf [accessed January 2026]; EAC, 2001–2005, 'The Second EAC Development Strategy', available at: http://www.eac.int [accessed July 2013].

36. EAC, 1999, 'The Treaty for the Establishment of the East African Community', available at: https: //www.eacj.org/?page_id=33 [accessed January 2026].

EAC cooperation in 1999, the EAC has witnessed a series of inter-company strategic mergers and acquisitions, thanks to national competition laws of the Member States. The EAC Common Market Protocol promulgated in accordance with Articles 1, 76 and 104 of the EAC treaty entered into force in 2010. Among some of the key competition policy provisions is Article 16 of the Protocol, which requires Member States to guarantee the free movement of services supplied by nationals within the EAC. Section 21 of the Protocol enjoins the EAC Member States to implement measures to prevent deceptive and fraudulent practices in the supply of goods and services within the EAC. Article 21 of the Protocol is subject to Articles 17 and 18 that deal with national treatment and most favoured nation (MFN) treatment principles, which promote open, fair and undistorted competition.

52. With the enactment of the law in 2006, which came into force on 1 December 2014 (hereafter),[37] efforts to strengthen competition within EAC were further boosted. According to the Preamble and Articles 3 and 37.1 of the Act, its purpose is to promote fair trade by prohibiting anticompetitive practices and removing market barriers that may hinder cross-border trade and economic transactions. The East African Competition Act has been implemented in most member states. It has been observed that despite this progress, the lack of competition culture in the EAC region has led to policy contradictions which may necessitate amendment to complementary laws.[38] So far, only Kenya and Uganda have national competition laws and fully functional institutions. The East African Competition Act was amended in 2023 by the East African Community Competition (Amendment) Act, 2023 (Amendment Act) took effect on 31 December 2024.[39] According to the preamble to the Amendment Act, its goal is to confer legal status on the East African Community Competition Authority (EACCA) and thereby to empower it to investigate and address anti-competitive behaviour, impose and collect fines for anti-competitive conduct, manage mergers and acquisitions, and protect the interests of consumers within the EAC regions. The EAC Competition Act also establishes EACCA, which is to function alongside national competition authorities in the Member States, and whose goal is to promote fair competition, protect consumer welfare, and prohibit anti-competitive practices. Article 44 of the EAC Competition Act gives the EACCA exclusive original jurisdiction in the determination of matters concerning the violation of the EAC Competition Act. Another objective of the amendment is to align merger provisions with global standards, in particular with regard to the assessment of mergers that could 'significantly impede' competition in the EAC market. Factors such as market structure, alternatives to competitors and pro-competitive benefits (e.g., efficiency gains, technological progress) are now explicitly taken into account.

---

37. EAC, 2006, 'EAC Competition Act, 2006', Legal notice no. 2/2007, Vol. AT; L-003.
38. Sixth Development Strategy 201/22-2025/26, pp. 133–134; available at: https://faolex.fao.org/docs/pdf/mul214454.pdf [accessed May 2025].
39. EAC, 2024, 'EAC Competition (Amendment) Act, 2023', Legal notice no. 33 of 31 Dec. 2024.

53. This jurisdiction connotes that national competition authorities have no parallel competence, and that such authorities, or even national courts, have no jurisdiction to make decisions or findings based on the EAC Competition Act. This reinforces the need for all the EAC Member States to promulgate competition laws and policies and set up institutions for regulating competition at national level.

II. Treaties

54. According to section 3 of the Judicature Act, as read with sections 2.5 and 6 of the Constitution of Kenya, general rules of international law, including treaties, become constituents of Kenya's laws upon ratification.

55. International sources of competition law are therefore limited to treaties Kenya has ratified. Thus, treaties ratified by Kenya, and which incorporate competition-related provisions, such as the Paris Convention, the General Agreement on Tariffs and Trade (henceforth 'GATT')[40] and the Trade Related Aspects of Intellectual Property Rights (henceforth 'TRIPS'),[41] are part of the laws of Kenya. For signatory Member States, the Paris Convention and the TRIPS have provisions for protecting competition in the market of products and services. The Paris Convention[42] adopted in 1883 is the very first international regulation of unfair competition. According to Article 1.2 of the Paris Convention, the protection of industrial property shall include, among other things, the repression of unfair competition. Unfair competition is defined in Article 10*bis* as 'any act of competition contrary to honest practices in industrial or commercial matters'. Kenya is a signatory to the Paris Convention.

56. Article 2.1 of the TRIPS incorporates the substantive provisions of the Paris Convention, including Article 10*bis* of the Paris Convention that deals with unfair competition. Article 8.2 of TRIPS gives the signatory states a broad discretion to enact TRIPS-compliant competition laws that are in their interests. Article 40 also makes it clear that licensing practices that hinder competition may have *adverse effects on trade and may* impede the transfer and dissemination of technology. It, therefore, permits Member States to specify in their national laws competitive practices that may have distort competition, and to put in place appropriate measures in line with TRIPS to prevent or control such practices.

57. The GATT 1947/1994 also embodies basic rules aimed at helping signatory states guard against anticompetitive practices. The Preamble and Articles XI, XII and XXVIII of the GATT obligate the GATT Member States to make efforts to

40. GATT, 1947/1994, 'General Agreement on Tariffs and Trade', available at: http://www.wto.org/english/docs_e/legal_e/gatt47_e.pdf [accessed July 2013].
41. TRIPS, 1994, 'The Trade Related Aspects of Intellectual Property Rights', available at: https://www.wipo.int/wipolex/en/treaties/details/231 [accessed Januray 2026].
42. Paris Convention, 1883, 'Paris Convention for the Protection of Industrial Property', available at: https://www.wipo.int/wipolex/en/text/288514 [accessed July 2013].

reduce, even if through negotiations, tariffs on traded goods, and to eliminate quantitative restrictions on imports and exports by signatory countries. Moreover, the MFN treatment dealt with in Articles I and XIII of the GATT, Article 4 of the TRIPS and Article II of the General Agreement on Tariffs in Services (GATS)[43] states that if a Member State grants benefits on a product, i.e., reduced tariffs or lower custom duties, it must immediately and unconditionally extend it to the like products of other countries. The national treatment clause encapsulated in Article III of the GATTand Article 3 of the TRIPS boosts the MFN principle by requiring signatories to these treaties to subject import products to a treatment no less favourable than that accorded to like domestic products.

§3. Secondary Sources

I. Secondary Legislations

58. A considerable amount of secondary legislation, executive orders and guidelines complements the Kenyan Competition Act. These include the Price Control (Essential Goods) Act, Consumer Protection Act,[44] the Sale of Goods Act,[45] the IPA and the Law of Contract.[46] While these secondary legislations could lower prices for consumers and provide them with more choices, potentially improving their purchasing experience and protecting them from unfair practices, they should be carefully drafted and implemented to avoid unintended consequences that could be detrimental to competition and overall health of markets in the EAC region.

II. Regulations

59. Among the competition regulations that apply to Kenya by virtue of its EAC membership are the EAC Competition Act, 2006,[47] the EAC Competition Regulations[48] passed in 2010 for the better carrying into effect of the provisions of the Act, and the COMESA Competition and Consumer Regulations, 2025.[49] According to

43. GATS, 1995, 'The General Agreement on Trade in Services (GATS)', available at: http://www.wto.org/english/tratop_e/serv_e/serv_e.htm [accessed July 2013].
44. KLR, 2013, 'Consumer Protection Act, No. 46 of 2013', available at https://new.kenyalaw.org/akn/ke/act/2012/46/eng@2022-12-31 [accessed January 2026].
45. KLR, 1931, 'Sale of Goods Act, Chapter 31 of the Laws of Kenya', available at: https://new.kenyalaw.org/akn/ke/act/1930/33/eng@1964-11-03 [accessed January 2026].
46. KLR, 1961, 'Law of Contract Act, Chapter 23 of the Laws of Kenya', available at: https://new.kenyalaw.org/akn/ke/act/1960/43/eng@2022-12-31 [accessed January 2026].
47. EAC, 2006, 'The East African Community (EAC) Competition Act of 2006' avaialable at: https://www.eacompetition.org/laws/category/competition-act [accessed May 2025].
48. EAC, 2010, 'EAC Competition Regulation', 2010, available at: http://www.eac.int [accessed July 2013].
49. COMESA, 2025, 'COMESA Competition and Consumer Protection Rules', 2025, available at: https://comesacompetition.org/resources/rules/comesa-competition-and-consumer-protection-rules-2025/ [accessed January 2025].

sections 3 and 4 of the EAC Competition Act, the Act applies to all economic activities and sectors having cross-border effect. According to section 3, the main objectives of the Act include, among others:

1. establishing the EAC Competition Authority (EACCA);
2. protecting consumers from unfair and misleading practices, ensuring they receive fair treatment and access to fairly priced and quality goods and service;
3. protecting the businesses of Partner States and making them more competitive in global markets by facilitating fair competition and removing interstate trade barriers;
4. ensuring that all market participants, regardless of their nationality or place of residence, have equal opportunities to compete within the EAC, and eliminating any discrimination by partner states on the basis of nationality or place of residence in order to create a level playing field for all companies operating in the region;
5. preventing anti-competitive practices such as price-fixing, collusion, and market allocation;
6. investigating and approving mergers and acquisitions to ensure they don't harm competition within the EAC bloc; and
7. promoting economic integration and development in the Community by:

a. enhancing the competitiveness of Community enterprises in world markets by exposing them to competition within the Community; and
b. bringing the Community's competition policy and practice in line with international best practices.

60. The EAC Competition Act requires Member States to enact and implement their own national competition laws to ensure that the EAC Competition Act's provisions are effectively enforced within their territories. The adopted national laws must be aligned with the EAC Competition Act, meaning they should share similar principles, prohibitions, and enforcement mechanisms. The EAC Competition Act also emphasises the importance of cooperation between the EAC Competition Authority (EACCA) and the Member States' competition authorities to ensure the consistent implementation of competition policy across the region. The EACCA is responsible for implementing the competition policy and the Act, with support from Partner States. National authorities of the EAC are responsible for investigating and prosecuting anti-competitive practices that occur within their borders, while the EACCA focuses on cross-border issues and broader regional enforcement.[50]

COMESA, 2025, 'COMESA Competition and Consumer Regulations, 2025', available at: https://comesacompetition.org/resources/regulations/comesa-competition-and-consumer-protection-regulations-2025/ [accessed January 2025].

50. *See* the Preamble and ss 3–4 & 38–44 of the EAC Competition Act.

61. Section 44 gives EACCA, once established, the exclusive jurisdiction over all mergers and enforcement matters with cross-border competition effects, and over matters relating to the violation of the EAC Competition Act. The provision further provides that the resolutions and decisions of the EACCA shall be legally binding upon EAC's Member States, authorities and subordinate courts. The EACCA will have jurisdiction over all eight EAC Member States, namely, Kenya, Somalia, Democratic Republic of Congo, South Sudan, Uganda, Burundi, Rwanda and Tanzania. National competition laws and regulations will cover competition transactions within and not beyond respective national boundaries. The main challenge the EACCA still remains the implementation of effective, efficient and dedicated national competition regulatory frameworks in the eight Member States that have the power to investigate, prosecute, and impose penalties on businesses that violate the rules.[51]

62. Chapter VI, Article 55.1 and 3 of the COMESA treaty lay out the foundation for the development of the COMESA competition policy and the subsequent COMESA Regulations. Article 55.1 states that:

> the member states agree that any practice which negates the objective of free and liberalised trade shall be prohibited. To this end, the member states agree to prohibit any agreement between undertakings or concerted practice which has as its objective or effect the prevention, restriction or distortion of competition within the Common Market.

63. Article 55.3 of the Treaty mandates the COMESA Council of Ministers to make regulations to regulate competition within the Member States. As a result, in 2004, the Council made and ratified the COMESA Competition Regulations of 2004, which entered into force in December 2014. The Regulations aimed to foster competition as an instrument for accelerating economic growth by requiring Member States to prohibit anticompetitive practices and other restrictions that may harm free trade and competition within the Common Market. COMESA Competition Regulations of 2004 was repealed by COMESA Competition and Consumer Regulations, 2025 (COMESA Regulations) and the COMESA Competition and Consumer Protection Rules 2025 (2025 Rules),[52] both of which entered into force on 5 December 2025 he Regulations have according to section 4 the purposes of:

> (a) promoting competition by preventing and prohibiting anti-competitive business practices, anti-competitive mergers and other restrictions that deter the efficient operation of markets, thereby enhancing consumer welfare in the

---

51. Sixth Development Strategy 201/22-2025/26, pp. 133–135; available at: https://faolex.fao.org/docs/pdf/mul214454.pdf [accessed May 2025].

52. COMESA Competition Commission, 2025, 'COMESA Competition and Consumer Protection Regulations 2025', available at; https://comesacompetition.org/resources/regulations/comesa-competition-and-consumer-protection-regulations-2025/ [accessed January 2026]; COMESA Competition Commission, 2025, 'COMESA Competition and Consumer Protection Rules 2025', available at; https://comesacompetition.org/resources/rules/comesa-competition-and-consumer-protection-rules-2025/ [accessed January 2026].

Common Market; and (b) enhancing consumer welfare by preventing and prohibiting unfair trade practices thereby protecting consumers against offensive conduct by market actors in the Common Market in all the member states. Regulation 8 of the Regulations mandates the COMESA Competition and Consumer Commission (CCCC) among other functions to promote and enforce compliance with these Regulations and monitor, investigate and assess anti-competitive business practices by undertakings within, or having an effect within, the Common Market in all the member states.

64. According to Regulation 3 of the COMESA Regulations protection are binding on the undertakings of all COMESA Member States.

65. Article 10.2 of the COMESA Treaty makes the regulations, directives, decisions and recommendations made by the COMESA Council binding on all COMESA nations and mandates the Member States to cooperate to ensure effective enforcement of competition laws within their borders. According to Article 8.3 of the COMESA Treaty, such directives, decisions and recommendations are binding only on the COMESA Member States they concern, and in respect to competition matters that they address. According to Article 29.2, decisions of the COMESA Court of Justice on the interpretation of the provisions of the COMESA Treaty are binding on the COMESA Member States; such decisions also take precedence over the decisions of national courts.

66. There are now two separate legal regimes which govern the enforcement of competition law and policy in the COMESA Member States, namely:

a. the domestic competition laws within each of the COMESA Member States; and
b. the COMESA Competition Regulations and Rules.

67. National competition laws apply to anticompetitive practices emanating at national level, and are thus enforced by the national competition authorities in their respective Member States. As already mentioned above, in accordance with Article 3.1 of the COMESA Regulations, the COMESA Competition Regulations and Rules apply to all commercial activities with a cross-border impact, which means that the Commission can essentially only intervene when predatory or unfair practices complained of affect regional players in the COMESA market sector.

III. Guidelines

68. There are several competition law Guidelines at national level aimed at helping the CAK in Kenya to deal with competition-related matters. These include Guidelines on market definition, merger thresholds, abuse of dominations and exemptions. The CAK applies market definition Guidelines to product and geographical markets in order to establish the limits of competition between trading companies and potential new entrants into a market, and also to set the framework for the application of the competition policy as mandated by the Competition Act.[53]

69. In line with section 21, which prohibits unfair agreements, decisions or concerted practices aimed at distorting competition and trade, the CAK has also developed exemption Guidelines, which set specific criteria and indicators for determining when a particular practice infringes the Competition Act. Competition lessening cartel practices, such as price coordination among players in the market, output limitations and sharing of markets and customers, collusive tendering, abuse of Intellectual Property (IP) rights, etc., are among the practices proscribed by the exemption Guidelines.[54]

70. Besides the exemption and market definition Guidelines, the CAK has also developed merger control Guidelines based on two criteria, namely, competition effects and public interest concerns. The merger thresholds provide an effective mechanism for controlling mergers and acquisitions at a national level. Section 46 of the Competition Act mandates the CAK to approve all mergers.[55]

71. These national Guidelines are supplemented by the COMESA Regulations. COMESA is the regional regulator charged with the responsibility of enhancing regional economic integration among the Member States by promoting fair competition and securing consumer protection. The merger assessment Guidelines help in clarifying COMESA's competition enforcement policies and practices, and in particular, how the merger provisions of the COMESA Regulations are to be construed when assessing mergers. For instance, the Guidelines have provided clarity on: (a) when to notify the CCCC of mergers; (b) what mergers with 'regional dimension' and what monetary thresholds should be applied to them mean; and (c) the category of transactions for which notification is required. The Guidelines also provide factors to consider when assessing the public benefit/public interest criteria in merger control.[56]

72. Regulation 6 of the COMESA Regulations refers to public benefit/public interest when authorising agreements thereunder, and when assessing mergers defined in Regulations 41 and 47 . Moreover, in order to enhance regional economic integration in the Common Market and reinforce intra-regional trade among

53. CAK of Kenya, 2014, 'Guidelines on Relevant Market Definition', available at: http://www.cak.go.ke [accessed July 2013].
54. CAK of Kenya, 2012b, 'Exemption Guidelines', available at: http://www.cak.go.ke [accessed July 2013].
55. CAK of Kenya, 2013, 'Proposed Merger Thresholds', available at: http://www.cak.go.ke [accessed July 2013].
56. COMESA, 2013, 'Draft Merger Assessment Guideline under the COMESA Competition Regulations (2004)', 'Draft Market Definition Guidelines', 'Guidelines on the Application of Public Interest Criteria', 'Draft Guidelines on the Application of Articles 16 and 19 of the COMESA Competition Regulations (2004) to Horizontal and Vertical Business Practices', and 'Draft Guidelines on the Application of Article 18 of the COMESA Competition Regulations (2004) Prohibiting Abuses of a Dominant Position', available at: http://www.comesacompetition.org [accessed July 2013].

COMESA Member States, COMESA plans to develop draft guidelines regarding the implementation of Article 18 of the COMESA Regulations dealing with abuse of dominant position.

§4. Sources of Law: Relation and History

73. The hierarchy of the sources of law in Kenya is spelt out in section 3 of the Judicature Act. Under this provision, the jurisdiction of the High Court, the Court of Appeal and all subordinate courts shall be exercised in accordance with:

a. the Constitution;
b. subject thereto, all other written laws, including the Acts of Parliament of the United Kingdom cited in Part I of the Schedule to this Act, modified in accordance with Part II of that Schedule;
c. subject thereto and so far as those written laws do not extend or apply, the substance of the common law, the doctrines of equity and the statutes of general application in force in England on 12 August 1897, and the procedure and practice observed in courts of justice in England at that date;
d. but the common law, doctrines of equity and statutes of general application shall apply so far only as the circumstances of Kenya and its inhabitants permit and subject to such qualifications as those circumstances may render necessary.

74. In underscoring the necessity of applying the English common law to the Kenyans only when 'local circumstances render it necessary', Denning L.J. held in *Nyali v. Attorney General*[57] that 'just as with an English oak, so with the English common law. You cannot transplant it to the African continent and expect to retain the tough character, which it has in England. It will flourish indeed, but it needs careful tending. So with the common law. It has many principles of manifest justice and good sense, which can be applied with advantage to the people of every race and culture every world over but also has many refinements, subtleties and technicalities, which are not suitable to other folks. These offshoots must be cut away. In these far of lands the people must have a law which, they will understand and which they will respect. The common law cannot fill this role except with considerable qualifications'.

75. Section 260 of the Constitution of Kenya, 'legislation' includes:

a. an Act of Parliament, or a law made under authority conferred by an Act of Parliament; or
b. a law made by an assembly of a county government, or under authority conferred by such a law.

---

57. *Nyali v. Attorney General*, [1956] 1 QB 7.

76. Section 2 of the Constitution of Kenya declares the Constitution as the supreme law of the land and voids all laws that are inconsistent with it. In accordance with section 3 of the sources of law in Kenya can be summed up in the hierarchy below:

a. the Constitution;
b. Statute law or Acts of Kenyan Parliament;
c. specific Acts of the Parliament of the United Kingdom cited in Part I of the schedule to the Judicature Act;
d. subordinate, subsidiary or delegated legislation;
e. judicial precedents;
f. English statutes of General application, in force in England on 12 August 1897;
g. the substance of Common law in force on 12 August 1897; the doctrine of Equity in force in England on 12 August 1897; procedures and practices observed by courts of Justice in England on 12 August 1897, in so far only as the circumstances of Kenya and its inhabitants; and
h. various customary laws, including African, Hindu and Islamic customary laws in so far as they are applicable and not repugnant to justice and morality or inconsistent with any written law.

77. Sections 2.5 and 2.6 of the Constitution of Kenya recognise two further sources of law in Kenya, namely:

1. the general rules of international law; and
2. any treaty or convention ratified by Kenya.

78. Section 3 of the Interpretation and General Provisions Act[58] defines 'written law' as spelt in section 3 of the Judicature Act as:

a. an Act of Parliament for the time being in force;
b. an applied law;
c. any subsidiary legislation for the time being in force; or
d. any county legislation as defined in Article 260 of the Constitution.

§5. Role of Precedents and Authorities

79. Judicial precedents, also known as *stare decisis* (to stand upon prior decisions), are a body of law formed through court decisions, as opposed to law formed through statutes. Kenya's legal system is based on the doctrine of judicial precedent. Judicial precedents are instrumental in helping judges lay down principles of law relevant to the cases before them. The judges of lower courts must observe the principles so laid down by adopting not the written and enacted law, but the judicial

58. KLR, 1956, 'Interpretation and General Provisions Act', Ch. 2 of the Laws of Kenya, available at: https://new.kenyalaw.org/akn/ke/act/1956/38/eng@2022-12-31 [accessed January 2026].

precedents set by superior courts. In other words, these precedents, once established, become mandatory, or rather the *ratio decidendi* to be followed in future cases involving the same facts.[59]

80. There are four types of precedents: original, distinguishing, reversing and overrule precedents. Original precedents arise where there is absolutely no decision on a particular point of law, and the courts have to develop a decision from cases that are closest in rules to the one under consideration. A distinguishing precedent is one that establishes whether or not the facts of an earlier decision are different from those in the case at hand in a material way, and determines whether or not the reasoning of a previous case applies and the extent to which it applies. Where a court reverses a decision of a lower court in the same case and replaces it with another, it creates a reversing precedent. Likewise, if a higher court overrules its own decision or the decision of a lower court on the ground that the decision was wrongly decided or that it was decided without regard to established principles of law, then an overruled precedent is created.

81. As already indicated before, Kenya's legal system is based on the Constitution, the Judicature Act and the common law precedents. Judges in Kenya play a significant role in shaping judicial precedents. It should be noted that under Kenya's new Constitution, the Supreme Court and not the Court of Appeal is the highest court in the land. Its decision/precedents are, according to sections 162 and 163.7 of the Constitution of Kenya, binding on the Court of Appeal, the High Court, the Magistrate's Courts, as well as specialised courts and tribunals. As a rule, the decisions of the Court of Appeal are binding on the High Court and the Magistrates' Courts, while those of the High Court are binding on the Magistrates' Courts. The Magistrates' courts do not create any binding precedents, and their decisions are thus not binding on any court.[60]

59. *Dodhia v. National Grindleys Bank Co. Ltd*, Journal of African Law, 14(1), 34, pp. 35, 39, 41, 49, and 54.

60. Andrews, H.N., 1985, 'Reporting Case Law: Unreported Cases, the Definition of a Ratio and the Criteria for Reporting Decisions', Legal Studies, 5(2), 205, pp. 216 and 227; Mullen, T., 2007, 'Reflections on Jackson v Attorney General: Questioning Sovereignty', Legal Studies, 27(1), 1, pp. 2, 7 and 15; Warner, K.A., 1990, pp. 63–67, 'Judicial Reasoning and Precedent: Negligently Inflicted Psychological Injuries', Legal Studies, 10(1), 63.

Chapter 2. Scope of Application

§1. Territorial Reach

82. According to section 5 of the Kenya's Competition Act, the Act applies across all business practices conducted in the entire Kenyan territory; extending in scope to private and public sectors and to economic operators in the national economy, including Government, state corporations, local authorities, importers and exporters in so far as they engage in trade. The Act incorporates most concepts and elements found in antitrust legislation of many countries. In accordance with section 6 of the Competition Act, the Act applies:

a. to Kenyans and non-Kenyans transacting business in Kenya;
b. to companies incorporated in, or conducting business in Kenya;
c. to any person supplying goods or services in Kenya or acquiring goods or services within Kenya;
d. and to persons or companies acquiring shares or other assets outside Kenya, which acquisition results in the change of control of a business, part of a business or an asset of a business in Kenya.

83. The liberalisation of trade and services in the EAC and COMESA bloc of countries has enhanced competition in the region and caused policymakers to adopt laws and policies aimed at promoting and enhancing competition among the various market players and protecting consumer welfare in the region. There are in fact some legislative conflicts between the Competition Act, the COMESA Competition Regulations and the EAC Competition Act. However, section 5.2 of the Competition Act, states that where there is a conflict between its provisions and those of any other written law with regard to matters concerning competition, the provisions of the Competition Act shall prevail. Section 4.3 of the EAC Competition Act further states that it shall not apply to restraints on competition imposed and resulting from Member States' regulation of specific sectors or industries to the extent that the anticompetitive conduct is required by such regulation within their own jurisdictions. Further Article 3.2 of the COMESA Competition Regulations provides that the latter shall prevail over the industry or a sector of an industry that is subject to the jurisdiction of a separate regulatory entity (whether domestic or regional) if that entity regulates anticompetitive business conducts and mergers and acquisitions dealt with in Parts 3 and 4 of the Regulations.

84. The reality on the ground, nevertheless, shows that the Competition Act applies to competition issues arising within a national border. The Act ensures that the Member States' sole jurisdiction over national problems is maintained. The EAC Competition Act and the COMESA Competition Regulations thus apply to competition issues of regional dimensions. Indeed, though there are some differences between the three competition regimes, the spirit of the national, EAC and COMESA Competition laws is the same, the objectives and scope of application are almost similar, and the legislations do complement each other.

§2. Special Sectors

I. The Energy, Electricity and Petroleum Sub-sectors

85. There are various policies, institutions and legal frameworks that regulate Kenya's energy sector. The energy sector has energy, biomass, petroleum and electricity as key sectors. The liberalisation of the energy sector started in 1997 with the promulgation of the Electric Power Act of 1997, and picked up later on with the enactment of the Energy Act, 2006 (hereinafter 'the Energy Act'). To facilitate private sector participation in electricity and energy service provision, under the Electric Power Act of 1997, the Kenya Power and Lighting Company (KPLC) was split to create the KenGen to carry out the generation function and the Electricity Regulatory Board (ERB) to regulate the power sector. KPLC was left with energy transmission and distribution functions. The Electric Power Act of 1997 and Energy Act led to the separation of the electricity transmission business from the distribution business, as well as to the liberalisation of procurement, distribution and pricing of petroleum products in Kenya.

86. The purpose of the enactment of the Energy Act was to amalgamate all the laws relating to electric power, renewable energy and natural gas (including petroleum) sub-sectors under one law. The Act repealed the Electric Power Act of 1997[61] and the Kenya Petroleum Act, Chapter 308 of the Laws of Kenya. It also established three bodies independent of State Influence; namely, the Energy Regulatory Commission (ERC) as a single sector regulator and the Rural Electrification Authority (REA), whose sole mandate is to accelerate rural electrification. The Energy Act, 2006,[62] also dissolved the ERB and replaced it with ERC, which, according to section 4.2 of the Act, is a body corporate and with an independent legal personality. The Act further established the Energy Tribunal, whose duties include the hearing of appeals from the decisions of the ERC. The ERC and the Energy Tribunal coordinate and advise the Ministry of Energy on policy and strategy relating to energy demand and supply. The new Kenya Energy Act, 2019,[63] amended multiple times and subsequently passed into law in 2019 as the Energy Act No. 12 of 2019 (hereafter 'Energy Act, 2019') consolidated all existing energy laws in Kenya. The Energy Act, 2019, repealed the Geothermal Resources Act, the Kenya Nuclear Electricity Board Order No. 131 of 2012, and the Kenya Energy Bill 2015 was enacted in 2016 to amend the Energy Act, 2006. The Energy Act, 2019, aims to promote efficient energy management, establish and empower relevant sector entities, and regulate various energy and petroleum-related activities, including the production, distribution and consumption of electricity and other energy forms, as well as consumption, consumer protection and competition in the energy market.

---

61. KLR, 1997, 'Electric Power Act, 1997, No. 11 of 1997 of the Laws of Kenya', (Repealed by the Energy Act, 2006, Act No. 12 of 2006.
62. KLR, 2006, 'Energy Act, 2006, Act No. 12 of 2006', available at: https://new.kenyalaw.org/legislation/, [accessed January 2026].
63. KLR, 2019 'Energy Act, 2019', available at : https://kenyalaw.org/kl/fileadmin/pdfdownloads/Acts/2019/EnergyAct__No.1of2019.PDF [accessed May 2025].

87. The ERC previously held the mandate over the energy sector in Kenya. The ERC has been succeeded by the Energy and Petroleum Regulatory Authority (EPRA), established according to section 9 of the Energy Act, 2019. According to the Preamble to, and section 4 of the Energy Act, 2019, EPRA is responsible for regulation of electricity, renewable energy, petroleum and coal sectors in Kenya. EPRA plays a crucial role in determining and adjusting prices of petroleum products, like super petrol, diesel, and kerosene, to reflect market conditions and supply chain costs. Section 25 of the Energy Act, 2019, establishes the Energy and Petroleum Tribunal, replacing the previous Energy Tribunal. According to section 36 of the Energy Act, 2019, Energy Petroleum Tribunal (EPT) has a wider scope to handle disputes and appeals within the energy and petroleum sectors arising from the act and related regulations, including those arising from the Energy Act and other related statutes. Section 36 of the Energy Act, 2019, gives the tribunal the power to grant various equitable reliefs and review its own judgments on all matters arising underthis Act or any other Act (The jurisdiction of the Tribunal does not include the trial of any criminal offence).

88. There are a few competition provisions in the Energy Act. Other than sections 3, 4and 5 that enable the EPRA to monitor, develop, and implement judicious policies and plans for the energy sector, which includes regulations for electricity, renewable energy, petroleum, and coal, section 9 empowers the EPRA to ensure significant improvement in market access through licensing. The EPRA is empowered, among other things, to:

a. renew, modify, suspend and revoke licences and permits in the energy sector;
b. enforce and review regulations, codes and standards for the subsector with the goal of protecting consumers from harmful products;
c. set, review and adjust electric power tariffs and tariff structures; and
d. approve electric power purchase and network service contracts for all persons engaging in electric power undertakings and investigating and resolving complaints and disputes on matters regulated under the Act.

89. In discharging the above duties, sections 6, 93.2, 131 and 207 of the Energy Act, 2019, state that the EPRA shall, in coordination with other statutory authorities, monitor and ensure implementation of, and the observance of, the policies that enhance competition, supply efficiency, increase reliability, and quality in the energy and related sectors. In Schedule 5 of the Energy Act, 2019, the roles and responsibilities of both the National and County Governments in the energy sector are clearly defined and aligned with the principle of devolution enshrined in the Kenyan Constitution. The Energy Act, 2019, empowers the national government to formulate policies and plans, while assigning county governments roles in regulating and enforcing energy efficiency within their jurisdiction. Some of the plans, policies and regulations prescribe practices or arrangements that have the object or the likely effect of preventing, restricting or distorting competition in the generation, transmission, distribution or supply of electrical energy.

II. Telecommunication Sector in Kenya

90. As a member of the World Trade Organization (WTO) and the GATS, which governs international trade in services, Kenya has been committed to liberalising services in a number of its sectors, including the telecommunications sector. The telecommunications sector in Kenya has transformed from a largely monopolistic and inefficient one to one of the most vibrant and expansive sectors of the Kenyan economy. Telecommunication services were introduced in Kenya in 1977, and were run jointly as part of the regional network with the then EAC counterparts, Uganda and Tanzania. At this time, the East African Posts & Telecommunications Corporation, established in 1967, was responsible for postal and other telecommunication services. With the disbandment of the EAC in 1977, the Kenya Posts and Telecommunication Corporation (KPTC) was established in accordance with section 3 as read with section 13 of the Kenya Posts and Telecommunications Act of 1977 (KPTA)[64] to run the postal, money, order, telephone and radio communication services at national level. KPTC had absolute monopoly over both postal and telecommunication services and enjoyed this monopoly until 1999, when the Government of Kenya launched sector deregulation by introducing competition in certain market segments and dissolving KPTC.[65]

91. To facilitate this, in 1998, the Parliament enacted the Kenya Information and Communications Act[66] as read with the Kenya Communication (Amendment Act), which laid out the framework for the reforms in the telecommunication sector. The Act, which repealed the Kenya Posts and Telecommunications Act of 1977 (hereinafter 'KPTA'),[67] is currently the framework for regulating the communications sector in Kenya, splitting KPTC into key bodies; namely, Communications Commission of Kenya (CCK), which is a statutory regulatory agency that licences and regulates telecommunications, radio communications and postal services.

92. The telecommunications sector in Kenya has become an important industry that currently encompasses mobile services, fixed-line services, courier services, broadcasting services, frequency spectrum management, electronic transactions, and cyberspace management. The sector has experienced strong growth, driven by fierce competition characterized by the spread of mobile technologies, rising demand for fast internet connections, and mobile payment services. This has led to innovation, efficiency gains, and strategic adjustments in order to survive and grow,

64. KLR, 1934, 'Telegraphic Press Messages Act', Ch. 512,]; KLR, 1977, 'Kenya Posts and Telecommunications Act of 1977', repealed. *See* s. 103 of the Kenya Information and Communications Act, all available at: https://new.kenyalaw.org/legislation/, [accessed January 2026].
65. OECD Global Forum on Competition, 2004, p. 6, 'Challenges/Obstacles Faced by Competition Authorities in Achieving Greater Economic Development Through the Promotion of Competition; Contribution from Kenya – Session II'; CCNM/GF/COMP/WD(2004)8.
66. KLR, 1998, Kenya Information and Communications Act, available at: https://new.kenyalaw.org/akn/ke/act/1998/2/eng@2022-12-31 [accessed January 2026].
67. KLR, 1999, 'Postal Corporation Act, 1999, Chapter 411', KLR, 2009, 'Kenya Communication (Amendment Act) No. 1 of 2009', all available at: https://new.kenyalaw.org/legislation/, [accessed January 2026].

resulting in the emergence of new market leaders such as Safaricom, the country's dominant market leader. Other players include Airtel Kenya and Telkom Kenya. In the2024/25, for instance, the country experienced a very high and adoption of smartphones. The demand for mobile money and mobile money services also increased during this period. In 2024/25, for example, the country experienced a significant increase in smartphone usage. Demand for mobile payment services and mobile money services also rose during this period. Of importance in this sector is M-Pesa, which as an alternative mobile money transfer service introduced in Kenya in 2007, and which enables people with our without access to banking services to store and transfer money on their cell phones, send and receive money, pay bills, purchase goods and services, and withdraw cash through a network of agents—all using their smartphones, without needing a bank account.Today, M-Pesa continues to drive innovation in other digital services, including mobile banking, e-commerce, and e-government, as well as empowering women. The CCK continues to promote competition in all areas of the telecommunications sector.[68]

93. The Kenya Information and Communication Act encapsulates provisions that deal with competition in the telecommunications sector. For instance, section 84Q of the Act prohibits business activities which have the goal of unfairly preventing, restricting or distorting competition. Section 84R of the Act mandates the CCK to ensure that there is fair competition in the sector, and to promote, develop and enforce fair competition and equality of treatment among licensees. Section 84S of the Act lists some of the business practices which may amount to breach of fair competition or equal access. It further empowers the CCK to make in accordance with section 84T of the Act, to declare anticompetitive such practices, and to declare the agreements or contracts associated therewith, null and void. According to section 84T of the Act, any person aggrieved by the decision of the Commission can appeal to the Tribunal dealing with telecommunications. The CCK also cooperates with the CAK in the investigation of restrictive trade practices in the sector and in the area of mergers and takeovers. The competition provisions for the sector include sections 5, 21 and part IV of the Competition Act. These provisions state that the Competition Act is applicable to all persons, including the Government, state corporations and local authorities, as far as they engage in trade. Through the CAK, the CCK limits state control on the licensing of participants in certain trades and professions by government agencies (e.g., telecommunications), promotes competition in the national economy and protects consumers from unfair market conduct.[69]

---

68. CCK, 2025, 'Fourth Quarter Sectors Statistics Report for the Financial Year 2024/2025' (1 April – 30 June 2025), available at https://www.ca.go.ke/sites/default/files/2025-09/Sector%20Statistics%20Report%20Q4%202024-2025_1.pdf [accessed January 2026]; Safaricom, 2025, Annual Report, 2025, available at: https://www.safaricom.co.ke/images/Downloads/Annual-2025-Reporrt.pdf [accessed January 2026].
69. Communications Commission of Kenya, 2012–2013, 'Annual Report 2012–2013', available at: https://www.ca.go.ke/sites/default/files/2023-05/Annual-Report-for-the-Financial-Year-2012-2013.pdf [accessed January 2026].

94. At international level, Kenya is a signatory to the WTO Agreement on Basic Telecommunications Services (BTA), which is an annex to the Fourth Protocol of the GATS. BTA was passed on 5 February 1998 with the goal of improving market access for telecommunications equipment suppliers, vendors and service providers by ensuring that all service suppliers seeking to take advantage of scheduled commitments have reasonable and non-discriminatory access to, and the use of, public basic telecommunications networks and services. BTA covers, among others, services such as voice telephony, data transmission, telex, telegraph, facsimile, fixed and mobile satellite systems and services, cellular telephony, mobile data services, etc. By acceding to the BTA, Kenya has committed to a set of definitions and principles on the regulatory framework for the BTA defined by the WTO, and in addition, consented to opening up its telecommunications services markets. The BTA is built into Kenya's competition policy of open and non-discriminatory market access by virtue of section 2.6 of the Constitution as read with section 5.4b of the Kenya Information and Communications Act.[70]

III. Tourism

95. Tourism, one of Kenya's pivotal service sectors, is the third highest contributor to GDP after agriculture and manufacturing and the largest foreign exchange earner after tea and horticulture. Initially, the entire tourism business was controlled and regulated by the Government. After the implementation of structural adjustment in the 1990s, the Government divested its interests in the industry and confined its role to providing an environment in which enterprises involved in tourism can thrive. Both the public and private sectors (comprising of local and foreign operators) play a significant role in the promotion of tourism. The public sector actors in Kenya include the Ministry of Tourism and Wildlife, Kenya Tourist Board and the Kenya Tourist Development Corporation (KTDC). These bodies play a significant role in marketing Kenya as a top tourist destination locally and globally. The KTDC owns the Bomas of Kenya, whose role is to promote, preserve and maintain Kenya's rich, diverse cultural values of the various ethnic groups of Kenya as a tourism product. The Kenya Wildlife Services (KWSs), created under the Wildlife Conservation and Management Act (WCMA), Chapter 376 of 1977,[71] conserves and manages wildlife in Kenya, and is responsible for formulating and enforcing the laws and regulations relating to sustainable conservation and utilisation of wildlife, fauna and flora, national parks and reserves. The other public players are the

70. WTO Reference Paper, 24 Apr. 1996, available at: https://www.wto.org/english/tratop_e/serv_e/telecom_e/tel23_e.htm [August 2013]; Owino, K., 2006, 'Kenya' in CUTS International, 2006, 'Competition Regimes in the World, A Civil Society', available at: https://competitionregimes.com/ [accessed August 2013]; Waema Mwololo, T., 2007, 'Kenya. Telecommunications Sector Performance Review: A Supply Side Analysis of Policy Outcomes', School of Computing and Informatics, University of Nairobi, Kenya; KLR, 1998, Kenya Information and Communications Act, available at: https://new.kenyalaw.org/akn/ke/act/1998/2/eng@2022-12-31 [accessed January 2026].

71. KLR, 2013, 'The Wildlife Conservation and Management Act, No. 47 of 2013', available at: https://www.kenyalaw.org/kl/fileadmin/pdfdownloads/Acts/WildlifeConservationandManagementActCap376_2_.pdf [accessed January 2026].

National Museums of Kenya, which manages and conserves monuments, sites, antiquities and historical resources, the Utalii College and the Tourist Police Unit. The Utalii College, the best training college for the tourism sector in Africa, established under the Tourist Industry Licensing Act Cap 381, provides training opportunities for frontline, supervisory and managerial personnel in the tourism and hospitality sectors, while the Tourist Police Unit is charged with ensuring the safety and security of tourists in the country.[72]

96. Indeed, the continuing liberalisation of the tourism sector, the creation of a borderless region that allows for the free movement of people and goods across the EAC countries, has significantly opened the sector to competition from foreign firms as well as investors from other EAC countries. In 2024, Kenya's tourism sector experienced a significant surge in international tourist arrivals, welcoming more visitors compared to 2023. This represents a growth of 14.6% in the sector. This growth has increased revenue from inbound tourism from KES. 377.49 billion in 2023 to KES 452.20 billion in the year 2024. This corresponds to growth of 19.79% in the industry. The significant improvement in the tourism sector can largely be attributed to a combination of sustainable tourism strategies, such as aggressive marketing strategies, improved infrastructure and a greater variety of travel options. In addition, the simplified electronic travel authorisation (ETA), the rise of package tours and a renewed global interest in travel to Kenya have further expanded the tourism market, to mention but a few. Though Kenya still faces stiff competition from regional players such as Rwanda, Tanzania, and South Africa, which have also intensified their tourism marketing strategies, Kenya is still one of the most popular tourist destinations in Africa. Tourism in Kenya is mainly based on natural attractions, which include its unique blend of wildlife reserves and beautiful clean beaches that allow visitors to enjoy the country's vibrant atmosphere.[73] For this reason, the management and conservation of wildlife continues to remain crucial in maintaining and improving Kenya's earnings from the tourism industry. The Government continues to underscore the importance of wildlife conservation through tougher conservation laws and Kenya has a considerable body of law (forty-four in total) regulating the tourism sector. This barrage of laws is complicated by the overlapping functions of more than fifteen public organisations regulating the sector and eleven associations and civil societies representing different markets. The most important of the laws includes the repealed Tourism Industry Licensing Act.[74] This Act establishes the Tourism Industry Licensing Authority (TILA) and licenses through the TILA, tourism-related businesses. It also regulates the private sector, which comprises of tour operators, travel agents, curio dealers, charter plans, etc.

72. Cuts International, 2008, 'Services Trade and Domestic Regulation in Kenya', Briefing Paper No. 5, available at: http://www.cuts-citee.org/pdf/Briefing_Paper08-Services_Trade_and_Domestic_Regulation_in_Kenya.pdf [accessed August 2013].
GATS, 1994, 'KENYA: Schedule of Specific Commitments', GATS/SC/47, 15 April.
73. Ministry of Tourism and Wildlife, 2024, 'Annual Tourism Sector Performance Report 2024' available at https://tri.go.ke/wp-content/uploads/2025/02/TRI-Tourism-Sector-Performance-Report-2024.pdf [accessed May 2025].
74. KLR, 1970, 'Tourism Industrial Licensing Act', Cap 381 of the Laws of Kenya, 1970, revised in 1990, available at https://new.kenyalaw.org/legislation/ [accessed January 2026].

The Hotels and Restaurants Act, Chapter 494 of the Laws of Kenya, revised in 1986, established the Hotels and Restaurants Authority to license hotels, lodges and restaurants, classify lodges, hotels and restaurants, and collect levies from them. It also processes work permits for foreign professionals in the industry. The Wildlife Conservation and Management Act[75] (hereinafter 'WCMA 2013') is the principal legislation that governs wildlife conservation and trade in Kenya. It repealed the previous legislation, Chapter 376 of the Laws of Kenya (WCMA 1989), and applies to all wildlife resources on public, community and private land, and Kenya's territorial waters. It is administered by the Ministry of Information and Tourism, which works together with the Kenya Tourist Board to develop, promote and coordinate a national tourism marketing strategy, market Kenya at local, national, regional and international levels as a premier tourist destination. The WCMA 2013 proscribes the hunting of game animals and trade in raw ivory by any person without a valid permit. The purpose of the Act is to consolidate and amend all the laws relating to the protection, conservation and management of wildlife in Kenya. The KWS is State Corporation established in 1990 under the WCMA 1989 to conserve and manage wildlife in Kenya, and to enforce related laws and regulations, including the WCMA 2013. It manages the biodiversity of the country, protecting and conserving the flora and fauna as well as all the national parks and reserves under its jurisdiction.[76]

97. The Competition Act does not contain provisions that directly apply to the tourism sector; its overall goal is still relevant to the tourism sector because its purpose is to promote and safeguard competition in the national economy and to protect consumers from unfair and misleading market conduct. Indeed, the Act plays a major role in shaping the structure of the tourism sector through its influence in shaping the structures of competition, and the setting forth of the rules necessary for the functioning of the market in which undertakings engaged in tourism or tourism-related businesses operate. Provisions that play a crucial role in the tourism industry include those that:

a. cover the market, i.e., the relationships between suppliers, wholesalers, retailers, and consumers;
b. the act applies to all economic activities within or having an effect within Kenya and to entities operating within the Kenyan borders, irrespective of what product or service such entities manufacture, sell, supply or offer; and
c. regulate restrictive agreements applicable to decisions and trade associations, abuse of dominant positions, mergers, unwarranted concentrations of economic power and consumer welfare.

---

75. KLR, 2013, 'The Wildlife Conservation and Management Act, No. 47 of 2013', available at: https://www.kenyalaw.org/kl/fileadmin/pdfdownloads/Acts/WildlifeConservationandManagementActCap376_2_.pdf [accessed January 2026].
76. UNCTAD, 2008, 'Services and Development: Implications for the Telecommunications, Banking and Tourism Services Sectors in Kenya', UNCTAD/DITC/TNCD/2007/2; The World Bank, 2010, 'Kenya's Tourism: Polishing the Jewel', Finance and Private Sector Development, African Region, World Bank, Washington DC.

98. Moreover, according to its GATS commitments schedule of 1994, Kenya made full commitment on the tourism and travel-related sector (hotels and restaurants, travel agencies and tour operators' services and tourist guides' services). Under these commitments, Kenya fully committed itself to almost full removal of tourism-related market access and national treatment restrictions that may hinder competition. Whereas these laws are likely to strengthen the enhance competition in the sector, they also have the potential of undermining the competitiveness of the players in the sector in Kenya.

§3. State-Owned Enterprises and Public Utilities

99. State-owned enterprises (hereinafter 'SoEs') or parastatals, as they are commonly known in Kenya, date back to the colonial period. They are also referred to sometimes as statutory bodies or statutory corporations and include semi-autonomous government agencies, trust funds and public enterprises. The British colonial masters used SoEs on the one hand as mechanisms for providing socially optimal levels of essential services to privileged white settlers, and on the other hand as a tool for locking out indigenous Kenyans from full participation in economic development processes. At independence, the government of Kenya decided to redefine its economic goals.

100. In its Sessional Paper No. 10 of 1965 on African Socialism and its Application to Kenya, the government of Kenya set as one of its objectives the re-invention of the SoEs into vehicles for economic empowerment and for increasing participation by Kenyans in the economy and promotion of indigenous entrepreneurship. As a result of this seminal paper, pre-independence SoEs then dominated by European administrators were strengthened and brought under the control of indigenous Kenyans. It was believed that this would help Kenyans to fully participate in the mainstream economic life. At the same time, new SoEs were established in sectors such as trade, transport, communications, manufacturing, education, agriculture, finance and banking sectors in which Kenyans were previously excluded. By 1990, the Kenya government not only held equity in 240 SoEs but also majority shareholdings in more than half of the newly formed SoEs.[77]

---

77. Atieno, Y., 2009, 'Corporate Governance Problems Facing Kenyan Parastatals: A Case Study of the Sugar Industry', available at: https://www.semanticscholar.org/paper/Corporate-Governance-Problems-facing-Kenyan-%3A-A-of-Atieno/8513d123efb7ab69525ca0fa6b395e95b9108a8d [accessed on January 2026]; Center for Governance and Development, 2005, 'A Decade of Parastatal Waste-A Study of the Audited Accounts of State Corporations Over the Period from 1993–2002', available at: https://books.google.de/books/about/A_Decade_of_Parastatal_Waste.html?id=3_y7AAAAIAAJ&redir_esc=yf [accessed on January 2026]; Whish, R., 2003, 'Competition Law', Lexis Nexis, Butterworths; Wambua, J., et al., 2005, 'A Decade of Parastatal Waste: A Study of the Audited Accounts of State Corporations over the Period from 1993 to 2002', a publication of Centre for Governance and Development/USAID, available at: http://openlibrary.org/books/OL21663250M/A_decade_of_parastatal_waste [accessed October 2013], Rubini, L., 2009, pp. 92, 93, 'The Definition of Subsidy and State Aid: WTO and EC Law in Comparative Perspective', Oxford University Press.

101. Though most of the SoEs are governed by the legal instrument under which they were set up, the State Corporations Act (hereinafter 'SCA')[78] remains the supreme law in all matters relating to management and control of SoEs in which the government has a direct or indirect controlling equity interest. Section 2 of the SCA defines a state corporation as:

a. a state corporation established under section 3 of the Act;
b. a body corporate established before or after the commencement of the Act by or under an Act of Parliament or other written law;
c. a cooperative society established under the Co-operative Societies Act, Chapter 490 of the Laws of Kenya; a building society established in accordance with the Building Societies Act; Chapter 489 of the Laws of Kenya; a company incorporated under Chapter 486 of the Laws of Kenya, which is not wholly owned or controlled by the Government or by a state corporation; the Central Bank of Kenya (CBK) established under the Central Bank Act, Chapter 491 of the Laws of Kenya;
d. a bank or a financial institution incorporated under the Banking Act, Chapter 488 of the Laws of Kenya; or other company incorporated under the Companies Act,[79] whose majority of the shares and stocks are owned by the Government or by another state corporation; or
e. a subsidiary of a state corporation.

102. SoEs operated under enabling laws under which they are established must, in accordance with sections 3 and 5A of the SCA, not only comply with the requirements of those enabling laws, but in addition, with the provisions of the SCA unless exempted therefrom by the President. Though the SoEs have continued to play an important role in the development process of the country, most of them have been performing so poorly mainly due to weak management, political interference, corruption and mismanagement. This has prompted the government to set up a task force to review their sizes, performance, relevance, viability and mandate duplication, and give a new policy direction as to how they can be privatised or rather weaned off so that they can become self-financing and beneficial to Kenyans. At the same time, the Government of Kenya recently announced the privatisation of 207 non-strategic SoEs and the merging of SoEs with overlapping functions with a view to smoothing service delivery.[80] The Privatisation Act,[81] which was expected to provide the legal framework for privatising SoEs in Kenya, became operational in 2008.

---

78. KLR, 1986, 'State Corporations Act, 1986, Chapter 446 of the Laws of Kenya', available at: https://kenyalaw.org/kl/fileadmin/pdfdownloads/Acts/StateCorporationsActCap446.pdf [accessed January 2026].
79. The SoEs such as those created under KLR, 1962, 'Companies Act, Chapter 486 of the Laws of Kenya', KLR, 1989, 'Banking Act Chapter 488 of the Laws of Kenya', and KLR, 1987, 'Insurance Act Chapter 487 of the Laws of Kenya' all available at: https://new.kenyalaw.org/legislation/, [accessed January 2026]., are required not only to comply with the requirements under the enabling Act, but also those of the SCA.
80. Office of the President, 2013, 'Report of the Presidential Taskforce on Parastatal Reforms', available at: http://www.cofek.co.ke [accessed October 2013], Mwaura, K., 2007, 'The Failure of Corporate

I. Banking Sector

103. Kenya Commercial Bank (KCB) has its roots in the National Bank of India, which opened its first outlet in Mombasa in 1896. In 1904, the bank extended its operations to Nairobi, where it continued running business until 1958, when it merged with Grindlays Bank to form the National and Grindlays Bank. After independence, the Government of Kenya acquired a 60% shareholding in National & Grindlays Bank in an effort to enable Kenyans to get access to credit and control their economy. In 1970, the Government acquired 100% of the National & Grindlays Bank shares and renamed the bank KCB. The Government has over the years reduced its holdings in KCB; for instance, in 2004, to 26.2% and in 2008 to 23.1%. The Government shareholding in KCB as of 2010 was 17.4%. Today, the KCB is one of Kenya's and Africa's largest commercial banks, giving financial services to all sectors of the economy, and with subsidiaries across EAC Member States, Burundi, Tanzania, Uganda, Rwanda and South Sudan.[82]

104. All banks in Kenya are licensed and regulated by the Central Bank of Kenya (CBK). According to section 4A of the Central Bank of Kenya Act, Chapter 491, as read with section 3 of the Banking Act, Chapter 488 of the Laws of Kenya, the CBK, which falls under docket of the Minister of Finance, is responsible for:

a. formulating and implementing monetary policy and fostering liquidity;
b. licensing of commercial banks, non-bank financial institutions, foreign exchange bureaus, mortgage finance institutions, as well as foreign banks; and
c. supervising the proper functioning of the financial system in Kenya.

105. The Companies Act, the Banking Act, the Central Bank of Kenya Act, the Microfinance Act, 2006 and various prudential guidelines issued by the CBK under section 33.4 of the Banking Act are the laws the latter uses to oversee the banking sector in Kenya. The prudential guidelines lay down a set of minimum rules that

Governance in State Owned Enterprises and the Need for Restructured Governance in Fully and Partially Privatized Enterprises: The Case of Kenya', Fordham International Law Journal, 31(1), Blanchard, P.L., 2013, 'U.S.-Kenya Relations: Current Political and Security Issues', 23 September, CRS Report for Congress Prepared for Members and Committees of Congress, R42967.

81. KLR, 2010, 'Privatisation Act, Chapter 485 of the Laws of Kenya', available at: : https://new.kenyalaw.org/legislation/, [accessed January 2026].

82. CGD Bills Digest, 2005, 'The National Social Security Pensions Trust Bill: The Making of a Better NSSF', Issue 03/05 August; David, M., 1981 'The Transition in Smallholder Banking in Kenya: Evidence from Rural Branch Bank Loans', The Journal of Developing Areas, 16(1), October, pp. 71–86; KCB undated, 'KCB Group History', available at: https://kcbgroup.com/our-history [accessed January 2026], Ministry of Finance Kenya, 1998, 'Policy Paper on Public Enterprise Reform and Privatisation', available at: http://www.pc.go.ke [accessed October 2013]; Ministry of Finance Kenya, 2012, 'State Corporations Annual Budget for 201/2014 Financial Year', DGIPE/A/1/10; Bird, N., and Kirira, N., 2009, 'Government Institutions, Public Expenditure and the Role of Development Partners: Meeting Kenya's Environmental Challenges', an Overseas Development Institute Report produced on behalf of the Danish Embassy – Nairobi.

are aligned with competition principles. These rules have to be adhered to by institutions in order to maintain a stable, competitive and efficient banking and financial system between banking institutions, individuals and corporations conducting banking business in Kenya.

106. Still, it would follow that in matters concerning competition and consumer welfare, the general rules of competition policy spelt out in the Competition Act and the Consumer Protection would apply with exceptions, especially due to the complex nature of the banking sector and its specificity. Special matters would have to remain within the framework of the numerous banking laws and the CAK would need to consider carefully which cases they take on and how and to what extent to apply the Competition Act and the Consumer Protection Act.

II. Insurance

107. The National Social Security Fund (NSSF) was established in 1965 under the National Social Security Fund Act.[83] The Fund mandates membership for all formal sector employers and salaried employees except for those exempted by the law. The aim of the fund was and still remains to provide benefits to retiring members as a lump sum rather than through periodic payments. An amendment to the Act in 1987 transformed NSSF into an autonomous State Corporation. The National Social Security Fund (NSSF) Act, No. 45 of 2013 was assented to on 24 December 2013 and commenced on 10 January 2014, thereby transforming NSSF from a Provident Fund to a Pension Scheme to which every Kenyan with an income must pay a defined percentage of his/her gross income so as to be eligible to social security benefits to workers, including retirement, survivor, invalidity benefits and a monthly life pension upon retirement. The Act establishes two funds, the Pension Fund and the Provident Fund, to guarantee contributions and the payment of benefits from both Funds. This provides social security for Kenyan workers and ensures their financial security throughout their working lives and in retirement.[84] NSSF remains a state-run pension scheme.

108. The insurance sector is regulated by the Insurance Regulatory Authority (IRA), a State Corporation whose mandate is to regulate, supervise and promote the growth of the insurance industry in Kenya. This includes safeguarding the interests of insurance beneficiaries through effective regulation and supervision. Insurance players regulated by IRA are, *inter alia*, insurance companies, reinsurance companies, microinsurance companies, insurance brokers, bancassurance intermediaries

83. KLR, 2013, 'National Social Security Fund Act, Chapter 258 of the Laws Kenya', available at: https://kenyalaw.org/kl/fileadmin/pdfdownloads/Acts/National_Social_Security_Fund_Cap._258_.pdf [accessed January 2026
84. *See* ss 3 and 4 of theNational Social Security Fund Act; Cytonn, 'The Kenya National Social Security Fund, March 2025', available at: https://cytonn.com/topicals/the-kenyan-national-3 [accessed May 2025].

and medical insurance providers. IRA works with various stakeholders, e.g., CAK locally, regionally and internationally, to develop guidelines and monitor insurance activities in the country to maintain a thriving, competitive and stable market. Due to cutthroat competition in the industry, which comprises fifty-eight licensed insurance companies, abuse of buyer power, price fixing and unscrupulous practices among insurers, improper marketing conduct, etc., are some of the competition issues that arise within the insurance industry. The IRA and the CAK, in acknowledging the interface between the two sectors, have signed a memorandum of understanding (MoU) that sets forth rules for the anticipated mergers and buyouts in the insurance sector to protect consumers from price fixing and insurance providers against anticompetitive behaviour. The rules will allow for mutual consultation and cooperation between IRA and CAK, who have concurrent jurisdiction with respect to the handling of mergers, potentially anticompetitive conduct, enforcement of and compliance with existing regulations, and issues concerning consumer protection. The MoU is expected to define the roles of CAK and IRA, minimise duplication of duties and eliminate any conflicting laws and policies by sharing information and enhancing the consistency in decision-making processes in matters of consumer protection and competition in the insurance market. The collaboration will also help both authorities to keep an eye on the challenges posed by the emerging local and global trends in the insurance sector and deal with the new trends in a competitive manner.[85]

III. Financial Aid from Public Authorities

109. The control by the Government of state provided aid is an integral part of competition policy in Kenya. Kenya has about 262 SoEs operating in different sectors of the economy. Most SoEs are funded differently, depending on how and why they were founded or depending on their functions or the sector under which they operate. Just like other SoEs in other countries, SoEs in Kenya are funded directly by the Government through economic resources provided directly by the Treasury as grants or equity, or loans borrowed from the government-on-government guarantee, or loans borrowed from foreign and local beneficiaries or obtained through bilateral arrangements. Others are required to internally generate their own revenue (i.e., through sales, licences and approval fees, levies for public services rendered by and/or user fee for use of facilities owned by the SoEs) after the first grant from

85. IRA, 2016, 'The Signing of the MoU Marks an Important Milestone That Strengthens the Work of Both the IRA and the CAK', available at: http://www.ira.go.ke/index.php/publications?layout=edit&id=237 [accessed August 2016]; Ombok, E., 2010, 'Kenya National Social Security Fund's Assets Fall 9.2% in Year to June '09', June 29, Bloomberg; *See* Insurance Act, Ch. 487 Laws of Kenya, available at: https://new.kenyalaw.org/akn/ke/act/1985/1/eng@2023-12-11 [accessed June 2025]; IRA, 2024, 'Insurance Industry Report for the Period Janaury- December 2023', Fourth Quater Release, February 2024, available at: https://www.ira.go.ke/assets/file/Q4_2023_Industry_Release.pdf [accessed June 2025].

the line ministry through the exchequer. Despite existing legal frameworks that guarantee accountability, governance and financial transparency in most SoEs in Kenya are still wanting. Most SoEs in Kenya can still administer the funds they collect or receive in form of loans in an unrestrained and unchecked manner. As indicated above, though most of the SoEs in Kenya are governed by the parent legislations under which they are established, the SCA is still the regulatory framework under which such SoEs are administered and managed.[86]

110. The SCA sets forth what the SoE responsibilities should be as regards the disbursement of funds they receive. For instance, sections 4 and 15 of the SCA, as read with sections 201d and e and 154 of the Constitution of Kenya, give powers to the Cabinet Secretary to give directions of a general character (including directions regarding finances) regarding the management of SoEs. These provisions dictate that the funds allocated to SoEs, being public monies, be disbursed prudently and aligned with the reasons for allocations, and further that reports submitted on fiscal outlays be clear and transparent. In effect, the Cabinet Secretary works together with the National Treasury not only to approve the establishment of the SoEs and their funding but also to defend their accounts before the Public Accounts Committee of the Parliament.[87] Moreover, section 5.2 of the Act empowers SoEs to borrow money in Kenya or from elsewhere, subject to approval by the Cabinet Secretary and limitations that the Treasury may impose upon them.

111. Part IV of the SCA directly regulates SoE finances. In particular, section 10A of the Act provides that the fiscal year of SoEs is to begin on 1 July in a year to 30 June in the next year. This corresponds to the nation's financial year and guarantees that during the reading of the annual budget, funds required by SoEs in a financial year are set aside. Section 11 of the SCA further requires every SoE to submit not later than February of each year, its estimates of revenue and of expenditure, as well as a list of projects to be undertaken in the following financial year and proposals for funding such projects to the Cabinet Secretary of the National Treasury and to the Treasury for approval. This system of checks and balances ensures that no SoE can, without the written approval of the Cabinet Secretary, incur expenditures beyond what it submitted in its estimates of expenditure for a given fiscal year. Section 14 the SCA requires each SoE to keep, *inter alia,* complete and accurate financial and property management records, and in accordance with Part III of the Public Audit Act, to submit on a yearly basis, their accounts to the Controller

86. Njiru, E., 2008, 'The Role of State Corporations in a Developmental State: the Kenyan Experience', 30th AAPAM Annual Roundtable Conference, Accra Ghana, 6th –10th October 2008; Obala, R., 2013, 'President Uhuru Kenyatta Unveils Team to Restructure Parastatals', Standard Digital, Kenya, 24 July; Okundi, B., 2013, 'There's a Need to Breath New Life into State Corporations Through Reforms, Daily Nation, Kenya, 25 September.
87. Friedrich-Ebert-Stiftung, 2012, 'Regional Disparities and Marginalisation in Kenya', available at: http://www.fes-kenya.org [accessed October 2013]; Migai-Akech, J.M., 2006, 'Development Partners and Governance of Public Procurement in Kenya: Enhancing Democracy in the Administration of Aid', IILJ Working Paper 2006/3; Global Administrative Law Series, available at: https://iilj.org/wp-content/uploads/2016/08/Akech-Development-Partners-and-Governance-of-Public-Procurement-in-Kenya-2006-2.pdf [accessed January 2026].

and Auditor-General (Corporations) for audit who accordingly to section 15 of the Public Audit Act[88] prepare a report on the examination and audit and submit the report to the Cabinet Secretary responsible for finance. The next paragraphs provide examples of SoEs whose mother Acts under which they are founded, and provide specifically how their funds are to be regulated. Indeed, since the Privatisation Act became law, a number of SoEs such as including those reviewed below, have been privatised.[89]

IV. The Kenya Tourist Development Corporation

112. Kenya Tea Development Agency (KTDA) is a corporation formed by section 3 of the Kenya Tourist Development Corporation Act.[90] Section 9 of the Act allows KTDA, subject to approval by the Cabinct Secretary for Finance, to borrow money from the government to enable meet its obligations and exercise its functions effectively and efficiently. However, the same section states that KTDA should at no given time have an overdraft of an amount above GBP 500,000, or an outstanding amount exceeding GBP 13,250.000 either received by way of advance from the government or borrowed from other sources. Moreover, section 10 of the Act permits the government to make advances to KTDA up to such amounts as may be provided by Parliament and guarantee the repayment of such sums by the KTDA. The same provision requires the Cabinet Secretary to present a statement to the Parliament, guaranteeing the repayment of the borrowed sums. Further, section 12 requires KTDA to create and maintain a reserve fund and ensure that the amounts in that fund are solely used to fulfil the corporation's obligations. Section 14 of the Act mandates the Corporation to maintain proper books of accounts and records in respect of business activities it undertakes in each fiscal year. Such records and accounts must be in accordance with Part II of the Public Audit Act, audited by the Auditor-General (Corporations). The application of antitrust laws to such records is as described in §3.III of this monograph.

88. KLR, 2010, 'Public Audit Act, Chapter 412b, Act No. 12 of 2003, Act No. 7 of 2007', available at: https://new.kenyalaw.org/akn/ke/act/2015/34/eng@2022-12-31 [accessed Janaury 2026].
89. Section 21 of the SCA entitles a person aggrieved by the decision of the Inspector to appeal in accordance to s. 11 of the Act to the State Corporations Appeal Tribunal. The Tribunal then considers and determines appeal, and may confirm, vary, or quash the decision of the Inspector and subsequently remit the case to the Inspector with such directions as it thinks fit. Section 23 of the Act states that further appeal against the Tribunal decisions lie in the High Court, whose decisions are final and not be subject to further appeal. Unfortunately, State Corporation Appeal Tribunal has never been constituted since the enactment of the Act 1986, and neither has the State Corporations Advisory Committee, whose function according to s. 26 of is administer the SCA ever been created.
90. KLR, 2010, 'The Kenya Tourist Development Corporation Act, 2010, Chapter 382 of the Laws of Kenya', available at: : https://new.kenyalaw.org/legislation/, [accessed January 2026].

V. The Kenya Broadcasting Corporation

113. Section 3 of the Kenya Broadcasting Corporation Act[91] (hereinafter 'KBC Act') establishes the KBC. Section 37 permits the government of Kenya to give the corporation financial grants, needed for day-to-day running of the company. Additionally, the Corporation can, pursuant to section 39 of the KBC Act, borrow money either by issuing loan stock or by taking credit from creditors in Kenya or outside Kenya on terms and conditions defined by the Minister for Finance. According to section 42.1 of the KBC Act, KBC must prepare estimates of revenue and expenditure for the following financial year before the start of every financial year. Such estimates must be prepared and approved by the Board and forwarded to the Minister for Finance for further approval. Section 42 prohibits the corporation from incurring any expenditure other than that proposed and approved. As with all other SoEs, KBC accounts must in accordance with section 43 be audited by the Auditor-General (Corporations). KBC being a broadcasting house is subject to competition.

§4. Appreciable Effect and De Minimis Rule

114. The maxim *de minimis non curat lex* is a Latin term that means the law does not concern itself with trifles. The *de minimis* rule, therefore, guides those applying the law in various sectors not to concentrate on matters that do not have any great significance or impact on the circumstances they are dealing with. The rule is applied in many branches of the law, including competition law, where its purpose is to save the time of competition authorities, which would otherwise unnecessarily involve themselves in investigating and adjudicating upon practices that do not have any tangible effect on a market.

115. In Kenya, the *de minimis* rule is used to describe small amounts of funding that do not require the approval of authorities. The rule is based on the assumption that small amounts of aid generally have negligible impact on trade and market competition and therefore do not need approvals.[92] There must be an appreciable effect on such amounts. Sections 21.1 and 2 of the Competition Act prohibit vertical and horizontal restrictive trade practices. Any agreements between undertakings, decisions by undertakings or concerted practices by undertakings (in horizontal and vertical relationships) whose *object* or *effect* is the prevention, distortion or lessening of competition in Kenya or a part of Kenya are prohibited. But that is as far as it goes. The Competition Act, the SCA and the Public Finance Management Act 2012 are all silent on the application of the *de minimis* rule to state aids granted to SoEs. The legislations do not also define the requirement of 'appreciability', meaning that there is no cap on state aid amounts, which may appreciably be provided to SoEs from public funds.

91. KLR, 2010, 'The Kenya Broadcasting Corporation Act, Chapter 221 of the Laws of Kenya', available at: : https://new.kenyalaw.org/legislation/, [accessed January 2026].
92. Hojnik, J., 2013, 'De Minimis Rule Within the EU Internal Market Freedoms: Towards a More Mature and Legitimate Market?' European Journal of Legal Studies, 6(1), 25–45.

Chapter 3. Overview of Substantive Provisions

§1. Restrictive Agreements

116. Sub-paragraphs 1, 3 and 4 of section 21 of the Competition Act define restrictive agreements as those between undertakings, decisions by associations of undertakings, decisions by undertakings or concerted practices by undertakings which have as their object or effect the prevention, distortion or lessening of competition in trade in any goods or services in Kenya, or a part of Kenya. An amendment to section 2[93] of the Competition Act states that the term 'agreement', when used in relation to a restricted practice, includes a contract, arrangement or understanding, whether legally enforceable or not. The same amendment provides that a concerted practice means cooperative or coordinated conduct between firms, achieved through direct or indirect contact, that replaces their independent action, but which does not amount to an agreement.

117. Section 21.8 of the Competition Act, however, exempts from the application of section 21. 1 of the Competition Act, all agreements entered into, or practices engaged in by companies, their wholly owned subsidiaries or wholly owned subsidiary of the subsidiaries. Restrictive practices are not just confined to situations listed in section 21.3 of the Competition Act. According to section 21.5 of the Competition Act, restrictive agreement also exist between two or more undertakings if any one of the undertakings owns a significant interest in the other, or has at least one director or one substantial shareholder in common. However, according to section 21.6 of the Competition Act, this presumption may be rebutted if a party, director or shareholder concerned establishes that a reasonable basis exists to conclude that any practice in which the parties engaged was a normal commercial response to conditions prevailing in the market.

118. For the purpose of this rebuttal, section 21.7 of the Competition Act defines the term 'director' to include:

a. a director of a company as defined in the Companies Act;
b. in relation to an undertaking conducted by a society, a person responsible jointly with others for its management;
c. a trustee of a trust;
d. or in relation to an undertaking conducted by an individual or a partnership, the owner of the undertaking or a partner of the partnership; and
e. in relation to any other undertaking, a person responsible either individually or jointly with others for its management.

119. Any undertaking that engages in the practices or enters into agreements described above is considered engaging in a prohibited restrictive trade practice, and

93. Finance Bill, 2014, Kenya Gazette Supplement No. 87 (National Assembly Bills No. 25), 12 Jun. 2014.

its directors and officers will be liable to large fines and/or jail sentences. Other than undertakings, section 22 of the Competition Act prohibits trade associations from entering into restrictive agreements or engaging in predatory trade practices that repress competition. Among the non-exhaustive practices, which are considered restrictive under section 22, are unjustifiable exclusion from a trade association of any person carrying on or intending to carry on in good faith the trade in relation to which the association in question is formed.

120. In determining whether an exclusion from such an association is unjustifiable, the CAK may, according to section 22 of the Competition Act, examine, in addition to any other relevant matters, the application of any rules of that association and the reasonableness of those rules. Recommendations (aimed at defeating or evading the application of the provisions of the Competition Act) made by an Association directly or indirectly to its members or to any class of its members may also be considered restrictive trade practices if they relate to:

a. the prices charged or to be charged by such members or any such class of members, or to the margins included in the prices or to the pricing formula used in the calculation of those prices; or
b. the terms of sale (including discount, credit, delivery, and product and service guarantee terms) of such members or any such class of members and which directly affect prices, profit margins included in the prices or the pricing formula used in the calculation of prices.

121. According to section 22.4 of the Competition Act, where a specific recommendation whether express or implied is made by, or on behalf of a trade association to its members or to any class of its members, concerning an action to be taken or not to be taken by them in relation to any matter affecting the trading conditions of those members, the provisions of Competition Act apply, as if membership of the association constituted an agreement under which the members agreed with the association and with each other to comply with the recommendations, notwithstanding anything to the contrary in the constitution or rules of the association.

§2. Dominant Undertakings

122. The Competition Act applies, according to its section 5, to all persons, including the Government, SoEs and local authorities insofar as they engage in trade. Section 4.3 of the Competition Act defines a dominant person as one who:

a. produces, supplies, distributes or otherwise controls not less than one-half of the total goods of any description that are produced, supplied or distributed in Kenya or any substantial part thereof; or
b. provides or otherwise controls not less than one half of the services that are rendered in Kenya or any substantial part of Kenya.

123. Section 23 of the Competition Act applies the same words used in defining a dominant person to define a dominant undertaking. According to section 2 of the Act, the word 'undertaking' means any business carried on for gain or reward by an individual, a body corporate, an unincorporated body of persons or a trust in the production, supply or distribution of goods or the provision of any service. Section 4.2 of the Competition Act lists down factors that can make person or an entity dominant in any given market. These include the importation into Kenya by persons resident in Kenya or abroad, of goods or services, the economic circumstances of the affected market and the market shares of the persons or entities supplying or acquiring goods or services in a given market. The dominance referred to in this section is about the position of economic strength an entity or person enjoys in a given market. This position must accord that entity or person such great market power over its competitors and consumers such that enable it to hinder competitive trade in that market. An amendment to section 2[94] of the Competition Act states that the term 'market power' is the power of a firm to control prices, to exclude competition or to behave to an appreciable extent, independently of its competitors, customers or suppliers.

124. Section 24 of the Competition Act prohibits persons or entities with a dominant position in their economic sector from abusing this position and from distorting competition in Kenya, and lists the following examples as abusive practices. Such practice must have an impact on trade:

a. imposing unfair purchase or selling prices or other unfair trading conditions;
b. limiting or restricting production, market outlets or market access, technical development, etc. through predatory or other practices;
c. applying dissimilar conditions to equivalent transactions with other trading parties.

125. According to the CAK factors, such as geographical price discrimination, customer loyalty, rebates and loyalty reprograms, price cuts aimed at eliminating a competitor from a particular market, unjustified refusal to supply goods or services, and refusal to grant licences are other forms of competitive tools that determine dominance in a market.[95] Entities with a dominant position are prohibited from contravening section 24 of the Competition Act, and are liable under section 24.3 to not more than five years or to a fine of not more than KES 10 million or both if they abuse their dominant positions.

94. *Ibid.*
95. CAK, undated, 'Consolidated Guidelines on the Substantive Assessment of Restrictive Trade Practices under the Competition Act', available at: https://cak.go.ke/arch/sites/default/files/Consolidated%20Guidelines%20on%20Restrictive%20Trade%20Practices%20.pdf [January 2026].

§3. Concentrations

126. Provisions on unwarranted concentration of economic power are found in sections 50–54 of Kenya's Competition Act. An amendment to section 2[96] of the Competition Act states that the term 'unwarranted concentration of economic power' means the existence of cross-directorship between two distinct undertakings or companies producing substantially similar goods or services and whose combined market share is more than 40%.

127. The concept can encompass a merger of two distinct and independent entities, an acquisition of an entity or entities by one or more persons or entities already established in business, or merger of two (or more) previously independent undertakings to form a joint venture. The Act makes mention of two types of mergers. Section 41.1 states that a merger occurs when one or more undertakings directly or indirectly acquire or establish direct or indirect control over the whole or part of the business of another undertaking. Section 41.2 states that a merger, as defined in section 41.1, may be achieved by:

a. the purchase or lease of shares, acquisition of an interest or purchase of assets of the other undertaking in question;
b. the acquisition of a controlling interest in a section of the business of an undertaking capable of being operated independently, whether or not the business in question is carried on by a company;
c. the acquisition of an undertaking under receivership by another undertaking situated either inside or outside Kenya;
d. acquiring by whatever means the controlling interests in a foreign undertaking that has a controlling interest in a subsidiary in Kenya;
e. in the case of a conglomerate undertaking, acquiring the controlling interest of another undertaking or a section of the undertaking being acquired capable of being operated independently;
f. vertical integration;
g. exchange of shares between or among undertakings which result in substantial change in ownership structure through whatever strategy or means adopted by the concerned undertakings; or
h. amalgamation, takeover or any other combination with the other undertaking.

128. In order to guard against unwarranted concentration of economic power, section 50 of the Competition Act endows the CAK with board powers that enable it to keep under review structures of production and distribution of goods and services supplied and distributed in Kenya. The goal is to determine where concentrations of economic power exist whose detrimental impact on the economy may outweigh the efficiency advantages of integration in production or distribution. Subsection 2 of section 50 as read with section 52 of the Act gives the CAK the authority to carry out investigations into any economic sectors, including persons whose

96. Finance Bill, 2014, Kenya Gazette Supplement No. 87 (National Assembly Bills No. 25), 12 Jun. 2014.

trade practices demonstrate unwarranted concentration of economic power. The CAK has power to make appropriate orders against such sectors/persons directing them to dispose of such portion of their interests in production, distribution or the supply of services as the CAK deems necessary to remove the unwarranted concentration. Section 52 allows institutions or persons aggrieved by the decision of the CAK to appeal to the Tribunal. The effect of sections 50–54 of the Competition Act is to leave the construction and implementation of these provisions to the CAK and the Tribunal. This has the advantage of enabling all cases regarding unwarranted concentration of economic power to be dealt with uniformly by the CAK and the Tribunal.

129. Section 42 of the Competition Act also prohibits the implementation of mergers without the approval of the CAK. The CAK affects the approval by way of an authorising order, without which no merger can have a legal effect in Kenya. Moreover, no rights or obligations imposed on the participating parties by an agreement in respect of the merger can be enforced by an action in any Kenyan court of law. This section helps CAK to control concentration in mergers between companies that fulfil the requirements laid down under the Competition Act. Respective laws regulate sector-specific mergers in the telecommunications, insurance, tourism and banking sectors.

§4. Other Prohibitions

130. The prohibitions regarding unwarranted concentrations have a broad palette that, under section 55 of the Competition Act, encompass safety standards for consumer goods and product-related services. The section prohibits the making of misleading representations in regard to standard, quality, value, grade, composition, history, previous use, value grade, place of origin or price, etc. of goods and services.

131. Other than these, sections 56 and 57 further prohibit unconscionable conduct by persons or entities in business transactions in all sectors, including sectors such as banking, micro-finance and insurance. Both sections contain a non-exhaustive list that the CAK should take into account when assessing whether conduct in relation to trade in connection with the supply or possible supply of goods or services to a person or undertaking in Kenya is unconscionable. For persons and suppliers of goods and services, these include:

a. the bargaining strength of the parties, i.e., the supplier and the consumer of goods and services;
b. whether any unreasonable conditions are imposed on the weaker party so as to protect the legitimate interests of the stronger party;
c. whether the consumer could understand the documentation used in supplying the goods and services in question;
d. the use of undue influence or pressure, or any unfair tactics, was used against the consumer;

e. the amount for which, and the circumstances under which a consumer could have acquired similar goods or services from a completely different supplier.

132. For supplier of goods and services, further unconscionable practices include:

a. the requirements of any applicable industry code;
b. other requirements, i.e., that a business consumer acted on the reasonable belief that the supplier would comply with that code;
c. failure by the supplier to disclose to reasonably disclose nature of the business to the consumer;
d. any other intended conduct of the supplier that might affect the interests of the business consumer;
e. willingness by the supplier to negotiate terms of the contract for supplier of goods and services with the business consumer; and
f. the readiness to act in good faith on the part of both parties.

133. Section 56.3 also prohibits persons or entities in the banking, micro-finance and insurance sectors from imposing charges and fees on customers not brought to the attention of the customer before the provision or supply of goods. In determining whether an unconscionable conduct exists in trade, the CAK can according to section 56.6 consider any circumstances that were not reasonably foreseeable at the time of the alleged contravention; and/or have regard to conduct parties engaged in, or circumstances existing, before the commencement of the Competition Act.

§5. Tests of Illegality

I. Per Se Prohibitions and Naked Restraints in Kenya

134. As already indicated above, sections 21 and 22 of the Competition Act prohibit agreements between undertakings, decisions by associations of undertakings, decisions by undertakings or concerted practices by undertakings or practices conducted on behalf of trade associations which have the effect of preventing, distorting or lessening of competition in trade in any goods or services in Kenya.

II. Balancing Tests

135. Balancing test or rule of reason determines whether a conduct should be classified as anticompetitive, and its effects, positive and negative, on consumer welfare are considered. The per se prohibition provisions of section 21 of the Competition Act apply to horizontal agreements between competing undertakings as well as to supplier-customer relationships in vertical agreements, and prohibit according to section 21.3 agreements and practices in which competitors agree to:

a. directly or indirectly fix purchase or selling prices or any other trading conditions;
b. divide or allocate customers, suppliers or territories among themselves with the goal of sheltering themselves from competition and denying business consumers the benefit of choice;
c. bid rig;
d. sell products or services at certain prices (resale price maintenance (RPM)) to prevent potential resellers from setting their prices independently; however, according to section 21.4, a supplier of goods and services may recommend a resale price to a reseller of the goods or a provider of the service, so long as the supplier expressly stipulates to the reseller that the recommended price is not binding, or if any product, or any document or thing relating to any product or service bears a price affixed or applied by the supplier, the words 'recommended price' appear next to the price so affixed or applied;
e. limit or control production, market outlets/access, technical development or investment;
f. apply dissimilar conditions to equivalent transactions with other trading parties, thereby placing them at a competitive disadvantage.

136. CAK may under section 50.4 of the Competition Act consider unwarranted concentration of economic power as prejudicial to the public interest if, having regard to the economic conditions prevailing in the country and to all other relevant factors, the effect such concentration leads to:

a. unreasonable increase of the costs relating to the production, supply or distribution of goods or the provision of services; or
b. unreasonably increase of:
   - the price at which the goods are sold; or
   - the profits derived from the production, supply or distribution of goods or from the performance of any services; or
c. lessening, distortion or limitation of competition in the production, supply or distribution of goods or the provision of any services;
d. deterioration in quality of any goods or in the performance of any services; or
e. inadequacy in the production, supply or distribution of any goods or services.

137. Individuals, entities and associations can, under sections 25, 28 and 29 of the Competition Act, apply to the CAK for exemption from restrictive practices in respect to any agreement or category of agreements; any decision or category of decisions; or any concerted practice or category of concerted practices that fall within the ambit of sections 21 and 22 of the Competition Act.

138. The CAK may grant the exemption if it is satisfied that there are exceptional and compelling reasons of public policy that justify the exemption of an undertaking or an association from the provisions of section 21 or 22 of the Competition Act.

139. In determining the exemption, section 25 of the Competition Act states that the CAK may take into consideration the extent to which the said agreement, decision or concerted practices:

a. contribute to or result in the maintaining or promoting exports;
b. improve or prevent decline in the production or distribution of goods or the provision of services;
c. promote technical or economic progress or stability in any industry; or
d. bring about a benefit for the public, which benefit should outweigh its anticompetitive detriments.

140. Section 27 of the Competition Act allows the CAK to revoke the exemption if it is satisfied that the exemption was granted on materially incorrect or misleading information, or if there has been a material change of circumstances since the exemption was granted, or if a condition upon which an exemption was granted has not been complied with. The CAK retains the discretion to grant an exemption subject to such other conditions and for such periods as it may consider appropriate.

III. Merger Tests

141. In considering the effects a merger may have on competition, the CAK applies the Substantial Lessening of Competition (SLC) and the Public Interest Test (PIT). SLC test focuses on economic efficiency and consumer benefits indicators such as markets and their structures, industry concentration, barriers to entry and exit, extent of countervailing buying power, efficiency gains or customer benefits, as well as the anticompetitive outcomes/out restrictions that the merger may generate. These indicators are gauged by looking into whether the merger or acquisition in question is horizontal, i.e., involving actual or potential competitors, whether the extant competitors in a given market or industry are likely to exert pressure on the merged entities and the extent of competitive struggles for market shares and position between such entities.

142. The PIT test, however, considers the extent to which a merger affects employment, the ability of other smaller entities to gain access or to be competitive in any sector or industry or the ability of national industries to compete in international markets or an industrial sector. The PIT test further takes into consideration the economic benefits the merger, takeover or acquisition is likely to bring in form of opportunities in research and development (R&D), technical efficiency, increased production, or improvements in systems of distribution of goods or provision of services, as well as market entry and exit of potential and existing competitors. The outcome of both tests depends on the thresholds applied.[97]

97. Hewitt, G., 2004, pp. 96–97, 'Substantive Criteria used for Assessment of Mergers: Background Note', OECD Journal of Competition Law and Policy, Vol. 6(3).

143. The Competition Act prohibits business deals whose probable anticompetitive consequences outweigh their likely benefits. Consequently, the CAK applies both the dominance and SLC tests when determining mergers. Section 41 of Kenya's Competition Act gives non-exhaustive examples of situations that the CAK has to take into consideration when deciding whether a merger is anticompetitive. These include cases where the person or entity controlling the undertaking being merged:

a. beneficially owns more than one-half of the issued share capital of the undertaking;
b. is entitled to vote a majority of the votes that may be cast at a general meeting of the undertaking, or has the ability to control the voting of a majority of those votes, either directly or through a controlled entity of that undertaking;
c. is able to appoint, or to veto the appointment of, a majority of the directors of the undertaking;
d. is a holding company, and the undertaking is a subsidiary of that company as contemplated in the Companies Act;
e. in the case of the undertaking being a trust, has the ability to control the majority of the votes of the trustees or to appoint the majority of the trustees or to appoint or change the majority of the beneficiaries of the trust;
f. in the case of the undertaking being a nominee undertaking, owns the majority of the members' interest or controls directly or has the right to control the majority of members' votes in the nominee undertaking; or
g. as the ability to materially influence the policy of the undertaking in a manner comparable to a person who, in ordinary commercial practice, can exercise an element of control referred to in paragraphs (a) to (f).

Chapter 4. Overview of the Main Notions

§1. Undertakings

144. According to section 5.1 of the Competition Act, all types of businesses engaged in the supply and acquisition of goods and or services, regardless of their legal status, and the way in which they are financed, are considered undertakings in context of section 2 of the Act.[98]

145. Section 2 of the Competition Act gives no definition of the term 'business'. Nevertheless, the definition of the term 'undertaking' is so broad as to enable the CAK to exercise control over all markets falling within and beyond the parameters of the Competition Act. Sections 21 and 23 of the Competition Act prohibit undertakings in horizontal, vertical or conglomerate relationships from engaging in restrictive trade practices or from attaining and maintaining a dominant position within the common markets.

§2. Relevant Market

146. A market is the geographical field of rivalry where producers, sellers and buyers meet to competitively trade or exchange their goods and services. The market power of undertakings operating in any given market is determined by the relevant market. The relevant market definition helps in analysing the area in the market where market participants' actions can impact both competition and the competitive conditions in the market. This definition is also used to identify the restrictions of competition that exist in these markets and to determine whether these restrictions are anti-competitive. The concept of relevant market has two dimensions: the product market and the relevant geographic market. This concept was first introduced by the US Supreme Court in the antitrust case *Standard oil*[99] decided in the mid-twentieth century, and has today become a fundamental part of market definition in many jurisdictions across the world, including Kenya.

147. Product and geographical scopes are considered when determining actual competitors of companies involved in a given market that are capable of constraining their behaviour and preventing them from exercising their commercial freedom. In determining the product dimension of the market, the relevant market definition puts together products (of the same class or that are closely related) that are essentially interchangeable or substitutable by the end customer, due to characteristics of the products or services, their intended use or their prices. The product market describes the market where the final goods or services are exchanged.

98. Finance Bill, 2014, Kenya Gazette Supplement No. 87 (National Assembly Bills No. 25), 12 Jun. 2014.
99. *Standard Oil v. United States*, 221 U.S. 1, 61 (1911).

148. The geographical aspect of a relevant market refers to the territory, national, regional or international in which entities involved supply their goods or provide their services, and in which the conditions of competition are sufficiently homogeneous. In other words, the geographical area deals with undertakings in the same area of operation whose individual prices are likely to affect all other undertakings. Every relevant market includes a geographic market for the obvious reason that entities operating in mutually exclusive geographic areas are not in competition, and thus do not limit each other's ability to increase price significantly. Identification of a relevant market is, therefore, an important aspect in the definition of a market.[100]

149. Section 4 of the Competition Act defines the term 'market' as meaning:

> a market in Kenya or a substantial part of Kenya and refers to the range of reasonable possibilities for substitution in supply or demand between particular kinds of goods or services and between suppliers or acquirers, or potential suppliers or acquirers, of those goods or services.

150. According to this provision, there are three requirements that must be satisfied in defining markets, assessing effects on competition or determining whether a person has a dominant position in a market. These include:

a. importation of goods or the supply of services by persons not resident or carrying on business in Kenya;
b. economic circumstances prevailing in the relevant market and the market shares of the persons/entities supplying or acquiring goods or services in the market, the ability of those persons/entities to expand their market shares and the potential for new entry into the market.

The CAK's role according to this provision is therefore to analyse the market based on the nature of the product or services available therein; the geographical area where they are sold ; the availability of substitute products and services and actual consumer preferences.

151. Under the same provision, an entity is considered to have a dominant position in the market if it:

100. Ten Kate, A. and Niels, G., 2009, pp. 300–302, 'The Relevant Market: A Concept Still in Search of Definition', Journal of Competition Law and Economics, 5(2); Melischek, A.C., 2013, pp. 29–33, 'The Relevant Market in Economic Law: A Comparative Antitrust and GATT Analysis', Cambridge University Press; Taylor, Martin, 2006, pp. 8–15, 'International Competition Law: A New Dimension for the WTO', Cambridge University Press; CAK, 2009 'Guidelines for Market Definition', available at: https://cak.go.ke/arch/sites/default/files/Guidelines%20on%20Relevant%20Market%20Definition%20(1).pdf [accessed January 2026].

a. produces, supplies, distributes or otherwise controls not less than one-half of the total goods of any description that are produced, supplied or distributed in Kenya or any substantial part thereof; or
b. provides or otherwise controls not less than one-half of the services that are rendered in Kenya or any substantial part thereof.

152. In the context of competition, a definition of the 'relevant market' for lines of commerce where healthy competition is vital is, therefore, not only a necessary precondition for determining whether an anticompetitive exists in a defined market but it would help the CAK and other competition authorities working with it to understand the market, calculate the market shares, assess market power, allocate markets to consumers thereby ensuring fair competition and preventing anti-competitive practice.[101] The CAK uses the concept of relevant market to identify and combat anti-competitive practices, including agreements between competitors (cartels), and the abuse of a dominant market position, and analyses their impact on consumers and the economy in general. Further, the CAK is able to define actual competitors in market, control their market behaviour and prevent them from behaving independently of their competitors, customers and suppliers. Moreover, a proper definition of the market also helps the CAK to determine which competitors in a given market fall within the prohibitions outlined in the Competition Act. This in turn increases transparency and predictability for entities trading in Kenya with regard to the application of the Competition Act, promotes and safeguards competition in the national economy, and protects consumers from unfair and misleading market practices. In *Airtel Kenya Ltd v. Safaricom Ltd,*[102] the CAK received a complaint from Airtel Kenya Limited against Safaricom Limited with regard to abuse of dominance practices contrary to the provisions of the Competition Act. Airtel claimed that Safaricom Limited had entered into agreements with its M-PESA agents to hinder them from offering mobile money transfer services to competing providers. The CAK in considering whether Safaricom Limited was a dominant undertaking as defined under the Competition Act and whether it abused its dominance by entering into exclusive arrangements with its M-PESA agents, contrary to sections 23 and 24.2(b) of the Competition Act, found that Safaricom Limited was dominant in the mobile money transfer service market and that the arrangement between itself and its agents restricted competition in the market in breach of the Competition Act.

---

101. *See* for example, Official Journal of the European Union, 2024, Communication from the Commission, 'Commission Notice on the Definition of the Relevant Market for the Purposes of Union Competition Law' (C/2024/1645), pp. 4–17, avaiable at: https://eur-lex.europa.eu/legal-content/EN/TXT/PDF/?uri=OJ:C_202401645 [accessed June 2025].
102. *Airtel Kenya Limited v. Safaricom Limited,* CAK/EC/05/34/A, 18 Jul. 2014, Competition and Consumer Protection Law Digest, 1st, Edition August 2011-June 2022.

§3. MARKET POWER AND DOMINANT POSITION

153. From the competition point of view, market power is the ability of an entity or entities to raise prices profitably above the competitive level for a significant period. Most competition authorities intercede only where it is clear that the market power is not just unilateral but also significantly impedes competition. Generally, market share is the single most important criterion used to determine the existence of market power. Market share can help an entity to achieve greater scale in its operations and improve profitability, and give it the advantage to manipulate prices and outputs in crucial markets. Market power, if wielded well, enables the entity enjoying the power to create over-capacity or other barriers to market entry that eventually restrict competition.[103]

154. The Competition Act does not define the term 'market power'. However, from the description of unwarranted concentration of economic power as given in section 50.4 of the Act, market power refers to the extent to which an enterprise can influence the quality, quantity and prevailing prices of goods and services by exercising control over their demand and supply thereof. Enterprises that exploit their market power in a way that hurts competition in the marketplace have dominant market positions. A definition of a dominant undertaking has been provided in this Part 1, Chapter 4, §2 of this monograph.

§4. AGREEMENTS AND CONCERTED PRACTICES

155. An agreement whether express or conditional is a concord between two or more people, each of whom intends to create one or more legal obligations between them. An agreement need not be in writing to be enforceable and binding. Section 21 of the Competition Act, which prohibits agreements whose purpose is to restrict, distort or prevent competition, has a very broad definition of the term 'agreement' that includes not just agreements but also decisions of undertakings and concerted practices. It defines the term 'agreements' as 'agreements between undertakings, decisions by associations of undertakings, decisions by undertakings or concerted practices by undertakings which have as their object or effect the prevention, distortion or lessening of competition in trade in any goods or services in Kenya, or a part of Kenya, are prohibited, unless they are exempted by the Act'.

156. According to section 21 of the Competition Acts, not just agreements, decisions and concerted practices are included in the word 'agreement', the term also refers to agreements concluded between parties in a horizontal relationship, being undertakings trading in competition; or parties in a vertical relationship, being an undertaking and its suppliers or customers or both. Section 21.3 of the Act contains

103. Office of Fair Trading UK, 2004, 'Assessment of Market Power', available at: https://www.gov.uk [accessed March 2015]; Kato, M., 2009, pp. 393–395, 'Transitoriness of Market Power and Antitrust Activity', Journal of Competition Law and Economics, 6(2), 393; Park, S., 2009, p. 571, 'Market Power in Competition for the Market', Journal of Competition Law and Economics, 5(3), 571.

a non-exhaustive list of agreements, decisions or concerted practices, which, for the purpose of the Act, have as their object or effect the prevention, restriction or distortion of competition in Kenya. These have already been defined vividly in Part I, Chapter 3, §5, II of this monograph.

§5. Restriction of Competition

157. As mentioned above, agreements, decisions or concerted practices that may prevent, distort or restrict competition either because of their object or their effects are prohibited unless exempted by the CAK as spelt out in section 25 of the Competition Act. According to section 21.3 of the Competition Act, the test for determining whether there is restriction in competition consists of first establishing whether the agreements, decisions or concerted practices are a restriction by object, and, if not, whether they qualify as a restriction by effect.

158. In short, whether such agreements, decisions or concerted practices are harmless trade ventures or whether they place trading parties thereto at a competitive disadvantage, an examination of the specific circumstances in which they are made is essential. Such a determination requires a detailed examination of the commercial purpose of the agreement, decisions or concerted practices (based on the factors outlined in section 21.3 of the Competition Act), as well as the legal and economic context in, which they are applied, the behaviour of the parties on the market, and whether or not the agreements have as their object the restriction of competition.

§6. Abuse of Dominance

159. According to section 23 of the Competition Act, an undertaking in a dominant position is one that uses its significant strength in a given market to eliminate or restrict competition. According to the provision, being in a dominant position is in itself not anticompetitive; however, the power such an undertaking wields in a market becomes predatory when the undertaking takes advantage of its market power to eliminate competition or deter potential competitors from entering the market. Abuse of dominance is dealt with in detail in Part II, Chapter 2 of this monograph.

§7. Concentrations

160. Concentration of economic power occurs when two or more previously independent undertakings in a market merge, or when one or more undertakings acquire control over the other. Section 41 of the Competition Act states that a merger 'occurs when one or more undertakings directly or indirectly acquire or establish direct or indirect control over the whole or part of the business of another undertaking'. Section 50 of the Competition Act gives the CAK the power to evaluate the effects of such concentrations of economic power on the production and distribution of goods and services in Kenya to determine where competition-hindering concentrations of economic power exist. The section empowers the CAK to investigate the unwarranted concentration of economic power in any economic sector to remove impediments to competition.

161. According to section 50.4 of the Competition Act, unwarranted concentration of economic power is prejudicial to the public interest if it unduly increases the costs of manufacture or distribution, selling prices of goods or services, lessens competition, or reduces the quality of goods and services or prevents or limits the supply thereof to consumers. Some of the factors the CAK considers in determining 'public interest' within the context of section 50.4 of the Act are the extent to which the unwarranted concentration of economic power is likely to affect a particular industrial sector, employment and the ability of small undertakings to gain access or to be competitive in any market. It also looks at how such power will affect the ability of national industries to compete in international markets.

162. Given that these factors are likely to change as the decisions on public policy change to align with new technologies, trade and economic progress, the CAK is constantly reviewing the factors behind the unwarranted concentration of economic power as well as their economic consequences, and coining measures to protect public interest.

§8. Joint Ventures

163. The term 'joint venture' describes a variety of business arrangements or individuals who identify a business opportunity and pull their resources together with the goal of exploiting a set goal or objective through a new entity, which they incorporate for that purpose. One of the most common features of a joint venture is the pooling together of resources between competitors. Once the joint venture comes into existence, the entities coming together no longer compete in the same market, but operate in the same market as a single outfit. The merged entities retain their legal and economic independence while still working hard to achieve an objective they could attain on their own. Depending on the arrangement, joint ventures may either handicap competition or promote economic efficiency and innovation.[104]

104. Kauper, E.T., 1996, 'The Problem of Market Definition', Fordham International Law Journal, 20(5), 1682, available at: http://ir.lawnet.fordham.edu/cgi/viewcontent.cgi?article=1804&context=ilj [accessed on July, 2014]; Competition Bureau Canada, 2012, 'Abuse of Dominance: A Serious Competitive Offence', available at: https://competition-bureau.canada.ca/en/how-we-foster-competition/education-and-outreach/abuse-dominance-enforcement-guidelines.pdf [accessed in January 2026]; Marth W.R., 2009, 'Antitrust Treatment of Joint Ventures: Analyzing Competitor Collaborations', available at: https://www.robinskaplan.com/newsroom/insights/antitrust-treatment-of-joint-ventures-analyzing-competitor-collaborations [accessed January2026].

164. Though the basic reason for joint ventures is normally to save money, time and effort and realise shared objectives, there are other reasons why entities enter into such partnerships. Smaller companies that are incapable of competing effectively with competitor that is well-established in a particular industry, that has well-known products and loyal customers and enjoys substantial growth may consider a joint partnership with such a competitor. Companies wishing to venture into untapped foreign markets opt for joint ventures as a business method, the overall goal being to pool money, personnel and investments and hedge costs and enhance their chances of developing advanced new technological products or increase their profit margins in the new markets. Joint ventures are also formed by two competitors wishing to exchange technology, i.e., to engage in R&D collaboration to enable them to access complementary knowledge research streams and share scientific skills of the entity with which they are collaborating.[105] According to CAK's Consolidated Guidelines on the Substantive Assessment of Mergers under the Competition Act (hereinafter 'Guidelines on the Substantive Assessment of Mergers'),[106] joint ventures can also involve the integration of parts of the business activities of the parties to the joint venture, including a contribution of productive assets to the new joint venture. This kind of merger can enhance or eliminate competition between the entities involved in the joint venture's field of activity. This however depends on the permanence of the joint venture and the degree of autonomy it enjoys from its parent company.

165. The Competition Act does not define what a joint venture is and applies to joint ventures only insofar as such ventures constitute a notifiable merger under section 41 of the Act. Section 2 as read with section 41 of the Competition Act defines merger as 'an acquisition of shares, business or other assets, whether inside or outside Kenya, resulting in the change of control of a business, part of a business or an asset of a business in Kenya in any manner and includes a takeover'.

166. For the CAK to approve any joint venture, a number of criteria must be met. The first, according to the Guidelines on the Substantive Assessment of Mergers, is that the merger must be full-function venture within the meaning of section 41 of the Competition Act. This means that it must have performed for a period of ten years or more all the functions of an autonomous economic entity, including:

105. Beamish, W.P. and Nathaniel C. Lupto, C.N., 2009, 'Managing Joint Ventures', Academy of Management Perspectives, available at: http://aom.org [accessed July 2014].
OECD, 2002, 'Competition and Co-operation in Innovation in OECD Science, Technology and Industry Outlook 2002', OECD Publishing; Shapiro, C., 2002, 'Competition Policy and Innovation', STI Working Papers, 2002/11, DSTI/DOC(2002) 11, 22 April.
Devlin, A and Jacobs M., 2011, p. 548, 'Joint Venture Analysis after American Needle', Journal of Competition Law and Economics, 7(3), 543; Dutoit, B., 1989, pp. 439 and 444, 'Joint Ventures and Intellectual Property', International Review of Intellectual Property 4, 407.

106. CAK, Undated, 'Consolidated Guidelines on the Substantive Assessment of Mergers under the Competition Act', available at: https://cak.go.ke/sites/default/files/downloads/2024-08/ConsolidatedMergerGuidelines.pdf [accessed January 2026].

a. operating on a market and performing the functions normally carried out by undertakings operating on the same market; and
b. having a management dedicated to its day-to-day operations and access to sufficient resources, including finance, staff and assets (tangible and intangible) in order to conduct its business activities for a long duration within the area provided for in the joint-venture agreement.

167. Second, it must be established for an indefinite period, and take over one specific function within the parent companies' business activities without access to the market. In Kenya, joint ventures are usually restricted to individual or small projects; major corporations also use the joint-venture strategy in order to diversify. A good example of a joint venture in Kenya is that one between Kenya Electricity Generating Company, a leading electrical power generation company in Kenya, supplying the country with about 80% of its electricity, and Kenya Power, a company charged with the responsibility of transmitting, distributing and retailing that transmits, electricity to customers throughout Kenya. The two companies merged to create new products and services, and to attract private sector investment.

168. In 2014, the CAK approved a merger by way of a joint venture between Equity Investment Bank and Exotix Partners LLP. As part of a strategy to expand their markets, the two companies entered into a collaboration agreement that would enable them to collaborate closely in research, sales and trading platforms. The CAK unconditionally approved the merger, arguing that it did not present any competition concerns.

Chapter 5. Consequences of Violations and Enforcement Institutions

§1. Administration Enforcement

I. The Antitrust Authorities

A. Formation and Composition

169. As already indicated, the Competition Act repealed and replaced the RTPMPCA, which was administered by the Monopolies and Prices Commissioner at the Kenyan Ministry of Finance. Just like the RTPMPCA, the Competition Act has the objective of promoting competition in the economy through prohibition of anticompetitive practices, and the controlling monopolies, concentrations of economic power and prices.

170. The Competition Act institutionalises competition law in thereby establishing a fair, modern and effective regime for regulating competition in Kenya. The Act applies according to its section 5 to all sectors that engage in trade, including state enterprises. Section 7 as read with section 9 of the Competition Act establishes the CAK and empowers it to deal with competition matters in Kenya. The CAK has the duty of, *inter alia*, promoting and safeguarding competition in the national economy, and determining safeguards needed to protect consumers from unfair and rapacious market practices. The CAK has the duty of enforcing competition law in Kenya, and enacting policies, procedures and legislations needed to protect and govern competition in the marketplace. The CAK is required to consult with national regulatory bodies in all matters relating to competition and consumer welfare, and to advise the government on such matters.[107]

171. The CAK is a corporate independent body that performs its functions and decides all disputes brought before it independently, impartially and without interference from the government or disgruntled litigants. The CAK is made up of ten members, which also form its Board. These include a non-executive Chairman, a Principal Secretary, a Permanent Secretary in the Ministry of Trade or his representative, the Attorney General or his representative, and five other members appointed from among persons conversant with competition and consumer protection matters. The Minister of Finance appoints all the members. The last member of the Board, who is also the head of the Board, the Director General of the CAK, is appointed by the Board. The appointment is according to section 12 of the Competition Act subject to the approval of the Parliament.

107. Karanja, J. and Maina, R., 2014, 'Issues and Challenges in Competition: Kenya Overview', Global Competition Review, World Edition, available at: http://globalcompetitionreview.com [accessed July 2014], The CAK Kenya, 2010, 'The Competition Act No. 12 of 2010', available at: http://www.cak.go.ke [accessed April 2014].

172. According to Parts III-VI of the Competition Act, the CAK is responsible for competition policy relating to restrictive trade practices, mergers and takeovers, control of unwarranted concentration of economic power and control and display of prices or rather, consumer protection. Section 19 of the Act empowers the CAK to establish one or more divisions as it may deem appropriate for the proper performance of tasks required of it under this Act. Section 71 of the Competition Act establishes the Competition Tribunal to deal with functions, which include, among other things, the hearing and determining appeals from decisions and orders of the CAK. All the litigants who are dissatisfied with the decisions of the Tribunal may appeal to the High Court. The judgments issued by the High Court are final.

B. Investigative Powers

173. According to section 31 of the Competition Act, the CAK may, on its own initiative or upon receipt of information or complaint from any person or Government agency or Ministry, carry out an investigation into any conduct or proposed conduct of any economic sector, which it has reason to believe may be prejudicial to public interests. Such conduct may include those regarding the prohibitions relating to restrictive trade practices or those relating to abuse of dominance. To enable the CAK to carry out investigations smoothly, the enterprise or person under investigation is required to furnish the CAK with the information, documents or records pertaining to the matter specified in the notice of investigations to be issued by the authority to that person or enterprise ordering appearance before the CAK.

1. The Duty of Disclosure

174. The Competition Act does not define the term 'duty to disclose', but imposes a disclosure obligation on all distributors and suppliers of goods and services to disclose 'material' information relating to matters arising out of the Act. According to section 20 of the Competition Act, the term 'material' includes information, document or evidence material to matters to which the Competition Act applies.

175. Any person disclosing or giving material information to the CAK, whether under compulsion of law or otherwise, may claim confidentiality in respect of the whole or any part of the material. Information can be disclosed orally by way of claims for confidentiality, or in writing, signed by the person making the claim, specifying the material and stating the reason for the claim. The Competition Act gives the CAK the discretion to determine which material or claim for confidentiality may be categorised as confidential. The CAK is expected to grant confidentiality for the material or claim if it is satisfied that the same material or claim is of a confidential nature and that:

a. its disclosure could adversely affect the competitive position of any person; or that it

b. is commercially sensitive for some other reason.

176. Regardless of the decision made, the CAK must notify in writing the entity or person who made a claim for confidentiality of its decision to grant or not grant confidentiality. If it has not granted confidentiality, the CAK is required to consider the material confidential for at least fourteen days after giving such notification. Under section 20.8 of the Competition Act, the CAK may disclose the material in its possession at any time without notice to any other person if the disclosure is:

a. made to person who is also performing a function under the Act;
b. made with the consent of the person who gave the material; or if
c. authorised or required under any other law; or required by a court or a tribunal.

177. The CAK can also disclose confidential material if its disclosure would not cause detriment to the person supplying it or the person to whom it relates, or if, although the disclosure of the material would cause detriment to the person supplying it or the person to whom it relates, the public benefit in disclosing it outweighs the detriment. The CAK must, in such cases, give fourteen days' prior written notice to the affected person of its intention to disclose the material.

178. According to section 31 of the Competition Act, the duty to disclose extends to infringements relating to restrictive trade practices or abuse of dominance. The provision mandates the CAK to carry out investigations into any conduct involving the previously mentioned infringements and, by notice in writing, order the affected person or enterprise to furnish it with all relevant information, documents, records or copies thereof in his/its possession relating to the subject matter of the investigation. Such a person or enterprise must also appear before the CAK to give evidence or to produce any document or article specified in the notice and relating to the transaction that the CAK is investigating.

179. Section 60 of the Competition Act mandates supplier of goods within Kenya not to make misstatements or materially incorrect statements in respect of any given consumer product information standard. In such cases of misstatements regarding a product, the CAK may prescribe a consumer product information standard requiring the supplier of the goods to disclosure of information relating to the performance, composition, contents, methods of manufacture or processing, design, construction, finish or packaging of the goods. The CAK has the discretion to determine the form and manner in which such information is to be disclosed to the end users of the goods are clearly informed about their quantity, quality and or value.

180. The CAK itself has also according to section 78.2 the duty to disclose its source of funding and any conflicts of interest that may impact its work as an ombudsman in competition matters. The details of such disclosures are, according to section 4 of the Schedule to the Competition Act, to be included in its annual report. Besides, section 85 of the Competition Act requires all employees of the CAK to act with due care and in good faith to protect corporate welfare and interests of the CAK. As part of the duty of care, all staff of the CAK are required to disclose any financial or private interest they may have in any matter, which is subject of investigations before the CAK. Employees with conflict of interest relative to a corporate interest are not allowed to participate or assist in investigation of matters in which they have a financial or personal interest. It is solely upon the CAK to determine whether the conflict of interest can interfere significantly with the proper and effective performance of the functions and duties of the member or the CAK. Those participating or assisting in investigations are not to use confidential information gained in the course of employment for corrupt personal or relational financial gains.

2. Dawn Raids

181. In order to increase competition in the economy and promote fair play through competition, the Competition Act contains provisions that allow the CAK to conduct dawn raids (surprise visits to business offices to acquire documents) anywhere in Kenya to curtail unlawful anti-cartel activities, and to compel the production of documents, information and oral testimonies, etc. Section 31 of the Act empowers the CAK either on its own initiative or upon receipt of complaint from an individual, Government Agency or ministry to, upon notice to the affected person or business, investigate cartel conducts, including those regarding restrictive business practices and abuse of dominance. In such cases, the individual or business is required to furnish the CAK with information, records or documents pertaining to any matter specified in the notice, which the CAK considers relevant to the investigation. A further tool for increasing transparency and competition in markets is the entry and search mandate by authorised persons provided for in section 32 of the Competition Act. The section gives the CAK power to enter premises of persons believed to be engaged in cartel conduct, or in possession of relevant information and documents and to inspect the premises and any goods, information, documents and records found in such a premise. In the *MEA v. CAK* and Another, the CAK exercised its statutory mandate and conducted a dawn raid on the premises of MEA to uncover anti-competitive practices on the part of MEA that were impeding competition in the fertiliser industry.[108]

182. The CAK must however inform the affected person or business premises in writing of its intention to conduct an inspection of the premises, goods, documents and records situated thereon. The persons authorised by the CAK to carry out inspections may with the help of police officers and other law enforcement agencies execute the mandate conferred by section 32, and for instance, use any computer system on the premises, or require assistance of any person on the premises to use that computer system, to:

a. search any data contained in or available to that computer system;
b. reproduce any record from that data;

108. HCCC Constitutional and Human Rights Division, Petition No. 99 of 2016.

c. seize any output from that computer for examination and copying;
d. attach and, if necessary, subject to the issuance of a receipt to that effect, remove from the premises for examination and safekeeping anything that has a bearing on the investigation.

183. Furthermore, the CAK is required not only to give a written notice to the Minister of Finance but also to commercial enterprises whose interests may be impacted by the outcome of the inquiry or sectoral study, as well as to undertakings, including industry and consumer organisations, who may have an interest in the matter. Despite the compulsion to provide data, section 20 of the Competition Act allows individuals or enterprises to file confidentiality claims in respect of information or documents that they consider material. If the CAK is satisfied that information or documents disclosed to it is of a confidential nature and that its disclosure is commercially sensitive or could affect competitive position of the disclosure, then it declares such material as confidential.

184. The problem however is that the Competition Act contains no sufficient safeguards for protecting the material information or documents disclosed to the CAK. According to section 20.8 of the Competition Act, even if CAK has declared disclosed material confidential, it may still disclose the material to the public if such a disclosure will not cause any damage to the person or enterprise disclosing the material. CAK can also disclose the material in cases where, though the disclosing undertaking or person may suffer damage because of the disclosure, the public benefit resulting from disclosure of the material outweighs the benefit to the public of withholding the information. Persons or undertakings aggrieved by CAK's decision may appeal to the Tribunal. While the appeal to the Tribunal is still pending, CAK must hold the material confidential until the appeal is determined.

C. Adjudicating Powers (Ascertaining and Sanctioning)

185. The CAK enjoys, thanks to the powers accorded to it under section 7 of the Competition Act, not just independence in its operations and decision-making but also, according to section 9 of the Act, clear, explicit segregation of functions in areas such policy, management, regulation and adjudication. As a result, the CAK is able to remain transparent in the enforcement process and thereby fulfil its mandate of promoting and safeguarding competition in the national economy and protecting consumers from predatory practices, while still exercising its role as the government's advisor on competition issues and consumer welfare matters. Section 5.3 of the Competition Act institutionalises the interaction between the CAK and other sector-specific authorities or policy makers. The CAK is required under this provision to work with these sector regulators to identify and establish procedures for management of areas of concurrent jurisdiction, promote cooperation, provide and protect confidential information and ensure the consistent application of the Competition Act to improve the effectiveness of competition policy in Kenya. This notwithstanding, section 5.3 provides that if in the course of cooperation with other stakeholders, there is any conflict, disharmony or inconsistency in matters concerning competition and consumer welfare, the determinations, directives, regulations, rules, orders and decisions of the CAK shall take precedence.

186. According to section 40, as read with sections 71 and 73 of the Competition Act, appeals against the decisions of the CAK lie with the Competition Tribunal. The High Court of Kenya has, according to section 77 of the Act, the mandate to adjudicate appeals by the CAK resulting from determinations of the Tribunal. Its judgments are final.

D. *Other Institutional Tasks (Consultancy to the Parliament or Government)*

187. Section 3 of the Competition Act gives the objective of the Act as being to enhance the welfare of the people of Kenya by promoting and protecting effective competition in markets. The Act is the primary law regarding all competition and consumer welfare matters in Kenya. Section 5 of the Act states that it applies to all private and public undertakings entrusted with the provision of all goods and services that are of general economic interest. Other than the power to review government's policies, regulations, procedures and legislations and assess their impact on competition and consumer welfare, section 9 of the Act accords the CAK further extensive powers that enable it not just to consult with entities but also with the Executive and the Parliament in respect to matters on consumer protection and competition. In this regard, CAK's further functions include the following duties:

a. promote and enforce compliance with the Act;
b. receive and investigate complaints from legal or natural persons and consumer bodies;
c. promote public knowledge, awareness and understanding of the obligations, rights and remedies under the Act and its duties, functions and activities;
d. promote the creation of consumer bodies and the establishment of good and proper standards and rules to be followed by such bodies in protecting competition and consumer welfare;
e. recognise consumer bodies duly registered under the appropriate national laws as the proper bodies, in their areas of operation, to represent consumers before it;
f. make available to consumers information and guidelines relating to the obligations of persons under the Act and the rights and remedies available to consumers under the Act;
g. carry out inquiries, studies and research into matters relating to competition and the protection of the interests of consumers;
h. study government policies, procedures and programs, legislation and proposals for legislation so as to assess their effects on competition and consumer welfare and publicise the results of such studies;
i. investigate impediments to competition, including entry into and exit from markets, in the economy as a whole or in particular sectors and publicise the results of such investigations;

j. investigate policies, procedures and programs of regulatory authorities so as to assess their effects on competition and consumer welfare and publicise the results of such studies;
k. participate in deliberations and proceedings of government, government commissions, regulatory authorities and other bodies in relation to competition and consumer welfare;
l. make representations to government, government commissions, regulatory authorities and other bodies on matters relating to competition and consumer welfare;
m. liaise with regulatory bodies and other public bodies in all matters relating to competition and consumer welfare; and
n. advise the government on matters relating to competition and consumer welfare.

II. Government Direct Enforcement Activities

188. Before the enactment of RTPMPCA, Kenya had a controlled economy in which, the prices of consumer goods and services were set by the Government. With the enactment of the Sessional Paper of 1986, the government of Kenya relaxed state control of such prices and shifted to free-market economy wherein goods and services could be freely exchanged with a minimum of government rules. Indeed, the Competition Act reflects this stance. As already indicated in sections 7 and 31 of the Competition Act, the CAK is an independent corporate body that discharges its functions without intimidation, hindrance or interference from any person, undertaking, ministry or government agency.[109]

189. The CAK is the only statutory body responsible for administering and enforcing the Competition Act in Kenya. As already stated above, according to section 5.3 of the Act, even if a public body has jurisdiction in respect of any matter regulated under the Competition Act, the CAK and that body must cooperate to ensure the consistent application of the Act. Still, the CAK has greater authority in matters of consumer welfare and competition and its decisions prevail in instances of conflict or inconsistencies.

190. Nevertheless, as much as state intervention in competition matters was reduced to a great degree, today, the government still intervenes in price setting and policy formulation. The intervention is however at a minimum. Indeed, section 68 of the Competition Act exhorts the CAK to refer consumer complaints to specialised government agencies, which are then required to make appropriate determinations without involving the CAK, and inform the CAK and the complainants of the decision(s).

109. Government of Kenya, 1986, pp. 24 and 100, 'Sessional Paper no. 1 of 1986 on Economic Management for Renewed Growth', Government Printer, Nairobi, Kenya; United Nations, 2005, 'Voluntary Peer Review on Competition Policy: Kenya', UNCTAD/DITC/CLP/2005/6.

III. Other Administrative Agencies Applying Antitrust Rules

191. Other than the CAK and the Tribunal, there are a number of other administrative institutions that have the mandate to apply antitrust laws in Kenya, but only to the extent specified in legislations that establish them. Section 58.3 of the Competition Act provides that the CAK may delegate to relevant specialised agencies of the Government some of its functions in order to smoothly discharge its functions under the Act. This is a recognition that the specialised agency may be better suited than the CAK to carry out certain specific functions. So, for instance, according to sections 68 through 69, the CAK can consult with the Kenya Bureau of Standards (on all matters involving definition and specification of goods and the grading of goods by quality), specialised Government agencies (on consumer complaints) or recognised consumer bodies (on infringement of the Competition Act).

192. The difficulty that arises with the duty delegation is how overlapping competition and consumer matters should be dealt with and which body has jurisdiction over such matters. For instance, section 8 of the Public Procurement and Disposal Act 2005 (hereinafter 'PPD Act'),[110] which prohibits collusive tendering by public institutions during the acquisition and disposal of materials, establishes the Public Procurement Oversight Authority, and gives it powers to regulate procurements by public entities. Under section 2 of the PPD Act, its purpose is to ensure that the procurement procedures established under the PPD Act are complied with, that local industry, economic development and competition are promoted and competitors are treated fairly. According to section 5.1 of the PPD Act, if there is a conflict between the PPD Act or any other regulations, or the Government's notices and guidelines, in matters relating to procurement and asset disposal, the PPD Act and the regulations made under it shall prevail.

193. Another example is the Consumer Protection Act,[111] which contains much more detailed and comprehensive provisions on consumer protection than the Competition Act came into force in March 2013. Like the Competition Act, its purpose is to promote and advance the social and economic welfare of consumers, promote fair and ethical business practices, and reduce the unfair disadvantages experienced by consumers in accessing any supply of goods. Section 89 of the Act creates the Kenya Consumer Protection Advisory Committee and accords it wide-ranging powers, including the power to protect consumers' interests and ensure fair market competition, take necessary actions to safeguard all the interests of consumers while maintaining effective competition among suppliers of essential goods and services and to draw up and review consumer protection directives. Section 84 of the Act allows an aggrieved consumer to file a claim in any court in Kenya.

---

110. KLR, 2005, 'The Public Procurement and Disposal Act 2005, Chapter 412A of the Laws of Kenya', available at: : https://new.kenyalaw.org/legislation/, [accessed January 2026].
111. KLR, 2012, 'The Consumer Protection Act No, 46 of 2012', available at: : https://new.kenyalaw.org/legislation/, [accessed January 2026].

194. The CAK faces the challenge of addressing the problem of overlapping responsibilities associated with cooperation amongst multiple authorities dealing with competition and consumer protection matters. Resolving this challenge could help avoid simultaneous complaints to competition and consumer authorities, and improve policy and decision-making capacities of all the affected authorities. Perhaps a single authority should be set up for each sector and granted the monopoly to enforce consumer and competition matters in their respective spheres of operation.

IV. Administrative Fines and Levels of Fines in Kenya for Undertakings and Individuals

195. The enforcement of the Competition Act in Kenya is bolstered by a number of remedies whose goal is to deter individuals and or undertakings engaged in trade from engaging in anticompetitive and deceptive activities. These remedies include not just sanctions, but also fines and prison sentences. Such fines depend on the type and gravity of the predatory conduct and can be imposed by either the CAK and/or the Tribunal on individuals, undertakings and trade unions. The fines provided for are payable by both categories, though imprisonment is a matter of necessity for individuals only. The CAK has powers under section 36 of the Competition Act to grant the following remedies:

a. a declaration that a conduct complained of amounts to an infringement of the prohibitions regarding Part A- Restrictive Agreements, Practices and Decisions and Part B-Restrictive Trade Practices Applicable to Trade Associations of Part III of the Competition Act;
b. a restraint order preventing an undertaking from engaging in the conduct complained of;
c. an order direction an action to be taken by the undertaking or undertakings concerned to remedy or reverse the infringement or the effects thereof;
d. under section 52 of the Competition Act, an order for partial disposal of interests in production, distribution or the supply of services as it deems necessary to remove the unwarranted concentration;
e. the CAK can also during or after its investigations enter into an agreement of settlement with the undertaking or undertakings accused of infringing the Competition Act;
f. a financial penalty and imprisonment; and
g. any other relief.

196. A vivid explanation of some of these remedies is given in section 5 below, titled 'Administrative Injunctions, Interim Measures and Other Restrictive Orders'. Regarding administrative fines, as a general rule, under section 91 of the Competition Act, any person convicted of an offence under the Act for which no penalty has been specified under the Act is liable to a fine not exceeding KES 500,000, or to imprisonment for a term not exceeding three years, or both. Under section 93, the Minister of Finance may, in consultation with the CAK, make rules for the better carrying into effect the provisions of the Competition Act. The said rules can under section 93.2 of the Act include 'anything' that can be prescribed under the Competition Act. This, in the opinion of this author, includes fines.

197. Otherwise, the CAK can levy punitive or exemplary damages, usually in the form of fines or imprisonment. Such fines are exclusively imposed to address various forms of cartel conduct regulated under the Competition Act. Thus, a prison term not exceeding five years or a fine not exceeding KES 10 million or both is imposed under sections 21.9, 22.6, 24.3, 42.5, 54.3 and 70 of the Competition Act respectively, against monopolistic trade practices, abuse of dominance, unwarranted concentration of economic power, false or misleading representations in respect to a product, and unconscionable conduct in business transactions. Section 42.6 further states that, in addition to a fine, a penalty of an amount not exceeding 10% of the preceding year's gross annual turnover in Kenya of the undertaking or undertakings in question may be imposed on the undertaking contravening the provisions of the Competition Act relating to mergers. Finally, section 91 of the Competition Act sums it all up by providing that a person convicted of an offence under the Competition Act, for which no penalty has been specified under the Act, shall be liable to a fine not exceeding KES 500,000.

198. For cases concerning mergers and acquisitions, section 42.5 of the Competition Act imposes a prison term not exceeding five years, or a fine not exceeding KES 10 million, or both. In addition to foregoing penalties, in mergers and acquisitions cases, the CAK can in accordance with section 42.6 impose a financial penalty in an amount not exceeding 10% of the preceding year's gross annual turnover in Kenya of the undertaking or undertakings in question.

199. So for instance, in *Competition Authority of Kenya v. Tuskys Mattresses Limited and Ukwala Supermarkets Limited*, in which Tuskys Mattresses Limited (TML),[112] which was in a horizontal relationship with Ukwala Supermarkets Limited (USL) in Nairobi, was in the process of acquiring the latter. The CAK on conducting investigation into the acquisition pursuant to section 31 of the Competition Act established that the two competing supermarkets were involved in price fixing and predatory conduct aimed at limiting and controlling production, market outlets and access to essential goods and services, in contravention of section 21 of the Competition Act. The CAK imposed an out-of-court settlement pursuant to section 38 of the Competition Act in the sum of KSH 53,000,000. In arriving at the penalty, the CAK took into consideration the affected turnover, the duration of the unconscionable conducts complained of, and the further evidence adduced by the parties.

200. As per section 51.1, if any undertaking in the economic sector under investigation so requests, or the CAK considers it appropriate, it may determine that a

112. CAK, 2013/2014, pp. 23–24, 'The Annual Report 2013/2014', available at: https://www.cak.go.ke/arch/sites/default/files/annual-reports/FY%202013-2014%20CAK%20Annual%20Report.pdf [accessed Januray 2026].

hearing be held in relation to a proposed determination regarding unwarranted concentration of economic power. Section 51.2 states that if the CAK determines that a hearing should be held, it shall give reasonable notice in writing to the undertaking or undertakings involved – convening the hearing; specifying the date, time and place for the holding thereof; and stipulating the matters to be considered thereat.

201. Further, section 52 provides that after completion of its investigation, the CAK may make an order directing any person whom it deems to hold an unwarranted concentration of economic power in any sector to dispose of such portion of his interests in production, distribution or the supply of services as it deems necessary to remove the unwarranted concentration. Under the same section, the CAK may order, separately or together with the order to dispose of interests made under that subsection, the person in question to observe such other conditions as may be deemed necessary to remove the unwarranted concentration. Section 52.4 of the Act prohibits the CAK from making orders which would have the effect of subdividing a manufacturing facility whose degree of physical integration is such that the introduction of independent management units controlling different components would reduce its efficiency and substantially raise production costs per unit of output. A party aggrieved by the decision of the CAK may in accordance with section 53 lodge an appeal with the Competition Tribunal and a final appeal may be lodged with the High Court. In this respect, section 54.3. guards against excessive concentration of economic power and any person who is convicted of unreasonably holding such power shall be liable to imprisonment for a term not exceeding five years, or to a fine not exceeding 10 million.

202. As regards inability to pay fines due to financial hardships or other reasons, fines imposed by CAK/Tribunal are considered fines in the context of section 28 of the Penal Code of Kenya (hereinafter 'the Penal Code').[113] Under section 28c of the Penal Code, in case of an offence punishable with imprisonment and a fine in which the offender is sentenced to a fine with or without imprisonment, and in every case of an offence punishable with fine only, in which the offender is sentenced to a fine, the High Court may in its discretion order that in default of payment of the fine the offending persons or directors of an undertaking be imprisoned for a defined term. Such imprisonment is in addition to any other imprisonment to which such persons or directors may have been sentenced or to which they may be liable under a commutation of sentence. The court can also issue a warrant for the levy of the amount on the immovable and movable property of the offender by distress and sale under warrant. A term of imprisonment imposed in default of payment of a fine shall terminate whenever the fine is paid.

203. A cartel participant can also benefit from the plea bargaining provisions under Kenya's criminal law, in which the defendant's pleads guilty to a lesser charge, or to only one of several charges, in exchange for an agreement in which the prosecutor drops one or more charges, reduces a charge to a less serious offence,

113. KLR, 1930, 'The Penal Code, Chapter 63 of the Laws of Kenya', available at: https://new.kenyalaw.org/akn/ke/act/1930/10/eng@2023-12-11 [accessed January 2026].

and recommends leniency in sentencing. The judge is not bound to follow the prosecutor's recommendation. An acquittal in criminal trial does not exempt from civil actions.

V. Administrative Injunctions, Interim Measures and Other Restrictive Orders

204. According to section 37 of the Competition Act, the CAK can give interim relief against an undertaking if it believes that, on reasonable grounds, that an undertaking has engaged, is engaging, or is proposing to engage, in conduct that constitutes or may constitute an infringement of the prohibitions on restrictive agreements, practices and decisions or the prohibitions on restrictive trade practices applicable to trade associations. The aim of such interim reliefs is to protect public interest or prevent serious irreparable damage to any person or category of persons.

205. In *British American Tobacco Kenya Ltd v. Cut Tobacco Kenya Limited,*[114] the court granted an injunction to restrain the defendants from passing off their goods as those of the plaintiff, arguing that such passing off was uncompetitive and could damage the plaintiff's reputation and trademark and cause it irreparable loss. Section 55 of the Competition Act prohibits enterprises trading in Kenya from making false or misleading statements about goods and services, their standards, quality, price or origin. Whether a representation is false or misleading will depend on the circumstances of each case, but once proved, such a representation is considered an invasion of proprietary rights and is actionable under the Act. In any case under section 37 of the Act, the CAK may in such instances by order in writing, direct the undertaking or undertakings to stop and desist from engaging in commercially injurious conduct until the ongoing investigation is concluded.

206. Section 25 as read with section 29 of the Competition allows undertakings and associations of undertakings to apply to the CAK for exemption from restrictive agreements, practices and decisions dealt with under sections A and B of Part III of the Act. In addition, according to section 28 of the Competition Act, an exemption can be granted in relation to any agreement or practice relating to the exercise of any right or interest acquired or protected in terms of intellectual property rights.

207. Section 27 of the Competition Act gives the CAK the power, upon notice to the affected persons or enterprises, to revoke or amend at any time, any of its exemption orders or certificates of clearances because of the following reasons:

a. material change in circumstances since the exemption in question was granted;
b. exemption was granted, or the certificate was issued on materially incorrect or misleading information; or
c. the non-compliance with the conditions upon which the exemption was granted.

114. HCCC 354 of 1999.

208. Section 31 as read with section 36 of the Competition Act allows the CAK to investigate conducts that allegedly infringes prohibitions relating to restrictive trade practices or abuse of dominance. After a detailed hearing of the matter, the CAK can protect public interests, prevent entities from suffering irreparable damage, and restrain the infringing entity from engaging in the conduct complained of.

209. As regards mergers, the CAK has powers to give approval for a merger or decline to grant such approval. In granting or declining such approvals, the CAK takes into consideration factors such as the extent to which the proposed merger can hinder or reduce competition, restrict trade or endanger the continuity of supply of products and services. The CAK also takes into consideration the extent to which the planned merger could enable any undertaking to acquire a dominant position or to strengthen its dominant position in the Kenya markets. Section 47 of the Act gives the CAK the power to revoke an approval of a proposed merger that had already been granted if it establishes that its decision was based on materially incorrect or misleading information for which a party to the merger is responsible. A merger can also be revoked under the same section if any condition attached to the approval of the merger that is material to the implementation is not complied with. The Competition Tribunal may according to section 48.1 of the Competition Act allow an aggrieved party to a merger to apply to the Tribunal for review of the merger decisions made by the CAK. When this happens, the Tribunal can according to section 48.3 overturn, amend or confirm the decision of the CAK, or refer the matter back to the CAK for reconsideration on specified terms.

210. Furthermore, under section 61, if the CAK establishes that the goods supplied may cause injuries to consumers or do not meet the prescribed consumer product safety standards, the CAK may, by notice, order the recall of the goods, or disclose to the public the nature of a defect in the goods in question.

211. Additionally, in accordance with sections 67–69 of the Competition Act, the CAK is required to cooperate with the Kenya Bureau of Standards and recognised consumer Authorities in investigating liability for unsuitable goods. It can also refer complaints about such goods to government agencies for further determination.

VI. Interim Measures

212. Besides, where a breach under the Competition Act is established, under section 37 of the Competition Act, the CAK can issue a written interim relief/ injunction in the form of cease and desist orders. The orders are issued against any person or undertaking suspected of engaging in practices that constitute an infringement of the prohibitions under the Competition Act, and remain effective until the CAK completes its investigations.

§2. CIVIL ENFORCEMENT

I. Competent Civil Courts

213. The Competition Tribunal established under section 71 of the Act is a quasi-judicial body headed by an Advocate of the High Court of Kenya and with powers resembling those of a court of law. The Tribunal's Chairman is appointed by the Minister for Finance. The Tribunal's responsibilities include hearing and determining appeals from the CAK, prescribing the manner in which appeals may be made to the Tribunal, determining the fees to be paid for such appeals, establishing the procedures to be adopted by the Tribunal when hearing appeals, and deciding where and when the Tribunal will convene its sittings. The Tribunal has power to adjudicate on competition policy disputes brought before it and to make decisions as it deems fit. Its decisions are legally enforceable, but can be challenged in the High Court of Kenya. Competition disputes are brought before the High Court just like civil disputes under the Civil Procedure Act,[115] the legislation applicable in civil proceedings in Kenya. In such disputes, the High Court is obliged to give the reliefs prescribed under the Civil Procedure Act.

214. Section 92 of the Competition Act provides that Magistrates' courts have no jurisdiction to impose any penalty provided for in this Act. However, other legislations dealing with competition and consumer matters give both the High Court and the Magistrates' courts criminal and civil jurisdiction over individual and corporate disputes involving partnerships, competition and consumer matters. For instance, section 84 of the Consumer Protection Act without defining which courts are included in the term 'appropriate court' provides that an aggrieved consumer who has a right of action under the Consumer Protection Act can commence such actions in the appropriate court. Section 2 of the Companies Act defines 'court' as the High Court, and gives it jurisdiction in many instances to deal with disputes arising out of the Act, including mergers, takeovers, acquisitions and winding-up. According to section 2.1 of the Partnership Act[116] of 2012, the term 'court' means the High Court or, where the gross assets of a partnership do not exceed KES 300,000, the Resident Magistrates' courts. It follows, therefore, that the pecuniary value of a claim determines jurisdiction of a trial court in the previously mentioned statutes.

215. Appeals against the decisions of the CAK's Tribunal touch on a number of varying competition issues. In *KTDA Management Services*,[117] in this case, the Applicants moved to court seeking to quash a Tea Inquiry report by the CAK. The High Court granted a stay order directing the CAK not to use the report against the applicants until the matter is determined. The CAK filed its response with KTDA

115. KLR, 1924, 'Civil Procedure Act, Chapter 21 of the Laws of Kenya', available : https://new.kenyalaw.org/legislation/, [accessed January 2026].

116. *Ibid.*

117. Kericho High Court Miscellanous Application No. 3/2015 – *KTDA Management Services v. Competition Authority of Kenya & the Attorney General.*

with the court, in which it demonstrated the validity and the procedural probity of the report. The High Court is yet to determine the matter.

216. Another matter that is yet to be fully heard by the court is *Consumer Federation of Kenya (COFEK) v. Nakumatt Holdings Ltd and Others.*[118] In this matter, the Consumer Federation of Kenya (COFEK) brought a constitutional petition against the CAK and two others, alleging that there were differences between the till and shelf price at Nakumatt supermarkets. COFEK sought a declaration that the CAK had failed to discharge its consumer protection duties, and moved the court for an order that, in future, CAK should consult it when dealing with consumer complaints and connected matters.

217. And finally, in *Republic v. Competition Authority of Kenya ex parte Airtel Networks Limited,*[119] Airtel Networks filed judicial review proceedings challenging the CAK's decision to enter into an out-of-court settlement with its competitor, Safaricom Limited, against whom it had filed a complaint under Part III of the Competition Act. Airtel, Safaricom and CAK eventually settled this matter out of court.

II. Sanctions

A. *Nullity*

218. The Competition Act does not provide for specific sanctions that court of law may impose for contravention of any of its provisions. However, in order to encourage competition in the Kenyan economy, Parts III–VI of the Competition Act prohibit, unless exempted under the Act, deceptive vertical and horizontal restrictive trade practices and abuse of dominant position by undertakings. Part IV of the Competition Act contains provisions that not only define the term 'merger' but also address the entering into mergers, amalgamations and acquisitions and revocation of mergers whose formation is based on materially incorrect or misleading information and the appeal process. It also prohibits unwarranted concentration of economic power that is prejudicial to public interest, and to protect consumer from predatory practices, proscribes misleading representations and deceptive marketing practices that may influence a consumer to buy or use an advertised product. The prohibitions in the Competition Act are aimed at protecting consumers and honest business competitors who are engaging in honest trade in goods and services in any given market. The Competition Act establishes the mechanisms that ensure that each of its provisions is enforced.

118. Constitutional Petition Number 239/2015 – *Consumer Federation of Kenya (COFEK) v. Nakumatt Holdings Ltd, Atul Shah*, Kenya Bureau of Standards, Competition Authority of Kenya & Attorney General.
119. Nairobi Miscellaneous Application No. 418 of 2013 – *Republic v. Competition Authority of Kenya ex parte Airtel Networks Limited.*

B. Damages

219. The Competition Act does provide for damages. Thus, parties aggrieved about the decisions of the CAK or the Tribunal may move to the High Court and file an action for damages. Damages being the primary kind of remedy in civil disputes, the High Court or whatever court is presiding over the matter may grant appropriate damages, including cases involving antitrust infringements. Generally, actual damages are compensatory and are measured by the loss sustained. In order to be recoverable, damages must be established with reasonable certainty. This means that damages for antitrust infringements, which are speculative, remote, imaginary, contingent or merely possible, cannot be recovered. It has to be established that such damages were reasonably foreseeable. A causative link between the losses and the breach and losses must also be established. The closest the Competition Act comes to providing for damages is section 63 of the Competition Act. Without giving guidance as to how damages are to be calculated, the provision states that an undertaking shall be liable for loss sustained due to the supply of unsuitable goods, and shall compensate the consumer who has suffered loss by using such goods. Section 63 further states that the aggrieved consumer may also recover the amount of the compensation by action against the undertaking in a court of competent jurisdiction. The cases that fall under the ambit of section 63 include instances where:

a. an undertaking in trade supplies goods manufactured by the undertaking to another person who acquires the goods for resupply;
b. a person (whether or not the person who acquired the goods from the undertaking) supplies the goods, otherwise than by way of sale by auction, to a consumer;
c. the goods are acquired by the consumer for a particular purpose that was, expressly or by implication, made known to the corporation, either directly, or through the person from whom the consumer acquired the goods or a person by whom any prior negotiations in connection with the acquisition of the goods were conducted;
d. the goods are not reasonably fit for that purpose, whether or not that is a purpose for which such goods are commonly supplied; and
e. the consumer or a person who acquires the goods from, or derives title to the goods through or under, the consumer suffers loss or damage by reason that the goods are not reasonably fit for that purpose.

220. Liability is also imposed on the manufacture of defective goods under section 64 of the Competition Act. Under this provision, if an undertaking in trade or commerce supplies defective goods manufactured and a consumer suffers injury as a result of that defect, then the undertaking must compensate that consumer for the loss. Such a consumer can also recover damages by an action against the undertaking in a civil court. Under section 5 of the Civil Procedure Act, any court in Kenya has jurisdiction to try all suits of a civil nature excepting suits of which its cognisance is either expressly or impliedly barred.

C. Interim Measures

221. As already mentioned in section B.2.c of this Part I, section 37 of the Competition Act gives powers to the CAK to issue interim reliefs, where such a relief is necessary for the prevention of irreparable damage to any consume, or for the protection of public interest.

§3. CRIMINAL ENFORCEMENT

I. Criminal Sanctions for Antitrust Violations

222. Other than the administrative fines discussed in section A.4 of this Part I, the Competition Act provides for fines and imprisonment as the primary forms of sanctions against contravention of the Act.

A. Leniency

223. Leniency programmes have been in use for almost two decades as a power tool for detecting, investigating, fighting, dismantling and deterring cartels. The first antitrust leniency programme was created in the United States in 1973. Other developed and developing countries quickly adopted the leniency programmes as part of their antitrust enforcement reforms after it became clear that they could be used to obtain crucial evidence needed to prosecute cartel members, to destabilise existing cartels, and to deter cartel formation. Leniency programmes are used in almost every jurisdiction, regardless of whether the cartel activity under investigation is considered by the antitrust authorities as a criminal, civil or administrative offence. Under the programmes, the confessors and conspirators who cooperate with competition authorities and provide the authorities with useful information in respect of cartel activities in different markets are exempted from fines, jail sentences or criminal and administrative sanctions.[120]

224. The Competition Act has been amended to include provisions regarding leniency programmes. In accordance with section 89A.1, the CAK may operate leniency programmes wherein undertakings can cooperate with the CAK and voluntarily disclose the existence of an agreement or practice that is prohibited under the Competition Act. Such undertakings are exempted from all or part of a fine that could otherwise be imposed under the Competition Act.

120. Borill, J.R., Jimenez, J.L., and Garcia, C., 2013, pp. 107–112, 'Evaluating Antitrust Leniency Programs', Journal of Competition Law and Economics, 10(1), 107; Hammond, D.S., 2004, 'Cornerstone of an Effective Leniency Program', ICN Workshop on Leniency Programs, Sydney, Australia, 22–23 November; Finance Bill, 2014, Kenya Gazette Supplement No. 87 (National Assembly Bills No. 25), 12 Jun. 2014.

225. Section 89A.2 mandates the CAK to determine guidelines applicable to the leniency programmes. The programme is supposed to enable undertakings involved in cartels to self-report and provide information about a cartel, or that will help the CAK in its enhanced role to break up cartels in which they were involved. In so doing, they will receive full or partial immunity from fines depending on the circumstances of their case. The introduction of a leniency programme in Kenya will help the CAK to uncover cartels in every jurisdiction in which it has been deployed, and at the same time, to obtain insider evidence of the cartel infringement. It will also help speed up the adjudication of ongoing and future cases.

II. Other Application of Criminal Law to Relevant Conduct

226. As can be seen above, the Competition Act provides for either a fine of KES 10 million or confinement in jail for not more than five years or both. For offences for which no penalty has been specified under the Competition Act, section 91 of the Competition Act prescribes, other than a fine, a prison term of not more than three years.

III. Role of Prosecutors

227. The Competition Act does not specifically provide for the role of prosecutors in matters arising under the Competition Act. However, if a matter is declared a criminal offence, the burden of proof always rests with the prosecution as was held in *Republic v. Fateh Ali Shah Mushhad.*[121] When a person or enterprise faces a criminal charge under the Competition Act, the prosecution must prove their version of the facts or rather every element of the alleged crime, beyond a reasonable doubt.[122] This is the general standard of proof. The Court on its own motion may also, according to section 22 of the Constitution of Kenya, invite a friend of the court to expound on the matters before it, and help it get a clear picture of the issues in dispute in order to arrive at an informed and just decision.[123]

IV. Competent Criminal Courts

228. As already indicated above, the High Court deals with appeals from the Tribunal referred to it. Section 92 of the Competition Act gives the Magistrates' Courts jurisdiction to determine matters arising of course depending on the pecuniary jurisdiction from the Act and to impose appropriate penalties.

121. *Republic v. Fateh Ali Shah Mushhad*, EACA 41.
122. Sections 107–109 of the KLR, 1963, 'Evidence Act Chapter 80 of the laws of Kenya', available at: : https://new.kenyalaw.org/legislation/, [accessed January 2026].
123. *Judicial Service Commission v. Speaker of the National Assembly and the Attorney General*, HCCC 518 of 2013.

Part II. The Application of the Prohibitions

Chapter 1. Restrictive Agreements

§1. Introduction

229. A horizontal agreement is cooperation between actual and potential competitors trading on the same level in a market to, among other things, provide goods or services to their customers. Undertakings that enter horizontal agreements often form a single block of operation in a market. What this does is to inhibit market operations of undertakings that are not part of that single block and to provide healthy relationships between competitors and lessen competition among them.

230. There are many economic benefits that flow from horizontal agreements. These include sharing of risk and know-how, cost savings, efficiency and increased innovation. The negative effects of such agreements on competition include situations where the competitors involved make agreements that touch on sensitive matters such as pricing, production, distribution or information exchange about a particular product or market that have the effect of restricting or preventing competition and interfering with prices, supply and quality of products and the well-functioning of the market. Section 21 of the Competition Act proscribes price fixing or market sharing cartels or any agreement that can be treated as a cartel or as an unlawful restraint of competition.

§2. Horizontal Agreements

231. The Competition Act distinguishes between horizontal blocks that restrict competition and the honest horizontal associations of undertakings. In Kenya, cartel prohibition is the responsibility of the CAK, which has made efforts since its inception in 2011 to develop regulations and guidelines with which to guide market actors on cartel formation and on how to identify cartel-like activities and bring them to the attention of the CAK. The CAK is in addition equipped with trained personnel whose roles include cartel regulation and enforcement of the provisions of the Competition Act.

232. Section 31 empowers the CAK to investigate possible cartel activities. CAK has, for instance, pursuant to this provision, investigated the matatus sector in

Kenya. This sector serves up to 70% of Kenya's population as the favoured daily means of transportation from their homes to places of work. A Presidential decree issued by the government in 1973 allowed the matatu sector to compete with public bus transport companies. This, coupled with the Government's reduction in licensing and the availability of financing, caused the sector to experience tremendous growth. As of 2014, there were about 60,000 matatus plying Kenya's roads. The growth of the matatu industry has unfortunately led to undisciplined route cartels that have hindered the entry into the sector of other potential matatu investors.

233. Recently, the CAK investigated cartels in the matatu industry, which were actually operating under the banner 'trade and welfare association'. The cartels were not only fixing route prices and colluding to impose route entry charges to ensure that each route had only a few matatus. The 'trade and welfare association' was also recommending commuter fares payable by the sector members. The CAK investigated this matter and found that the price fixing and sector control by the 'trade and welfare association' hindered other matatu entrepreneurs from accessing the market, and accordingly issued the cartels with a 'cease and desist' order mandating them to desist from their antitrust activities.[124] In an appeal recently filed by the *East African Trade Association*[125] against the CAK's decision in the Competition Tribunal, the issues raised *included* whether:

- price fixing within a trade association constituted a horizontal restriction; in the context of section 22 of the Competition Act;
- the setting of warehouse prices and commission brokerage by a trade association was a restrictive trade practice and constituted a hardcore restriction; and
- when an exemption should be granted for certain restrictive trade practices.

The Competition Tribunal ruled that the fixing of brokerage commissions and storage fees constitutes a horizontal core restriction and that an exemption from such practices, which are considered restrictive of competition, can only be granted under section 25 of the Act if there are exceptional and compelling reasons of public policy. It also emphasised that horizontal price fixing constitutes a serious violation of competition law and is a practice that is strongly condemned. Price fixing restricts competition between service providers to the detriment of consumers.

124. UNCTAD, 2013, 'The Impact of Cartels on the Poor', [TD/B/C.I/CLP/24/Rev.1]; OECD, 2013, 'Competition and Poverty Reduction: Contribution from Kenya', Session I, DAF/COMP/GF/WD(2013)36, Chitere, P. and Kibua, T., 2004, 'Efforts to Improve Road Safety in Kenya: Achievements and Limitations in the Matatu Industry', Institute of Policy Analysis and Research, available at: http://www.ssatp.org [accessed September 2014], ICLG, 2015.

125. Competition Tribunal, 2017, 'East African Tea Trade Association v Competition Authority of Kenya', pp. 190–195, CT/001 of 2017, pp. 190–194, available at: https://cak.go.ke/sites/default/files/2024-02/CAK_COMPETITION_AND_CONSUMER_PROTECTION_LAW_DIGEST.pdf [accessed June 2025].

I. Cartels

A. *What Is a Cartel*

234. Cartels occur when firms agree not to compete with each other in an open market, but to come together to eliminate competition. Factors such as market concentration, degree of rivalry, product differentiation in a market or maximisation of profits are some of the reasons that influence cartel formation.[126]

235. In fact, unless exempted in accordance with procedures laid out in sections 25–28 of the Competition Act, section 21 of the Competition Act proscribes cartels, and considers as illegal any restrictive trade agreements and practices undertaken by such cartels. According to section 21, restrictive trade practices include horizontal agreements between independent undertakings, or decisions by associations of undertakings, decisions by undertakings or concerted practices by undertakings at the same level of production or distribution network. Such agreements are prohibited under section 21, if they have as their object the repression of competition between competitors, bid rigging, market allocation, production regulation and restriction of choice of goods and services, and anticompetitive price fixing.

236. Common horizontal agreements include joint purchasing, R&D development agreements and information exchange agreements. Cartels operate in disregard of the existing laws, and in many countries are considered the most serious form of competition law violation. Section 22 also prohibits restrictive practices by trade associations that include the unjustifiable exclusion of a competitor or the exclusion of a potential competitor from a trade association, or a price recommended by trade association to its members.[127]

237. According to section 21 of the Competition Act, one of the most common forms of cartel conduct includes output restrictions in which market operators covenant to:

a. reduce or restrict the supply of essential products and goods with the goal of creating scarcity;
b. bid rig and agree on who should win the tender and at what price;
c. fix the price of products or services;

---

126. Heimler, A., 2012, pp. 849–851, 'Cartels in Public Procurement', Journal of Competition Law and Economics, 8(4); OECD, 1993, 'Recommendation of the Council Concerning Effective Action Against Hard Core Cartels', C(98)35/FINAL; Ashurst LLP, 2014, 'Cooperation Agreement Between Competitors', available at: www.ashurst.com/doc.aspx?id_Resource=4712 [accessed September 2014]; Kaplow, L., 2011, 'On the Meaning of Horizontal Agreements in Competition Law', available at: http://ssrn.com/ [accessed September 2014].
127. OECD, 1993, 'Recommendation of the Council Concerning Effective Action Against Hard Core Cartels', C(98)35/FINAL; Weishaar, S., 2013, pp. 23–24, 'Cartels, Competition and Public Procurement: Law and Economics Approaches to Bid Rigging', Edward Elgar Publishing House, Office of Fair Trading UK, 2004, 'Trade Associations, Professions and Self-Regulating Bodies: Understanding Competition Law', available at: https://www.gov.uk [accessed March 2015].

d. parcel markets and limit or control the supply of essential. This occurs when the cartelists divide markets by allocating customers, suppliers and territories;
e. force;
f. engage in practices involving collusive tendering, minimum RPM and abuse of IP rights.

238. The cartelists working together generally appoint on a case-by-case basis one company that assumes the role of a price leader. Indeed, in *Directline Assurance Company*,[128] the High Court of Kenya observed that the cartel problem in Kenya is an issue of concern to the industry, the Government and the public. The court further stated that competition law authorities must fight cartels by ensuring that effective sanctions against individuals and undertakings involved in cartel activities, putting in place adequate antitrust enforcement policies, and an institutional framework for dismantling hard-core cartels.

B. Price Fixing

239. Price-fixing agreements include those between undertakings whose goal is to fix, maintain and control the price of goods or services. Such agreements also extend to conducts that interfere with how prices of products and services are set by competitors in a particular sector. Price-fixing schemes help those involved to ascertain with accuracy what the pricing policy of their competitors is or will be. By joining forces to fix target prices, entities involved improve their bargaining position and gain leverage that enables them not only to extract great value in negotiations with other competitors but also to dictate terms and secure price of inputs at prices below competitive levels. Too much buying power if left unchecked may hinder competition. In horizontal arrangements, price fixing refers to situations where several competing undertakings agree to set prices for their products at a certain level in order to prevent real competition. Price fixing is considered the most blatant form of restrictive trade practice.[129]

240. According to section 21. 3 of the Competition Act, price fixing includes agreements, decisions or concerted practices between competitors that involve direct or indirect fixing of purchase or selling prices or any other price-related trading conditions that place other trading parties at a competitive disadvantage, or that cause competitors to collude on pricing structure and to decline to compete against each other. Under section 25 of the Competition Act, parties to an agreement or a concerted practice can apply to CAK for an exemption from the application of the

128. *Directline Assurance Company v. Attorney General of the Republic of Kenya and the Ministry for Transport*, HCCC, Petition No. 103 of 2010.
129. OECD, 2010, 'Collusion and Corruption in Public Procurement', Policy Roundtables, DAF/COMP/GF(2010)6; Ezrachi, A., 2012, p. 47, 'Buying Alliances and Input Price Fixing', Journal of Competition Law and Economics, 8(1), 47; Bulmash, H., 2012, pp. 361–365, 'An Empirical Analysis of Secondary Price Discriminations and Motivations', Journal of Competition Law and Economics, 8(2), 361.

provisions of Parts A and B of the Act, both of which prohibit restrictive trade practices. Section 26 of the Act empowers the CAK to grant an exemption if it is satisfied that there are exceptional and compelling reasons of public policy as to why any agreement, decision, concerted practice ought to be excluded from the application of the Competition Act. The CAK has to determine the period and conditions for such exemption.

241. In recent years, the CAK has dealt with a number of price-fixing cases.[130] Under investigation is, for instance, the *Kenya Tea Development Agency* (KTDA), which has been unilaterally serving sixty-five small-scale tea factories in the country for fourteen years. The Agency is currently under investigation for engaging in cartel-like activities, dictating and manipulating tea prices and auction commissions. The CAK is also investigating *Lafarge* for possible manipulation of cement prices, a charge that the global manufacturer, which has significant ownership in two Kenyan companies, has denied.

242. In 2012, the CAK dealt with a case involving the *Macadamia Nut Processors Association* for restricting nut farmers from selling their produce to specified buyers. The CAK handed over its report to the Ministry of Agriculture to take action against the association.

243. In 2015, the CAK began investigating the Cereal Millers Association (CMA) and other stakeholders for colluding to fix and anticompetitively hike the prices of flour contrary to section 21.3a of the Competition Act, and this, despite low cost of white maize and wheat. The Consumer Federation of Kenya, which named three major millers as the firms holding Kenyans at ransom by manipulating prices of flour, also lodged price-fixing claims against the CMA. After thorough investigations, the CAK cleared the millers of price-fixing claims and ruled that it found no form of anticompetitive practices on the part of the millers.

244. In 2015, the CAK initiated investigations into complaints lodged by the *National Intelligence Service (NIS)*[131] against the Association of Kenya Reinsurers (AKR) for collusion, price fixing and generally unfair trade practices. AKR had, via a circular dated 2 October 2013, advised insurance companies on the minimum applicable premiums upon renewal of the NIS Group Life Scheme for 2013/2014. The Regulatory Authority (IRA) mandates insurance companies to use an independent actuary to define individual premium rates, which they are then required to file with IRA for approval. Investigations by CAK revealed that AKR's setting of the minimum premium rates and the request to insurance companies to charge a fixed rate amounted to collusion and price fixing contrary to sections 21.3.a and c and 22.b and c of the Competition Act. The CAK argued that this conduct had an impact

130. CAK of Kenya, 2012/2013, 'Annual Report', pp. 21, 48–50, available at: https://www.cak.go.ke/arch/sites/default/files/annual-reports/FY%202012-2013%20CAK%20Annual%20Report.pdf [accessed January 2026].

131. CAK, 2014/2015, *National Intelligence Service (NIS) against the Association v. of Kenya Reinsurers (AKR)*, available at https://www.cak.go.ke/arch/sites/default/files/annual-reports/FY%202014-2015%20CAK%20Annual%20Report.pdf [accessed January 2013].

on upstream and downstream insurance markets. The CAK, pursuant to sections 36 and 38 of the Competition Act, imposed on AKR a fine of KES 721,715 based on the affected turnover or rather the total re-insurance premium for the NIS Group life cover, which could have benefited the members for the preceding years. CAK further ordered AKR and its members to desist from any similar anticompetitive conduct. In 2018, the CAK conducted investigations, searches and seizures at the business premises of Crown Paints PLC (Crown), Basco Products Kenya Limited (Basco), Kansai Plascon Kenya Limited (Plascon) and Galaxy Paints and Coatings Limited (Galaxy),[132] all members of the Kenya Paints Association, pursuant to sections 31 and 34 of the Competition Act. Upon completion of the investigations, the CAK requested Crown, Plascon and Galaxy to respond to the allegations that they had violated sections 21.1 and 3 (a) and 22.1(b) of the Competition Act, which prohibits agreements whereby undertakings in vertical or horizontal relationships directly or indirectly fix prices (either when buying or selling) or other trading conditions. The CAK found that Crown Paints PLC, Kansai Plascon Kenya Ltd and Galaxy Paints and Coatings Ltd were involved in practices amounting to an agreement on prices and transport costs, and that these agreements were likely to distort competition in the paint manufacturing industry.

1. Bid Rigging

245. Bid rigging or collusive tendering is a type of price fixing that occurs when two bidders agree on which one of them should win. Such bidders may also agree not to bid against each other, or agree to place phantom bids to trick legitimate bidding competitors into bidding more than they would have bid otherwise. Examples of bid rigging schemes include acts such as:

a. dividing markets by submitting bids only in certain geographical areas or to certain public organisations, or refusing to sell to or quoting intentionally high prices to buyers in geographic areas allocated to competing entities;
b. suppressing bids in which one or more bidders who otherwise would be expected to bid, or who have previously bid, agree to refrain from bidding or to withdraw submitted bids from consideration. In such a way, the designated winning bidder's bid is accepted without competition;
c. entering into subcontracting arrangements whereby bidders who agree not to bid or to submit a losing bid are rewarded with supply contracts in exchange, from the successful low bidder;
d. rotating bids by ensuring that all conspirators submit bids but take turns being the low bidder; and or
e. placing complementary bids, in which some competitors agree to submit bids that contain either special terms or that are too inflated to be accepted by the buyer. Such bids are generally fake and merely designed to give the appearance

132. CAK, 2019 '*Competition Authority of Kenya v Crown Paints*, PLC and 3 others', CAK/EC/05/166/A 17 Jun. 2019, pp. 6–8, available at: https://cak.go.ke/sites/default/files/2024-02/CAK_COMPETITION_AND_CONSUMER_PROTECTION_LAW_DIGEST.pdf [accessed June 2025].

of genuine competitive bidding when in fact they are meant to conceal secretly inflated prices.[133] The CAK has recently ruled that bid-rigging is harmful to competition.[134]

246. Almost all forms of bid rigging schemes have one thing in common: an agreement among some or all of the bidders does not disclose their agreement to the person calling for bids. In so doing, they manipulate the direction competition takes in the affected market and, in most cases, eliminate competition among the participants and deny them the freedom to trade under competitive prices and terms. Bid rigging is very subtle and takes place mostly behind scenes, and therefore, very difficult to detect.[135] Section 21.3 of the Competition Act prohibits collusive tendering of any form.

2. Market/Client Allocation

247. Market sharing is a kind of scheme in which undertakings enter into agreements whereby they divide defined particular markets between themselves by geographic areas, products or services, or even by customers (corporations and retailers). Market/client allocation patterns may, for example, involve situations where competitors agree to sell defined products and services only to customers in certain geographic areas and refuse to sell to those in undefined geographic areas. Alternatively, it can also include the selling of products and services at exorbitantly high prices to customers in geographic areas allocated to competing undertakings.[136]

248. In *Jamii Telkom v. Runda Association*,[137] Jamii Telkom filed a complaint with the CAK in which it alleged that it had been barred by Runda Association from installing fibre networks in the area. The CAK resolved the matter by allowing Jamii Telkom into the market.

---

133. OECD, 2012, 'Recommendation of the Council on Fighting Bid Rigging in Public Procurement', available at: http://www.oecd.org [accessed December 2014]; OECD, 2010, 'Collusion and Corruption in Public Procurement', Policy Roundtables, DAF/COMP/GF(2010)6.
134. In CAK; 2021, '*Inter Tropical Timber Trading Ltd vs Top Range Ventures and 5 Others*', CAK/EC/05/188/A, pp. 2–4. available at: https://cak.go.ke/sites/default/files/2024-02/CAK_COMPETITION_AND_CONSUMER_PROTECTION_LAW_DIGEST.pdf [accessed June 2025].
This case concerned bid rigging in a tender procedure for the supply of electricity poles, where it was established that the parties had entered into collusiive agreements contrary to ss 21.1 and 21.3(c) of the Competition Act,and exchanged commercially sensitive information, practices which harmed competition.
135. Heimler, A., 2012, p. 849, 'Cartels in Public Procurement', Journal of Competition Law and Economics, 8(4).
136. CAK of Kenya, 2012/2013, 'Annual Report', p. 49, available at: https://www.cak.go.ke/arch/sites/default/files/annual-reports/FY%202012-2013%20CAK%20Annual%20Report.pdf [accessed January 2026].
137. *Jamii Telkom v. Runda Association* in CAK of Kenya, 2012/2013, 'Annual Report', p. 49, available at: https://www.cak.go.ke/arch/sites/default/files/annual-reports/FY%202012-2013%20CAK%20Annual%20Report.pdf [accessed January 2026].

249. Market sharing definitely prevents, distorts or restricts competition. However, on the face of it, one cannot fail to see its potential advantages. It would reduce costs for market research and even for distribution. This notwithstanding, section 21(3)(b) of the Act prohibits any agreement or concerted agreement that divides markets by allocating customers, suppliers, areas or specific types of goods or services.

3. Production/Innovation Limitation

250. Every market economy, wherein there is production of goods and services, needs competition. Competition, coupled with well-developed competition rules and policies, plays a great role in ensuring market functions properly and efficiently, and in providing consumers with the benefits of a free-market system. It is also one of the key drivers for improving productivity and encouraging innovation.

251. Section 3 of the Competition Act has its object, among other things, the enhancement of the welfare and the protection of the people of Kenya by promoting and protecting effective competition in markets and preventing unconscionable and predatory market conduct in order to increase efficiency in the production, distribution and supply of goods and services and to promote innovation. Section 24.b of the Competition Act prohibits abuse of dominant position through market conduct that limits or restricts production, market outlets or market access, technical development or technological progress through deceptive practices.

252. In determining merger cases, section 46.h of the Competition Act mandates the CAK to take into consideration factors including any benefits relating to R&D, technical efficiency, increased production, efficient distribution of goods or provision of services and access to markets that are likely to be derived from the merger under consideration.

253. Section 50 of the Competition Act further mandates the CAK to review the structures of production and distribution of goods and services in Kenya in order to regulate concentrations of economic power that may increase production and consumer prices and thereby prejudice public interest or be detrimental to competition. The provision prohibits unwarranted concentration of economic power that may in any manner limit production, supply or distribution of any goods or the provision of any service, or that may result in the inadequate production, supply or distribution of any goods or services. Section 52 of the Competition Act allows the CAK to order entities or individuals that are holding unwarranted concentration of economic power in any sector to dispose of interests in production, distribution or the supply of services as it deems necessary to remove the unwarranted concentration.

4. Group Boycott

254. Group boycott is a strategy used by two or more competitors in a given market to coerce those who are not members of a particular group to follow prescribed course of action as for example, not to conduct business with an entity/person unless the entity/person consents to stop doing business with an actual or potential competitor of the entities organising the boycott, or meets certain trading conditions. Boycotts not only give the organisers a competitive advantage but also create negative publicity against the targeted entity/person and impact on their bottom-line profits.

255. Group boycotts are either vertical or horizontal. Horizontal boycott situations occur in cases where cartel members agree amongst themselves not to sell or buy from certain customers. Boycotts are vertical if they involve agreements between entities operating at different levels of production and supply chains in different markets or agreements in which entities refuse to deal with competing entities. Vertical group boycotts may also be used to implement an illegal price-fixing agreement, wherein the competitors agree not to engage in commercial dealings with others except on agreed-upon terms. This result is price increases. Whatever form they take, boycotts are methods used to shut out a competitor from a relevant market or to prevent entry of new entities into a specific market. In Kenya, boycotts are a violation of antitrust laws and are considered illegal under section 21 of the Competition Act, in particular, the boycotts that are, among other things, aimed at promoting collective RPM, fixing purchase or sell prices, or promoting collective exclusive dealings.

256. The CAK has successfully fought off group boycotts in two key sectors, namely, the maize and transport sectors. In the maize sector, the removal of self-regulations within millers association allowed for greater competition, resulting in lower prices of maize flour, an essential good for poor families in Kenya. Due to concentration of milling business in the hands of 'families' and to the fact that maize millers association 'recommend' minimum prices to be charged by their members, CAK has had to intervene and demand a review of the association's internal regulations.

257. To guide business behaviour and discourage anticompetitive practices that may harm consumers, the CAK has also been quite active in the Matatu sector. The sector is crucial for economic growth as Kenyans use matatus as a daily transport means. The CAK has eliminated restrictions to competition by way of cease-and-desist orders against price fixing by Matatu Owners Associations (MOA), and has vehemently fought to eliminate cartels levying route entry charges. To facilitate collusion, these cartels ensure there are as few as possible matatus on key routes and further use exclusionary anticompetitive tactics to bar the new entrants into the business. MOA has desisted from engaging in anticompetitive practices, a fact that has considerably reduced and stabilised commuter fares. Without the CAK's intervention, the cartelisation would have continued affecting Kenyans, particularly the poor.[138]

5. Collusion on Other Objects

258. Section 21.3.f and g of the Competition Act prohibit collusive tendering, the imposition of supplementary pricing conditions that by their nature or according to commercial usage have no connection with the subject of the contracts that entities enter into. It also outlaws the application of dissimilar conditions to equivalent transactions with other trading parties, placing such parties at a competitive disadvantage. Section 22.1b of the Competition Act prohibits trade associations from directly or indirectly making recommendations to their members relating to prices or terms of sales, such as discounts, credit, delivery, and product and service guarantee terms, which may directly impact prices, profit margins or pricing formula used in the calculation of prices.

II. Information Exchange Practices

259. The question that arises is whether exchange of information between undertakings is harmful to competition. If so, why, and what type of information should not be shared. There are proponents for either side of the argument. Some argue that it is not only beneficial to share information but also that it is necessary because undertakings cannot operate in a statistical vacuum. Information exchanges among competitors take place through different channels. Information exchange has its benefits and disadvantages. It can, for instance, remove market pressures from undertakings by increasing transparency in the market and removing uncertainty as to other firms' business strategies. Such a move can enable undertakings to predict each other's behaviour and thus seek to coordinate their actions on the market. However, it should be noted that it may also present a number of anticompetitive effects depending on the type of information exchanged, the way it is exchanged and the market characteristics. On the negative side, information exchange can lead to anticompetitive foreclosure of access to the market in which the exchange of information takes place or of a related market.

260. The nature of the information exchanged determines the impact on competition. Conducts likely to be considered anticompetitive include cases involving the exchange of information relating to future price, standard terms and conditions or quantities, output (including future sales, market shares, territories and sales to defined category of customer). They also include status or outcome of negotiations with suppliers and customers, or situations where undertakings transfer critical

138. OECD, 2013, pp. 161–164 'Policy Round Tables: Competition and Poverty Reduction', 2013, DAF/COMP/GF(2013)12; UN, 2004, pp. 161–163 'Model Law on Competition, UNCTAD Series on Issues in Competition Law and Policy'.

information with the help of customers (non-competitors) and suppliers acting as intermediaries. The Competition Act does not have specific provisions dealing with information exchange. Information exchange is dealt with indirectly within the framework of restricted trade practices. The furthest the Competition Act goes is to oblige, in its section 5.3, the CAK to cooperation with other entities involved in trade in ensuring exchange of information and protection of confidential information.[139]

A. *Trade Associations*

261. Information exchange is rapidly gaining importance, especially in the information-driven society that we live in. Today, human and economic development depend largely upon the exchange of information and its exploitation. Information exchange has also greatly increased the levels of competition so that even among competitors, information exchange relating to price, market shares, price or negotiations with common customers and suppliers is done quite restrictedly. Firms that are members of the trade association are thus careful about information they exchange at trade association meetings.

262. Generally, some of the trade associations representing the Government and other public bodies not only champion the interests of members on legislation, regulations, taxation and policy matters likely to affect them, but they also promote and protect the interests of members in the media by promulgating standards, codes of practice or standard terms and conditions. The motive for exchange of information, especially through trade associations, remains unclear. Perhaps this is because some trade associations are directly or indirectly seen as forums for anticompetitive, or even collusive, activities. In many countries, any decision, rule or recommendation of a trade association or agreement between its members, which has an appreciable effect on competition, is prohibited. In the Kenyan context, section 22 of the Competition lists activities of trade associations that amount to restrictive trade practices. These include:

a. unjustifiable exclusion from a trade association of any person carrying on or intending to carry on in good faith the trade in relation to which the association is formed. It is important to note that in determining whether an exclusion from such an association is unjustifiable, the CAK examines the application of any rules of that association and the reasonableness of those rules;
b. the direct or indirect making of recommendations by a trade association to its members or to any class of its members regarding: (i) the prices to be charged by such members or the margins to be included in prices, or (ii) the terms of sale discounts, credit, delivery and product and service guarantee terms.

139. OECD, 2010, 'Information Exchanges Between Competitors under Competition Law', DAF/COMP(2010)37; CAK, 2012, 'Exemption Guidelines for Horizontal Practices, 2012', available at: http://www.cak.go.ke [accessed October 2014].

III. Cooperation Agreements

263. Cooperation agreements on competition whether vertical or horizontal provide an avenue for competitors to enter into mutually beneficial agreements that may result in substantial economic benefits without contravening competition laws. These agreements can have different effects in different market scenarios. Cooperation is horizontal if actual or potential competitors enter into an agreement and vertical if agreements are concluded between entities operating at different levels of production or distribution chain. Such agreements can also involve non-competitors trading in the same product markets, but operating in different geographic markets without being potential competitors. Cooperation agreements can be used as tools to save costs, share market risks, increase investments, enhance product/service quality and variety and pool expertise, and bringing new innovations to market faster. At the same time,such agreement can be used to address product and service shortages in the supply chains and to reduce dependencies on certain products, services, and technologies. However, such agreements, if used to fix prices, allocate markets or enhance market power, may have anticompetitive effects or lead to loss of competition, especially if allowed to evolve into cartels.[140]

264. Still, whether horizontal or vertical cooperation agreements have an effect on competition, or whether their benefits outweigh the anticompetitive effects, will often depend on the market structure, the position of the entities in the markets affected by the cooperation and area and objectives of a given cooperation. Because vertical cooperation agreements are concluded between competitors, the same guidelines used to assess horizontal agreements are applied to them as well. To be exempted from the application of the provisions of the Competition Act, cooperation agreements whether vertical or horizontal must meet a number of cumulative conditions set forth in section 26.3 of the Competition Act; they have to be able to contribute to:

a. maintaining or promoting export;
b. improving or preventing decline in the production or distribution of goods or the provision of services;
c. promoting technical or economic progress or stability in any industry; and
d. obtaining a benefit for the public, which outweighs or would outweigh the lessening in competition that would result, or would be likely to result, from the agreement, decision or concerted practice or the category of agreements, decisions or concerted practices.

140. European Commision, 2023 Guidelines on the applicability of Article 101 of the Treaty on the Functioning of the European Union to Horizontal Co-operation Agreements' ', available at: https://competition-policy.ec.europa.eu/system/files/2023-07/2023_revised_horizontal_guidelines_en.pdf [accessed January 2026].

265. The CAK has released Exemption Guidelines[141] that are expected to streamline the implementation and enforcement of the Competition Act and thereby enable the CAK to fulfil its mandate of protection competition in Kenya. The Exemption Guidelines outline the criteria and define the indicators to be used to assess whether agreements, decisions and concerted practices pertaining to horizontal or vertical cooperation should be exempted from the application of the Competition Act.

266. The goal of the Guidelines is to help the CAK expand its mandate to protect competition process in Kenya, and reduce frictions between the competition and consumer protection objectives. The CAK has also developed Guidelines that govern cooperation between it and other competition or consumer bodies in line with section 9 of the Competition Act, which encourages cooperation with other consumer and competition bodies. The Guidelines contain principles that guide the CAK when entering into a cooperation arrangement with any consumer or competition body. The Guidelines also highlight the responsibilities of the cooperating parties and the criteria for identifying the consumer bodies to cooperate.

A. Research and Development

267. Cooperation agreements may also take the form of R&D, purchasing, production and distribution, specialisation or joint-venture efforts. Under the Competition Act, cooperation agreements of whatever form are not to contain any of the expressly prohibited anticompetitive practices under the Act. Specific exemptions may benefit certain categories of agreements due to their purpose – such as R&D agreements and joint ventures. Cooperation through R&D agreements can promote technical progress in Kenya by allowing undertakings to share financial risks and costs, share the costs and risks associated with the development of new products, bring together complementary technologies that may trigger further innovation and enable parties to the agreements to exploit the results of that research together.

268. Where the undertakings participate in complementary activities, this approach helps infuse healthy economic growth. The parties are left to agree as to whether entering into such an agreement will entitle each party to utilise and access the results of the work of the joint R&D and any pre-existing know-how for the purposes of further research or exploitation independent of the other party. R&D agreements have often been criticised for having the potential to endanger continual innovation and competition in product markets, particularly in industries where undertakings primarily compete on innovation, leading to fewer or poor quality products. There are also concerns that that R &D agreements may reduce the freedom of the participating entities to conduct R&D activities independently or in cooperation with third-party undertakings in a field unconnected with that to which the R&D relates.

---

141. CAK of Kenya, 2014, 'Guidelines on Engaging with other Consumer Organisations', available at: http://www.cak.go.ke [accessed December 2014].

269. The CAK exempts R&D agreements from competition rules, but considers the following factors:

a. the nature and extent of the collaboration;
b. whether the agreement dampens or deters innovation and its diffusion;
c. the features of the market in which the collaboration takes place;
d. whether the terms of the agreement restrict exploitation of the outcomes of the project;
e. whether there is evidence of improper information sharing beyond the scope of the project; and
f. at what stage of development the agreement applies; and whether the agreement involves non-competitors.

B. Specialisation and Standardisation Agreements

270. Specialisation agreements, which can be done in the context of either unilateral or reciprocal specialisation, or joint production, are aimed at encouraging cooperation between undertakings in the area of specialisation in the production of goods and the provision of services. Reciprocal specialisation agreements are those between two or more parties, which are active in the same market, through which two or more parties agree on a reciprocal basis, to cease production of certain products or to refrain from producing those products and instead purchase these products from the other parties, which agree to produce and supply them. Unilateral specialisation agreements are those in which one undertaking agrees to cease or refrain from the manufacture of certain products or the provision of certain services in favour of another participant.

271. The CAK considers cooperation in the area of specialisation as critical to improvement of the production or distribution of essential goods and services, the enhancement of technical and economic progress, and encouraging the production of quality products for end user. Consequently, specialisation agreements are exempted from application of the Competition Act, so long as they do not have as their objective price fixing, collusive tendering, market allocation, limitation or control of production and similar monopolistic practices.

272. According to the Exemption Guidelines developed by the CAK, standardisation agreements are essential for promoting technical and economic progress and encouraging the development of new markets and improved supply conditions. Technical standard agreements relate mostly to the technology-driven sectors of the economy. These agreements delineate the technical or quality requirements with which current or future products, production processes, services or methods may comply. However, standard setting through such agreements can give rise to restrictive effects on competition when they price competition, stifle innovation, limit or control products and services an undertaking can provide, fix prices or unlawful information exchange.

273. The CAK considers the following factors in analysing an agreement amongst competitors to establish standard terms and conditions: (a) whether adoption of the terms and conditions by members is mandatory; (b) whether the terms relate to terms of sale or purchase; and (c) whether they are widely adopted by the industry.

274. In determining technical standards, agreements can be exempted under the Competition Act. The CAK considers, among others: (a) whether standardisation promotes innovation; (b) whether standardisation indirectly fixes prices, quantity or quality; (c) whether the process of standardisation results in unlawful information exchange; and (d) whether standardisation is a mechanism to support collusion.

C. Joint Production

275. Undertakings are allowed to enter cooperation agreements for joint production. In joint production agreements, the participating undertakings agree to produce certain products or provide certain services jointly. Often, this is done by way of a joint venture or by way of horizontal or vertical subcontracting. Joint production agreements vary in form depending on the nature of products and services being offered.

276. As with specialisation agreements, horizontal subcontracting agreements include unilateral specialisation agreements between two entities which trade in the same product market or markets. They also cover reciprocal specialisation agreements between two or more undertakings, which have commercial dealings in the same production market or markets, on a reciprocal basis, as well as subcontracting agreements with third parties whose goal is to expand production. Since alignment between the parties in joint production agreements, especially in matters of the output or product quality and prices, can give them a market power that can lead to anticompetitive foreclosure of potential competitors from a particular market, the rules set forth in the Competition Act, which prohibit agreements that have the object or effect of restricting competition, apply.

D. Joint Purchasing and Joint Selling

277. Joint purchasing/selling agreements can be used to achieve economies of scale and to drive productivity growth by improving the development, production, distribution and marketing of goods and services. Such agreements also provide the modalities through which undertakings can organise business in any industry, and negotiate joint purchases and sales with several of the industry's dominant companies. Once organised in this manner, they can form a self-protective network of counterbalancing forces.

278. It is generally recognised that joint purchasing can often be procompetitive because it permits smaller undertakings to achieve similar purchasing power to larger competitors, which can lead to enhanced competition, for example, in the form of lower prices and/or better quality products or services.

279. This concept involves both horizontal and vertical arrangements: the horizontal arrangements between the competitors which are purchasing jointly, and the vertical supply arrangements between the suppliers and the cooperating purchasers' group, and in some cases, the downstream supply arrangements between the purchasing group and its members.

280. However, in situations where such agreements are used by undertakings to exclude certain members of the industry from an agreement to jointly purchase or sale goods and services, the agreements can increase the costs of those excluded undertakings and therefore, adversely affect competition.

281. Undertakings in this kind of arrangement should be careful not to practice price fixing because it is very likely to occur in such a situation. Price fixing is regarded as one of the evils against which competition law exists to protect. The Exemption Guidelines provide that in analysing a joint purchasing or selling agreement, the CAK must consider the extent to which the parties to the agreement retain their commercial autonomy. Parties should be willing to demonstrate the extent of any efficiency generated by the agreement.[142]

§3. Vertical Agreements

I. Distribution

A. *Introduction*

282. Vertical cooperation agreements (or concerted practices) for the sale and purchase of goods or services are entered into between entities doing business at different levels of the market or production or distribution chains. They include, for instance, distribution agreements between manufacturers and wholesalers or retailers on matters of common interest that impact competition, franchising, exclusive distribution, and resale and price restriction agreements. Section 21.2.b of the Competition Act states that vertical agreements are those concluded between an undertaking and its suppliers or customers or both that are in a vertical relationship. The case[143] concerned an application for exemption for a vertical agreement between Coopers K-Brands (CKL), a manufacturer, and its Strategic Business Partners

142. CAK of Kenya, 2014, 'Exemption Guidelines', available at: http://www.cak.go.ke [accessed December 2014]; Jephcott, M., 2005, p. 133, 'Horizontal Agreements and EU Competition Law', Anthony Rowe Ltd.
143. CAK, 2018, In the matter of Cooper K- Brands Limited CAK/EC/05/136/A, pp. 34–36, available at: https://cak.go.ke/sites/default/files/2024-02/CAK_COMPETITION_AND_CONSUMER_PROTECTION_LAW_DIGEST.pdf [accessed June 2025].

(SBP), one of its distributors. They applied to the CAK for exemption for the conclusion of exclusive distribution agreements for a period of five years. The SBPs had undertaken to distribute CKL's products to specialist retailers in allocated territories. Both companies applied for an exemption in respect of restrictions on territory allocation, product exclusivity, non-compete obligations and price fixing. In determining whether granting an exemption for anti-competitive practices such as territorial allocation, brand exclusivity and and RPM would result in negative competition, the CAK found that given CKL's strong market presence, the exemption would significantly restrict intra-brand market penetration and reduce the associated benefits for consumers in terms of prices.

283. The Competition Act distinguishes between restrictive practices that are outcome of vertical restraints, and those that arise from horizontal relationships. Vertical agreement helps to obtain the synergies needed to bolster efficiency of the undertakings involved. They are strategic alliances aimed at ensuring that resources and capabilities are shared at different stages of the value chain in order to create a competitive advantage for the different players in that chain. Furthermore, vertical agreements also have the effect of boosting competition if they simplify market entry for undertakings or allow one distributor to 'free ride' on the promotional efforts of another distributor. They are further critical if concluded in the interests of the undertakings concerned and the public as a whole, or if they, through the resulting improved supply and distribution chain, promote efficiency among the consumers. Under the Competition Act, vertical agreements are illegal and thus anticompetitive if they dictate price or quantity of goods and services. The Act also prohibits vertical agreements that contain restraints on the supplier or the buyer, for instance, those with an obligation on the buyer not to purchase competing brands. Vertical agreements that reduce possibilities for innovation, or result in anticompetitive market foreclosure that amounts to an abuse of dominant position, are illegal under the Competition Act.[144]

284. Though the Competition Act does not define the term 'distributor', the term can be defined to mean a person who participates in acts of distribution that are subject to the Act. The term 'distribution' therefore means the act by which goods and services are sold and or distributed by one person to another. The chain of distribution is, therefore, the path through which goods go before getting to the consumer. According to section 2 of the Competition Act, the term 'undertaking' is defined to include those businesses involved in the distribution of services and goods of any kind. They come in many configurations.

285. A producer of goods that are not for his own use always needs to put them in the market. The producer has the power to decide how to distribute his goods; he

144. WIPO, 2015 'Linking Universities and R&D Institutions to the Public and Private Sector for Management and Promotion and Commercialization of IP Assets', available at: http://www.wipo.int [accessed August 2016]; Whish R. and Bailey, D., 2012, 'Competition Law' (7th ed. Oxford University Press); Jones, A. and Sufrin, B., 2010, 'Texts Cases and Materials', 2010, 'EU Competition Law: Text, Cases & Materials', 4th Edition, Oxford University Press; Goyders, J. and Albors Llorens, A., 2009, 'EC Competition Law', 5th Edition, Oxford University Press.

could do his own distribution, or he could deliver them to an independent distributor. Sometimes, a wholesaler comes between the distributor or producer and the retailer. Under section 50 of the Competition Act, the CAK constantly reviews the structure of production and distribution of goods and services in Kenya to determine if there are anticompetitive activities in Kenya that may have a detrimental impact on competition. According to this section, agreements that are concluded with the goal of unreasonably increasing the costs of distribution of goods and the provision of services, the price at which goods and services are sold, or the profits derived from the distribution of goods are illegal. section 50 also prohibits agreements that lessen competition or create monopoly in the distribution, sale and purchase of goods and services, or that result in adequacy in the distribution of goods and services.

B. The Prohibition Against Resale Price Maintenance

286. RPM refers to a vertical agreement between a supplier and a distributor by virtue of which a manufacturer and its distributors agree to set maximum or minimum prices for entities trading in a defined geographical market. RPM can take the form of either a fixed, minimum, maximum or recommended price ceiling at which the products of the relevant manufacturer should be sold. RPMs do not permit price competition, and are mostly imposed by manufacturers to restrict the demand of their products at retail level. Thus, a price ceiling may be imposed on the retailer by the manufacturer, or it may be a joint agreement between them on the pricing floor.

287. Price maintenance cuts prices in several ways: it prevents discount negotiations on the prices of products and services being sold, it may also cause elimination or reduction of intra-brand competition, leading to price disadvantages for the consumer, and increases in price transparency that might facilitate horizontal collusion upstream or downstream. It is an effective tool used to minimise free riding. RPM can also be detrimental to competition as far as it supports cartels operating at manufacturer and retail levels. Colluding cartels may then increase prices, exclude competitors from the market and give those colluding power to exploit competitors in affected markets. When used well, RPM can help increase combined profits of upstream and downstream undertakings involved in price maintenance.[145]

288. The Competition Act prohibits all forms of cartel conducts, including RPM. Section 21.3.d of the Competition Act specifically prohibits an agreement, decision

145. Choi, Y.S., 2011, p. 573, 'The Per Se Rule on Minimum Resale Price Maintenance in Korea: A Time to Change', International Review of Intellectual Property and Competition Law, 2011, 570, Ewald, C., 2012, pp. 300–305, 'The Economics of Resale Price Maintenance: Why Europe Is Right Not to Follow the USA on the Slippery Slope of Leegin', Journal of European Competition Law and Practice, 3(3), 300; Buttigieg, E., 2010, p. 397, 'Lingering Uncertainty over the Antitrust Approach to Resale Price Maintenance', Journal of European Competition Law and Practice, 1(5), 397, OECD, 2008, 'Resale Price Maintenance: Series Roundtables on Competition Policy, available at: https://www.oecd.org/content/dam/oecd/en/publications/reports/2009/09/resale-price-maintenance_bd8c934a/126ecbc8-en.pdf [accessed January 2026].

or concerted practice which involves maintenance of minimum resale price. In *CAK v. Crown Beverages Ltd,*[146] Crown Beverages was fined an 'administrative penalty' of KES 2.4 million for engaging in restrictive trade practices by allocating territories for its distributors and setting minimum price rules for distributors in Kenya for distributors selling its products (Redds, Castle Lager, Nile Special, Peroni, Miller and Keringet mineral water). The CAK argued that setting of minimum prices was in contravention of section 21 of the Competition Act, and pointed out that such a practice has the dual effect of benefitting the manufacturers and distributors in the production and supply chain, and of causing detriment to consumers.

C. Exemptions from the Prohibition Against Resale Price

289. The exemption in section 21.4 of the Act provides that subsection 3.d of section 21 (which deals with agreements, decisions or practices involving RPM) shall not prevent a supplier or producer of goods or services from recommending a resale price to a reseller of the goods or a provider of the service, provided:

a. the supplier or producer makes it clear to the reseller or provider that their commended price is not binding; and
b. if products or services bearing a price affixed or applied by the supplier or producer, such products or services must contain the words 'recommended price' appearing next to the price so affixed or applied.

1. Books

290. RPM for newspapers, books and related articles is prohibited in most countries, and when allowed, is subject to defined exemptions. Some countries have in place guidelines that specify the procedure to be followed in allowing RPM for books, and especially in cases where the advantages of such practice are shown to outweigh its disadvantages. The Competition Act prohibits, subject to certain exemptions, agreements involving RPM. Section 5.1 of the Competition Act states that the Act applies to all persons, including the Government, state corporations, and local authorities in so far as they engage in trade. Section 5.3d gives the CAK the power to adjudicate on all matters concerning competition and consumer welfare. This certainly includes the purchase and distribution of books. As previously indicated, unless exempted by the Competition Act, sections 21.3.a and d prohibit agreements between undertakings that directly or indirectly fix purchase or selling prices of the books. Section 55.d of the Competition Act outlaws the giving of false or misleading representations with respect to prices of goods and services in Kenya.

---

146. *CAK v. Crown Beverages Ltd*, 31 Mar. 2014, available at: https://www.cak.go.ke/arch/sites/default/files/annual-reports/FY%202013-2014%20CAK%20Annual%20Report.pdf[accessed January 2026].

291. The Competition Act does not expressly provide for an exemption for RPM for books. Kenya has a strong wholesale and retail bookshop network, which has been instrumental in supplying books and other instructional materials to all parts of Kenya. Kenya is reputed to have the lowest secondary textbook prices mainly because of the powerful primary and national secondary textbook approval process and a national approved textbook list and price for selected teaching and learning materials used in primary and secondary schools (the Orange book) provided by the Ministry of Education. For all other books, publishers are required to indicate on the cover page of each book the recommended retail price as stipulated under section 21.4. This fixed price represents a certain security for the publisher when he decides to publish a book, and makes it possible to publish special interest literature, valuable but less popular literature and books of new authors. In addition, the fixed price allows publishers to refuse too high rebates to big retail chains, which would endanger the publishers' possibility to cross-subsidise less popular books. In a cultural dimension, publishers and booksellers say that a wide network of bookshops preserved by retail price maintenance brings books as cultural products closer to the population.[147]

2. Newspapers and Magazines

292. Kenya has more than one hundred newspapers and magazines. This includes four daily and weekly newspapers in English and one in Kiswahili, weekly and monthly magazines. The key media regulators are the Ministry of Information, Communication and Technology (MICT), CCK, and the Media Council of Kenya. The CCK was established under the Kenya Information and Communication Act, Chapter 411 of the Laws of Kenya, licences and manages services in the communications Industry. In practice, the prices of newspapers and magazines are fixed by the MICT based not just on the potential earnings by the publishing houses from sales but also on what the readers are willing to pay. Transportation, price of paper and publishing costs are also built into the final prices of the newspapers and magazines. The general motto is that if the newspaper price is too low, circulation might be healthy, but profits could decline. However, if the price is too high, circulation could decline or drop altogether. All newspapers and magazines must obtain a licence from the MICT through CCK. The Kenya Information and Communication Act has no restrictions on RPM, but prohibits, in its section 84S, the direct or indirect fixing of purchase or selling prices or any other trading conditions.

147. Ministry of Education, 2014, 'Approved List of School Textbooks and Other Instructional Materials for ECDE, Primary Schools and Teachers Training Colleges', Revised 13th Edition, Vol. 1, January 2014; Ministry of Education, 2014b, 'Approved List of School Textbooks and other Instructional Materials for Secondary Schools', Revised 13th Edition, Vol. 2, January 2014.

D. Exclusive Distributorship

1. Exclusive Distribution and Customer Allocation

293. Exclusive distribution is generally an agreement between suppliers and distributors, in which only one distributor is appointed as a sole distributor in a particular marketplace. The appointed distributor is then obligated not to distribute the products in other markets or appoint any third party to distribute the products in the defined market. Distribution agreements can be national or international in scope. Most exclusive distribution agreements often result in restraints that promote competition in the marketplace. For instance, the effect of such agreements may be that intra-brand competition is reduced and the market ends up being partitioned. Exclusive distributorship may, however, raise some competition concerns. Though the granting of exclusivity rights to a sole distributor to sell the products within a particular geographic region could boost inter-brand competition, it may foreclose other distributors from the market and eliminate intra-brand competition. Usually, the greater the degree of territorial protection granted to a particular distributor, the more serious the infringement on competition. Increased prices of goods and services are also the norm in cases where a distributor is conferred the exclusive right to distribute products in one or multiple markets or regions.

294. Just like exclusive distributorship, exclusive customer allocation is also a common vertical restraint. In exclusive customer allocation, a supplier enters an agreement to sell out its products or services to a single distributor who in turn is required to resell only to a specific class of customers. Exclusive customer allocation may not only result in collusion at both the suppliers' and the distributors' level but may also lead to market partitioning and therewith, price discrimination.

295. Section 21.3 of the Competition Act prohibits restrictive practices aimed at dividing the markets by allocating to suppliers specific types of goods or services. The section also prohibits any act that would result in limiting market access. Exclusive distribution and customer allocation therefore fall squarely within these prohibitions. However, under Part D of the Act, an association of undertakings can apply to be exempted from the prohibitions on restrictive trade practices. The CAK can grant the exception based on whether the trade practice is meant to prevent the decline in the production or distribution of goods, improve production and distribution, promote economic or technical progress of an industry or obtain a benefit for the public in a better way, outweighing the effects of reducing competition. The Competition Act provides that the practices that are prohibited are those that have as their object or effect the restriction of competition. Whether or not exclusive distribution and customer allocation agreements have negative effects on competition is a matter that is to be explored on a case-by-case basis. The CAK plans to publish Guidelines on exemptions on vertical practices, which will, among other things, provide directions in respect to exclusive distribution and customer allocation agreements.

2. Agency Agreements

296. An agent is an economic operator who acts on behalf of another entity called the principal, and has authority to create legal relations between the principal and third parties. Agency agreements bring about a very close legal interrelationship between the agent and the principal, the agent and the third parties with whom the agent transacts on behalf of the principal, and the principal and third parties with whom the agent makes commitments in the name of the principal. The close economic links may mean that the agent forms an integral part of the business of the principal, making the relationship characterised as one of economic unity. An agent may operate in two major forms. One such form is operation as an auxiliary organ that is part of the undertaking of the principal. In this case, the principal determines the price at which the agent should sell the goods and services, imposes restrictions or limits on the geographical areas in which the goods and services entrusted to the agent may be sold, and sets limits on the type of customers the agent should deal with. The second form is operation as an independent economic operator, in which case the agent assumes financial and commercial risks that are linked to the sale or performance of contracts entered into with third parties, or costs relating to the supply or distribution of goods and services.

297. It is under this second form that the independent operator can be found to be in breach of the Competition Act, especially in cases where the agent and the principal are acting independently of each other and can therefore, legally not be considered one entity under the Act. The economic reality of the relationship between an agent and a principal is what is determinative of the consequences of their actions and not the characterisation that the parties give to the arrangement. Aspects that are indicative of the nature of the agreement include assumption of risk, both financial and commercial, during sale of goods to third parties. If there is an element of taking of risk on the part of the agent, the agent can be treated as an independent undertaking. However, if the agent and the principal are working closely together, any foreclosure effect on the relevant market that results from their relationship will infringe competition law where, for instance, the relationship acts as a barrier to potential entrants to the market and softens competition.[148]

3. Exclusive Supply Obligations

298. This encompasses cases where a supplier is under the obligation to supply products to a specific buyer or for a particular use. Exclusive supply obligation is a vertical restraint that more often than not results in exclusive supply obligation or quantity forcing on the supplier. In fact, vertical agreements in which a supplier is expected to sell to one buyer or a limited number of buyers may lead to foreclosure of other buyers in the upstream market or to collusion between buyers.

148. Zhang, H.A., 2013, pp. 579–580, 'Toward an Economic Approach to Agency Agreements', Journal of Competition Law and Economics, 9(3), 553.

299. When evaluating exclusive supply agreements, the Competition Act requires the CAK to determine on a case-by-case basis whether such agreements have the effect of restricting competition. Under the Competition Act, the agreements can either be categorised as those respecting abuse of dominance, in cases where one of the contracting parties has dominant market power, or simply as anti-competitive. Factors such as the definition of the relevant market and the suppliers operating within a given market are also taken into consideration by the CAK when evaluating such agreements.

300. A good example of an exclusive supply agreement in Kenya was the competition case brought before the Kenya CAK by Zuku, a satellite pay-TV provider, against MultiChoice.[149] MultiChoice is a digital satellite TV service in Africa, which provides, *inter alia*, various general entertainment, movies, documentaries, news, etc. MultiChoice owns several subsidiaries, including Digital Satellite Televiison (DSTV), which is a competitor of Zuku. Zuku protested against MultiChoice's exclusive rights over broadcast of sporting events (in this case English Premier League). In so doing, Zuku argued that MultiChoice had foreclosed it from the upstream broadcasting market, and denied it a 'must have' premium content for any pay-TV. This conduct, Zuku further argued, amounted to a restrictive trade practice in violation of the Competition Act, Part III of section A, in particular sections 21 and 24.2.b of the Competition Act. It further accused Multi-Choice of selling such rights solely to DSTV, a vertically integrated retail distributor. Investigations have been concluded and hearing of the matter before the CAK.

E. Exclusive Dealing

301. Exclusive dealing involves vertical arrangements that require a buyer to obtain all or most of its goods and services from a single seller for a defined period of time, and from an exclusively defined territory. Forms of exclusive dealings include arrangements forbidding a buyer from purchasing products or services from a seller's competitors, from selling the products of a different manufacturer, or requiring a seller to purchase all, or a substantial portion of its total requirements of specific goods or services from one supplier.

302. Exclusive dealing arrangements can provide benefits and, at the same time, impede the ability of a seller's competitors to compete effectively in a market. One of the key benefits of exclusive dealing is that it places the buyer and the seller in a complementary role that ensures, for example, that free riders are kept at bay, and the downstream customers are effectively served. It also gives the participating enterprise the guarantee that there will be competition from rivals in the geographical area parcelled out cit. Vertically aligned buyers and sellers can also participate in joint promotions, marketing, pre-sale customer service and expansion into new

149. CAK, 2014/2015, 'Annual Report', p. 104. *CAK v. Multichoice*, Case No. 1 of 2012, avaialbleat: https://www.cak.go.ke/arch/sites/default/files/annual-reports/FY%202014-2015%20CAK%20Annual%20Report.pdf [accessed January 2026].

areas or products. These pro-competitive factors result in greater sales and enhance efficiency in the relevant market. Nevertheless, exclusive dealing can be anticompetitive in circumstances where it enables one manufacturer to monopolise efficient distribution services and thereby thwart entry or inhibit the growth of existing competitors. Under the Competition Act, exclusive dealing arrangements are illegal if they lead to the placing of key outlets or sources of supply in the hands of a single entity, thereby making it difficult for new, potentially competing firms to penetrate the market. Exclusive dealing agreements that facilitate price discrimination are also illegal under the Competition Act.

1. Non-Compete Clauses ('Single Branding')/Exclusive Purchasing

303. Single branding includes those agreements that require a buyer not to manufacture, purchase, sell or resell products, which compete with the products listed in the single branding agreement, or to purchase a good percentage of the products listed in the agreement from one particular supplier. Non-compete obligations and exclusive purchasing obligations are some examples of single-branding agreements.

304. Exclusive purchasing is a requirement placed on an undertaking to purchase all of its supplies of another undertaking from a specific undertaking. In order to determine whether such agreements are antitrust compliant, it is essential to gauge whether they eliminate competition in the relevant or affected markets during the time of their validity.

305. Single branding and exclusive purchasing agreements have certain advantages to the manufacturer and the distributor. For instance, the manufacture in such arrangements is able to predict the likely demand for a particular product during the term of the agreement. The distributor is also likely to get preferences where there are shortages, special prices and sometimes financial or technical assistance from the manufacturer. The possible competition risks are foreclosure of the market to competing rivals, facilitation of collusion between suppliers in case of cumulative use and, where the buyer is a retailer, restriction of inter-brand competition. The CAK is yet to formulate Guidelines for single branding and exclusive purchasing agreements.

F. Selective Distribution

1. Introduction

306. Selective distribution is a system in which a producer gets into vertical agreements with a certain number of limited dealers operating in the same geographical region or network. The distributors bound by such agreements have to sell specific products to defined distributors. Selective distribution agreements are often used by producers who deal in common or rather branded final products. Essentially, the producer puts in place a system in which the products can only be bought and resold by distributors and retailers who are authorised. Those who are not authorised are not in a position to obtain the products. The authorised distributors must resell the products to specified distributors who fall within the system or to the final consumer as possible buyers. Selective distribution agreements are mostly based on qualitative and quantitative criteria defined by manufacturers for all possible resellers. A qualitative selective distribution system is generally based on criteria that are:

a. only qualitative in nature;
b. required by the nature of the contract goods or services;
c. laid down uniformly for all distributors;
d. not applied in a discriminatory manner; and that
e. do not directly limit the number of distributors.

307. Notwithstanding these criteria, the products subject to selective distribution system must be of a kind that makes it necessary to use selective distribution system. For such products, it is justifiable to suppress price competition in favour of non-price competition. Moreover, the criteria a producer uses to limit the distributors of its products should be uniform for all possible resellers and must be applied in a manner that does not discriminate against the resellers involved. This makes it possible for any distributor, not just specific ones, to satisfy the criteria set out. Besides, any restrictions put in place by the producer should not go any further than is necessary to protect the quality of the product. The second category of selective distribution systems is those that are not purely qualitative. These systems do not satisfy some or all of the requirements for a purely qualitative selective distribution system, and are, for this reason, prohibited in competition law.[150]

308. From the competition law standpoint, the effects of such systems on competition are that they may facilitate collusion between suppliers or buyers, foreclose access to the market for certain category of distributors and thereby reduce intra-brand competition or minimise competition altogether. Selective distribution falls under the prohibition on restrictive practices arising out of limiting market access or outlets under section 21.3 of the Competition Act. The CAK is yet to release guidelines shedding light on how the section would apply to a selective distribution system or agreements associated therewith.

2. Resale of Motor Vehicles and Spare Parts

309. Kenya's automotive sector has undergone major transformations since the advent of Structural Adjustment Programs (SAP) in the 1990s. The sector includes

150. Lianos, I., 2007, p. 661, 'Commercial Agency Agreements, Vertical Restraints and the Limits of Article 81.1 EC: Between Hierarchies and Networks', Journal of Competition law and Economics, 3(4), 625.

car assemblers such as Kenya Vehicle Manufactures and General Motors East Africa; franchise dealers who have licences to import, assemble and distribute motor vehicles on behalf of car manufacturers in Japan, China, United Kingdom, Germany, etc.; second-hand car dealers; spare parts dealers retailing new assembly and used replacement parts, service, and repair garages that repair vehicles and briefcase businessmen who solicit for orders and source goods on demand. Kenya's leading motor vehicle dealers include Toyota (East Africa), DT Dobie, Cooper Motor Corporation, General Motors and Simba Colt. In addition, there are four vehicle assembly plants/body fabricating in the country, which concentrate on the assembly of pick-ups and heavy commercial vehicles.

310. Kenya offers a lucrative market of about 70% of used vehicle imports, resulting in tough competition for the established motor vehicle dealers whose sales have steadily declined due to stiff competition from second-hand imported vehicles, mainly from China and Japan. Stiff competition from second-hand vehicle parts is a problem that started when liberalisation of the economy was introduced in 1993. Massive importation of after-market vehicles has led to high demand for second-hand spare parts and related accessories. The demand for new vehicles as compared to second-hand vehicles is also very low in Kenya because Kenya is generally a low-income country. In order to reverse this trend, the Kenya Motor Industry Association (KMI), the representative body of the corporate participants in the motor industry, has imposed strict criteria on second-hand car imports and formulated incentives aimed at promoting local assembly of motor vehicles and encouraging vehicle manufacturers. The rapid expansion of the East African economy and the prospects of South Sudan joining the EAC have fuelled growth in the regional auto industry, new vehicle constructing plants have been constructed, and new car designs and new car manufacturers and sellers have been launched into the market.

311. Selective distribution in the motor vehicle industry is very common in Kenya, and involves transactions in which manufacturers of vehicles (from other countries) deal with specific distributors locally. The manufacturers of motor vehicles get into agreements with specific dealers who are the exclusive distributors of their vehicles and spare parts in Kenya. The Toyota brand of vehicles, for example, is distributed exclusively by Toyota Kenya, an entity that has branches in several parts of the country in order to reach the buyers. DT Dobie, an exclusive distributor of Chrysler/Jeep/Dodge, Nissan, Mercedes-Benz Benz and Renault, distributes vehicles via its three dealership-based in Nairobi, Nakuru and Mombasa. DT Dobie also sales spare parts, maintains and repairs its brand of cars that it distributes. These distributors are the exclusive dealers in new motor vehicles from the respective manufacturers, who have entered into contracts with them not to sell new vehicles to other distributors in the country. The extent to which selective distribution agreements entered into by car distributors and manufacturers limit competition is debatable, especially given that buyers have shown a preference for cheaper second-hand motor vehicles purchased directly from persons who have used them in other countries.[151]

G. *Franchising*

1. Introduction

312. This is an arrangement involving two distinct firms in which the franchisee pays the franchisor for the right to distribute or sell the franchisor's products, and for using the franchisor's IP rights, including the logos, and know-how for a defined period of time. Franchising is a kind of middle ground between vertical integration and outsourced distribution. For there to be an effective franchise system, every franchisee has to comply with the IP rights of the franchisor during and after the termination of the franchise agreement. The rights to use the franchisor's IP rights distinguish the franchisee from ordinary distributors. In addition to rights to Franchisor's IP, the franchisee receives from the franchisor during the life of the agreement, commercial or technical assistance, for example, training, financial planning, expertise and procurement of services that enable the franchisee to operate as an independent business. In return, the franchise pays a fee to the franchiser for the use of whatever business method the franchiser offers. Though the franchisee is a residual claimant, its rights to decide how the franchised business is run are restricted.[152]

2. Voluntary Chains

313. From a competition angle, other than provision of the business method, franchise agreements, whether selective distribution and/or non-compete and/or exclusive distribution, often have a number of vertical restraints touching on the products or services offered. In Kenya, there are a number of local and international franchisors with established operations in the market. The Kenya Franchise Association (KEFRA) is a private initiative formed by and for franchisors and franchisees doing business across a vast array of industries and assorted vertical markets. KEFRA's goal is to promote the interests of franchisors and franchisees, and to make and set policies for their benefit.

151. Kinoro, A.J., 2013, 'Factors Affecting New Vehicle Sale in the Kenya Motor Industry: A Case of General Motors (East Africa) Limited', International Journal of Social Sciences and Entrepreneurship, 1(2) 664–687; UK Trade and Investment, 2013, 'Automotive Sector in Kenya'. February 2013; KPMG, 2014, 'East Africa's Changing Auto Industry', 23 June; Mapenzi Bahati, E, 2009, 'The Influence of Marketing Strategies on Popularity of Toyota and Nissan Brands in Kenya', available at: https://erepository.uonbi.ac.ke/bitstream/handle/11295/22970/MAPENZI_BAHATI_E._MBA_2009.pdf [accessed January 2026].

152. Syekei, J., Coulson, P. and Märzheuser-Wood, B., 2014, 'Kenya', Franchise Law Review, 1st Edition, pp. 360.

314. In general, a franchise agreement, including voluntary chain agreements, is essentially a contract between the franchisor and the franchisee, and falls under the ambit of the contract law or rather the Contract Act. However, due to lack of franchise-specific provisions in the Contract Act, franchisees and franchisors may mutually agree on the terms and conditions to govern the franchise agreements they enter into. So, for instance, in the case of *Skoda Export Limited v. Tamoil East Africa Ltd*,[153] the court held that parties to a franchise agreement are free to determine the jurisdiction in which they want their franchise disputes resolved. Nevertheless, franchise arrangements that have as their object the fixing of purchase or sale prices, the limiting or controlling of production or investment, the distorting or restricting of competition, etc., are prohibited under section 21 of the Competition Act, unless exempted under section 25 of the Competition Act from the application of the Act.

315. Depending on the industry the franchise parties are from, some franchising agreements may also be subject to the laws and or be supervised by regulatory bodies responsible for the respective industries. Besides, the franchisor and franchisee have to comply in addition with the provisions of the Anti-Counterfeit Act,[154] which prohibits trade in counterfeit goods. The Anti-Counterfeit Act establishes the Anti-Counterfeit Agency, whose duties include, *inter alia,* informing the public on matters relating to counterfeiting and combating counterfeiting trade and other dealings in counterfeit goods. Moreover, franchisees and franchisors doing business using the e-commerce platform have to adhere to the data protection and confidentiality provisions set out in the Kenya Information Communications Act 2010.[155] Local and international franchisors have, in addition, the obligation to pay taxes under the Value Added Tax Act.[156] The franchising business in Kenya is growing fast with new entrants entering the market every day, and eventually the CAK will be required to coin a legal framework or guidelines to govern the franchising business in the country.

II. Technology Licensing

316. The comprehensive policy framework for science, technology and innovation and the establishment of the institutions supporting innovation development have led to remarkable progress in technology licensing in Kenya. Section 64 of Part X of the IPA permits licensing contracts in respect of any inventions in any field of invention. Parties to the licensing contract have the freedom to determine the terms and conditions of such a contract. Section 69 of the IPA contains thirty-three

153. High Court of Kenya Civil Case No. 645 of 2007.
154. KLR, 2009, 'Anti-Counterfeit Act Cap 130A the Laws of Kenya', : https://new.kenyalaw.org/legislation/, [accessed January 2026].
155. KLR, 1999, 'Kenya Information Communications Act 1999, Chapter 411A of the Laws of Kenya', available at: : https://new.kenyalaw.org/legislation/, [accessed January 2026].
156. KLR, 2009, 'Value Added Tax Act, No. 35 of 2013', available at: : https://new.kenyalaw.org/legislation/, [accessed January 2026].

unconscionable terms, which may render a licensing contract void and therefore, not registrable under the IPA. Some of the voidable contracting clauses include those that:

a. require the licensee to sell products produced by him/her under the contract exclusively or principally to persons designated by the licensor;
b. limit the volume of the products produced by the licensee with the help of the technology to which the contract relates;
c. prohibit or restrict the use by the licensee of any technology other than the technology to which the contract relates;
d. fix prices for the sale or resale of the products produced by the licensee with the help of the technology to which the contract relates;
e. prohibit or restrict the use by the licensee, after the expiration of the contract, of the technology acquired as a result of the contract;
f. restrict the licensee from entering into sales, representation or manufacturing agreements relating to similar or competing technologies, when such restrictions are not needed for protecting the legitimate interests of the licensor;
g. impose restrictions on territories, quantities, prices, customers or markets in which the licence should sell or distribute his/her product; and
h. make the contracts subject to acceptance of supplementary obligations which, by their nature or according to commercial usage, have no connection with the subject of such contracts.

317. Section 7.d of the IPA allows the Board of KIPI to cooperate with authorities in Kenya and abroad on matters relating to the furtherance of the objectives of the IPA.

318. To further promote and increase awareness of IP rights in the country, in 2013, the Parliament of Kenya passed the Science, Technology and Innovation Act (hereinafter 'Science & Technology Act'),[157] which is gradually transforming Kenya's innovation and licensing landscape. The Science &Technology Act establishes three institutions in the Department of Education, Science and Technology that will be responsible for reviving innovation systems in Kenya. The newly established institutions include the National Commission for Science, Technology and Innovation, the successor to the National Council for Science and Technology, the Kenya National Innovation Agency, and the National Research Fund.

319. The Kenya National Innovation Agency is responsible for promoting development in the areas of science, technology and innovation, and increasing the awareness of the economic benefits of technological innovation and IP rights among investors, universities, research institutions, government policy makers and the public. Part IV of the Science &Technology Act regulates the licensing of technology in, from and into Kenya. According to section 12.5 of the Science & Technology Act, no licenses shall be granted for technologies that:

157. KLR, 2015 'Science Technology and Innovation Act', available at: https://new.kenyalaw.org/akn/ke/act/2013/28/eng@2022-12-31[January 2026].

a. have negative influence on the cultures of people of Kenya;
b. may use IP rights as a tool for illegally exploiting the traditional knowledge of the people of Kenya; or that
c. have adverse effects on the lives of Kenyans.

320. Section 15.3 of the Act further states that all technologies imported into, or exported from Kenya under any law, including the IPA, are technologies under the Science &Technology Act. Sections 9 and 21 of the Competition Act allow the CAK to cooperate with KIPI and other competition, innovation and consumer protection authorities on matters relating to consumer protection and competition policy.

A. *Patent, Trademark, Know-How and Trade Secret Licensing*

321. Section 54 of the IPA, which regulates both product and process patents, gives the patent owner the right to prevent third parties from using, making or disposing of a product which is the subject of the patent or which is derived from it, or making use of the process itself. Section 55 of the IPA gives the owner of a patent the right to prevent, by way of injunction, or claim damages from anyone using, selling or licensing his technology without his consent. The rules governing licensing of all innovations, including patents, are discussed in section 9 titled 'technology licensing'.

322. There are, however, exceptions to the exclusive rights conferred on patent owner. Under section 72 of the IPA, any person or company seeking to use a rights holder's patented technology without his consent can apply to the Tribunal to allow him to exploit the patented invention on the grounds that a market for the patented invention is not being supplied on reasonable terms in Kenya. Under section 75.2e, such an individual or company must pay the patent holder a reasonable remuneration for the license. Section 77 of the IPA allows the Tribunal to cancel a compulsory licence if the licensee fails to comply with the licensing terms, or if the conditions under which the license was granted have ceased to exist, or are unlikely to occur. In Kenya, compulsory licensing is an effective mechanism for facilitating access to cost-effective lifesaving medicines. The compulsory licensing provisions in the IPA allow generic drug producers to manufacture essential medicines covered by patents without the authorisation of the patent holder, and thereby create a mechanism for cheap generic drugs to be made available at significantly lower prices than their on-patent equivalents. Compulsory licensing has helped design an IP system in Kenya that appropriately balances incentives for patent holders and technology diffusion.[158]

158. Mey, B., 2013 pp. 230–235, 'The Legal Duel: The TRIPS Agreement and Drug Access Issues: Is the Agreement Actually the Cunning Manoeuvre It Has Been Dubbed?', Peter Lang GmbH, Internationaler Verlag der Wissenschaften; New edition edition (16 Aug. 2013).

323. The Exemption Guidelines on Horizontal Practices provide some further guidance on IP rights licensing. The CAK will consider a number of factors in determining whether an agreement limits competition, including the nature of competition in the market, the kind of restrictions in the agreement on the IP rights, benefits accruing to consumers and how the benefits could or could not be attained but for the agreement. Under section 28.1 of the Competition Act, though certain IP agreements including those relating to licensing may be restrictive or may bear some risk of distorting competition, the CAK will grant exemption if they are beneficial. The benefits may include clauses that support improved production or supply of new products and services, enjoyment of IP rights or other benefits for the consumers.

324. In Kenya, the Trademarks Act governs trademark registration.[159] Trade secrets protection is done mostly by way of non-disclosure agreements and non-compete contracts because of the fact that traditional IP rights, such as patent, copyright, and trademark cannot adequately protect them. The legal status of trade secret as a protectable IP right is upheld if the owner(s) can prove the trade secret was not generally known and reasonable steps were taken to preserve its secrecy. KIPI is solely responsible for the regulation of all IP rights, including trademarks, in Kenya. So far, there have been no reported decisions with regard to the licensing of trademarks, expertise and trade secrets by the CAK.

B. Vertical Exchanges of Information

325. Vertical exchange is the exchange of information between enterprises (for example, a retailer and a manufacturer) that operate at different economic levels in the supply chain. Vertical communication can help to enhance the overall efficiency of distribution systems, improve consumer supply and welfare, stabilise and or reduce prices, improve product positioning in multimarket industries, and therewith increase transparency in the market. Information exchange also helps new competing enterprises entering the market to evaluate the business opportunities awaiting them in a given market.

326. However, in the competition law context, information exchange may give rise to competition concerns if the participating enterprises align their business strategies and use information exchange as a tool to encourage collusive implicit market outcomes prohibited under the Competition Act. This may include, for instance, information exchanges that facilitate price setting, quantity setting or market sharing arrangements within a defined sector. Information exchanges may also lead to market foreclosure, especially in situations in which potential new entrants into a market are placed at a significant disadvantage because they lack the information available to the incumbent competitors involved in an information exchange scheme.

159. KLR, 1957, 'Trademarks Act, Chapter 506 of the Laws of Kenya', available at: https://new.kenyalaw.org/akn/ke/act/1955/51/eng@2022-12-31 [accessed January 206].

327. Kenya, like most countries, does not have specific provisions dealing with exchanges of information. Section 5.3.c of the Competition Act merely empowers the CAK to exchange information and provide protection to confidential information with regard to any business conduct governed by the Competition Act. Information exchange can, therefore, fall within the framework of the prohibitions against cartel agreements and/or concerted practices outlined in the Competition Act. According to the CAK's Consolidated Guidelines on the Substantive Assessment of Restrictive Trade Practices (hereinafter 'Guidelines on Restrictive Trade Practices'),[160] market competitors can exchange information that is non-price and that is aimed at boosting competition in the market as whole. This may for instance include information such as collaborations on technical, safety and education standards for the industry.

328. According to the CAK,[161] information exchange, whether horizontal or vertical, regarding the allocation of customers or markets to specific undertakings, exchange of labour and research costs, specification on services, or the exchange of any confidential business secrets, can be construed as information aimed at eliminating competition amongst the entities exchanging such information. The CAK assess the impact of each information exchange on competition on a case-by-case basis. The frequency of information exchange among such entities is also likely to have a significant impact on competition. In addition, the exchange of information between competitors, if not disclosed to the customers, is also likely to have a significant adverse effect on competition. The CAK has promised to deal with any exchange of information relating to price.

329. In order to determine the legality, or the extent to which, information exchange affects competition, the CAK has to deal with the anticompetitive concerns raised by information exchange on a case-by-case basis. Nevertheless, factors such as the type of information exchanged, the manner in which it was shared, the structure of the affected market, and its particular economic context, the age, level of aggregation and subject matter of the information exchanged, and the manner in which the information is exchanged have to be taken into consideration.

160. CAK, Undated, 'Consolidated Guidelines on the Substantive Assessment of Restrictive Trade Practices', available at: http://www.cak.go.ke [accessed August 2015].

161. CAK, 2013, 'Annual Report' 2012/2013, available at: https://www.cak.go.ke/arch/sites/default/files/annual-reports/FY%202012-2013%20CAK%20Annual%20Report.pdf[accessed Januray 2026].

Chapter 2. Dominant Undertakings' Prohibited Practices

§1. Abuse

330. Under the previous competition law regime, the Prices and Monopolies Commission dealt with a number of cases on abuse of dominant undertaking. One such case involved the sale of *NSSF shares in East African Portland Cement Company Ltd. (EAPCC)*[162] and Athi River Mining Company Ltd (ARM) to Blue Circle Industries Plc (BCI) of the United Kingdom. Kenya has three cement-manufacturing companies, which are all quoted in the NSE. Bamburi Cement Ltd. has a capacity of 1.2 million tonnes annually and sells about 600,000 tonnes in Kenya annually (50% of the annual domestic consumption). The EAPCC has a production capacity of 800,000 tonnes annually and sells about 500,000 tonnes annually (about 40% of the annual consumption). ARM has a production capacity of 100,000 tonnes annually and caters for about 10% of the annual domestic consumption. In June 2000, BCI applied for authorisation to acquire 9,300,000 and 870,000 N.S.S.F shares in EAPCC and ARM, respectively. NSSF, which is a public pension fund, had agreed to sell the stock and BCI had agreed to purchase the same. Investigations revealed that BCI and La Farge of France owned directly and indirectly through their International Holding Company, Bamcem, 73%, 42% and 19% of the shareholding in Bamburi Cement Ltd, EAPCC and ARM, respectively. The proposed transaction would result in Bamcem, which is owned by BCI, La Farge and Costal of Switzerland, 40%, 40% and 20%, respectively, and its principals owning 72%, 52% 21% in Bamburi Cement Ltd, EAPCC and ARM, respectively. The implication would then be that Bamce, its principals, BCI and La Farge would have substantial influence in decision-making and corporate policies of all three cement-manufacturing companies in Kenya if authorised to acquire 9,300,000 and 870,000 shares in EAPCC and ARM, respectively. Given the strategic importance of the cement sector in Kenya, BCI was most likely going to abuse dominance in the production and marketing of cement in Kenya if the deal went through, a move that could reduce competitive benefits in the production and supply of cement. The application was, therefore, rejected by the Minister for Finance.

331. In the *Transglobal* case, the logistics company Transglobal Cargo Centre filed a suit against Kenya Airports Authority (KAA) and Others, accusing KAA of discriminating against competitors engaged in ground handling services at the Jomo Kenyatta International Airport (JKIA) and abusing its dominant position contrary to sections 21 and 24 of the Competition Act. Transglobal alleged that it had lost KES 7 billion worth of business following delay by KAA in awarding it ramp handling services. The case fizzled out after Transglobal suddenly dropped the case. In the

162. CAK, 2014/2015, Transglobal Cargo Centre Ltd and KAA and Competitors at JKIA, Case No. 13 of 2014, p. 106, 'The Annual Report 2014/2015', available at: https://www.cak.go.ke/arch/sites/default/files/annual-reports/FY%202014-2015%20CAK%20Annual%20Report.pdf [accessed AJanuary 2026]; NSSF shares in East African Portland Cement Company Ltd. (EAPCC) in CAK of Kenya, 2012/2013, 'Annual Report', p. 21, available at: http:// https://www.cak.go.ke/arch/sites/default/files/annual-reports/FY%202012-2013%20CAK%20Annual%20Report.pdf [accessed January 2026].

case filed against a synthetic hair supplier, Styles Industries Ltd (Styles), that manufactures a popular brand of hair extensions and wigs by a competitor, Solpia Kenya (makers of Sistar hair), Styles was found guilty by the CAK for abuse of dominance in contravention of section 24 of the Competition Act. Following a complaint filed by Solpia, in which it accused Style of engaging in restrictive trade practices, including imposing unfair selling prices and conditions on suppliers, and threatening clients with account closure if they stocked Solpia's products, the CAK launched an investigation into Styles and found that Styles had indeed abused its dominant market position by imposing unfair trading conditions on its downstream suppliers. The case ended when Styles entered into financial settlement negotiations with the CAK to resolve the matter.[163]

§2. Exploitative Practices

332. These practices, which may also be exclusionary practices, occur or arise from conduct of dominant enterprises that take advantage of their market power to exploit their customers, competitors or other trading partners directly. The goal of such practices is to harm the dominant undertaking's competitors. Examples of exclusionary and exploitative practices include imposition of predatory prices, foreclosure of market entry, putting limits on production, discounts and refusal to supply essential goods and services.

I. Excessive or Unfair Pricing

A. *Determining Whether Prices Are Excessive*

333. The cost-of-production theory of value is the theory that the price of services and goods is determined by the sum of the cost of the resources that went into making such goods and services. Other than resources, the cost of commodities and services can include factors of production such as labour, capital, or land, raw materials and taxation. In particular, it is the marginal value and the marginal cost of the last unit traded that jointly determine a price. From the perspective of neo-classical economists, the 'fair' value of a good or service is given by its 'competitive' market price, which is the equilibrium price that would result from the free interaction of demand and supply in a competitive market. In competitive markets, the price of a good or a service should equal its marginal cost of production.[164]

334. The price of goods and serviced is thus considered excessive or predatory if the goods or services are sold far below or well above the cost of production in

163. African Antitrust Competition Law, 2019, Styles Industries (Darling) Kenya, available at: https://africanantitrust.com/category/distribution/ [accessed January 2026].

164. Lianos, I., 2007, p. 661, 'Commercial Agency Agreements, Vertical Restraints and the Limits of Article 81.1 EC: Between Hierarchies and Networks', Journal of Competition law and Economics, 3(4), 625.

a bid to drive smaller firms out of the market. This was reflected in the decision of the European Court of Justice in *United Brands Co. v. Commission,*[165] in which the Commission found that United Brands Company (UBC) had abused its dominant position in the market for bananas by, amongst other things, charging unfair (excessive) prices for the sale of Chiquita bananas to customers in Belgium-Luxembourg, Denmark and Germany. The court reiterated that a price is excessive if it is unrelated to the economic value of the product. The court further said that this can be determined if it can be shown that: (i) the price-cost margin is excessive, and (ii) the price imposed is either unfair in itself or when compared to competing products.

335. The CAK has dealt with a few cases involving predatory pricing. For instance, in *Telkom Kenya Ltd v. Airtel Kenya Ltd & Essar Telkom Kenya Ltd,*[166] CAK dismissed the case Telkom Kenya had filed against Airtel and Essar, claiming that the latter's off-net calling rates were predatory as they were below the normal market rates. Likewise, in *CAK v. Kenya Private Health Care Providers (PHP) Consortium,*[167] the CAK issued a cease and desist order against the Private Health Care Providers Consortium for recommending the percentage by which to increase fees in private hospitals. The order in question had prevented healthcare providers in Kenya from adjusting their fees upwards by 20%. Section 24.2 of the Competition Act states that it is an abuse of dominant position to impose predatory or selling prices and other anticompetitive trade conditions in business transactions.

B. Price Orders

336. A price order is an instruction from the CAK on how an undertaking should price its products and services, particularly in cases where such prices are predatory. Usually, a direction from a CAK towards a specific undertaking on pricing is in itself viewed as an interference with competition. Therefore, this power is cautiously exercised, on case-by-case basis, and in limited circumstances. Neither the CAK nor the Prices and Monopolies Commission before it has issued a price order.

C. Other Aspects Connected to Excessive Prices

337. The most common concept falling under this category is the regulation of prices by the government. In Kenya, a good example is the regulation of fuel prices

165. *United Brands Co. v. Commission*, Case C-27/76 [1978].
166. *Telkom Kenya Ltd v. Airtel Kenya Ltd & Essar Telkom Kenya Ltd. (6/7/2012)* in CAK of Kenya, 2012/2013, 'Annual Report', p. 49, available at: http:// https://www.cak.go.ke/arch/sites/default/files/annual-reports/FY%202012-2013%20CAK%20Annual%20Report.pdf [accessed January 2026].].
167. *CAK v. Kenya* Private Health Care Providers (PHP) Consortium: 26/07/2012, in CAK of Kenya, 2012/2013, 'Annual Report', pp. 23 and 50, available at: http:// https://www.cak.go.ke/arch/sites/default/files/annual-reports/FY%202012-2013%20CAK%20Annual%20Report.pdf [accessed January 2026].

by the government, mandated Energy Regulatory Commission (ERC) was established under the Energy Act, 2006. Some of the objectives of the ERB are to regulate the electrical energy, petroleum and related products, renewable energy and other forms of energy, and to protect the interests of consumers, investors and other stakeholders. Petroleum and fuel prices are regulated through price capping. So, for instance, 'Super' and 'Regular' petrol, 'automotive diesel' and 'kerosene' are some of the fuel brands whose prices are capped. The ERC review the prices of products that fall under its responsibility on a monthly basis. Other than price capping, crude oil and other petroleum products are purchased through the open tender system of the Ministry of Energy. Under this system, the oil company that quotes the lowest price gets to import for the whole industry. The importing cost forms the basis of the price capping formula.

II. Other Unfair Trading Conditions

338. The test for whether an undertaking engages in unfair trading conditions is the determination of whether an undertaking in a dominant position would impose the conditions it presently imposes if it were in that position. Further anticompetitive practices that include the requirements to provide a guarantee/ advance payments or to pay market entrance fees, or threats of termination/ annulment of contracts. Generally, the area of exploitative practices is yet to receive attention from the CAK.

III. Discrimination

339. Price discrimination is a strategy whereby customers in the same market are charged different prices for the same services or products. In some cases, the seller exploits the customer by charging the maximum price that each customer is willing to pay. Price discrimination is prohibited under section 24.c of the Competition Act, which states that the application of dissimilar conditions to equivalent transactions with other trading parties is an abuse of dominant position. Price discrimination occurs where a similar commodity is sold at different prices to different customers despite identical costs. In essence, the sales have varied ratios of price to marginal cost. Price discrimination also covers sales at the same price despite different costs. This activity can be consistent where a supplier maintains a policy of obtaining a higher rate of return from some customers than from others.

340. In some situations, price discrimination can result in a positive result when it increases allocative efficiency, thereby increasing output. However, in some situations, it does not and actually ends up transferring wealth from poor consumers to wealthier ones, and putting weaker and emerging enterprises in a given market at a competitive disadvantage.[168]

IV. Exclusionary Practices

341. As already said before, section 24 of the Competition Act prohibits the use of both exploitative and exclusionary pricing practices directed against market rivals with the goal of limiting the rivals' ability to compete. Exclusionary abuses include practices by dominant firms which are likely to have a foreclosure effect on the market, i.e., which are likely to prevent profitable expansion in or access to a market for already existing or potential competitors and which finally spill over and hurt consumers. In other words, exclusionary practices discourage entry of new firms into the market on the one hand, or hasten the exit from the market of those already there on the other. Exclusionary abuses of dominance may be both price-based and non-price-based. Examples of non-price-based abuses are contractual tying, single branding contracts and 'naked' refusals to supply. In these situations, it is clear that some 'foreclosure' takes place; the question is whether this foreclosure may be characterised as anticompetitive. Similar effects are achieved through pricing. High stand-alone prices in comparison to a bundled price for two products may 'tie' these two products together as effectively as contractual tying. High rebates given on condition of single branding may have the same effect as contractual exclusive dealing. Asking a very high price for a product or combining a high upstream price with a low downstream price may amount to a 'constructive' refusal to supply. Predatory pricing is a good example of a price-based exclusionary abuse. The concepts mentioned above are explained in the next paragraphs.

A. *Rebates*

1. Legal Framework

342. Rebates are discounts paid from the standard price paid by the seller to the buyer after the transaction has already occurred. Rebates are reductions in the list price of a relevant product, which a seller or supplier offers to a buyer or distributor as an explicit or implicit reward in exchange for a relationship of substantial exclusivity. Rebates also include bonuses or discount schemes to customers willing to buy products or services from a dominant supplier in the market, which enables a supplier to charge a different price for different units of a buyer's demand. The welfare effects of rebates depend on whether the rebate is unconditional or conditional. Unconditional rebates are those granted to specific consumers for each purchase they make, independent of their purchasing behaviour. Unconditional rebates amount to exclusionary practices when granted to consumers who are likely to

168. Geradin, D. and Petit, N., 2006, p. 526, 'Price Discrimination under EC Competition Law: Another Antitrust Doctrine in Search of Limiting Principles', Journal of Competition law and Economics, 2(3), 479.

switch loyalty to another supplier. This kind of situation may be triggered by the geographical advantage of a seller over the one the buyer currently buys from, and may result in the affected buyer moving to the seller that is geographically closer to them.[169]

343. Conditional rebates are granted to customers to reward customer fidelity and readiness to purchase products and services exclusively from a dominant supplier. Rebates lie somewhere between anticompetitive conduct and legitimate competition. They enable customers to buy products or access services that they would under ordinary circumstances not afford. Rebates can, however, raise competition concerns when an enterprise that is dominant utilises them to pre-empt market share that may be critical for rivals, to exclude new entrants from competing with the dominant rivals, or when they are used as tools for reallocating or accessing new critical markets or softening inter-brand competition. Rebate-trapped customers are usually prevented from making purchases from alternative suppliers, as doing so would in effect penalise the customers through the denial of the discount. This strengthens the position of the dominant undertaking and amounts to horizontal foreclosure of market access possibilities to upstream or downstream potential competitors.[170]

2. Kenya's Approach

344. The Competition Act does not directly address the subject 'rebates' and this has cast a significant uncertainty into the use of rebate schemes, but the CAK can investigate to determine if they lead to anti-competitive agreements. However, one can argue that under section 24.2 sub-paragraphs A, C and D of the Competition Act, rebate schemes employed by dominant companies are an abuse of their strong market position. Section 24.2.a of the Act prohibits all forms of agreements or concerted practices with competitors, potential competitors, suppliers or customers, whether oral or written, that directly or indirectly fix purchase or selling prices or any trading conditions with the goal of preventing, restricting or distorting competition. Section 24.2.c of the Act prohibits the application of dissimilar conditions to equivalent transactions with other trading parties, whereas section 24.2.d proscribes unconscionable contracts subject to supplementary un-negotiated boilerplate terms that have nothing to do with the subject matter of the contract. These provisions can be interpreted as prohibiting rebates.

169. Faella, G., 2004, p. 375, 'The Antitrust Assessment of Loyalty Discounts and Rebates', Journal of Competition law and Economics, 4(2), 375.

170. Geradin, D. and Petit, N., 2006, pp. 479–482, 'Price Discrimination under EC Competition Law: Another Antitrust Doctrine in Search of Limiting Principles', Journal of Competition law and Economics, 2(3), 479; Zenger, H., 2012, p. 719, 'Loyalty Rebates and the Competitive Process', Journal of Competition law and Economics, 8(4), 717.

3. The Legal Assessment

345. Rebates involve pricing of products that are tied to a consumer's purchasing trends and behaviour. In determining whether a rebate is abusive, it must be established whether that rebate has the effect of tying consumers to the dominant undertaking and whether the rebate is discriminatory. If neither of these can be proved, then the rebate is nothing but a normal competition tactic applied in the market.

4. Kenyan Cases

346. At the time of writing this monograph, the CAK had not expressly dealt with any case involving rebates.

B. Exclusivity

347. Exclusive dealing involves an arrangement in which two parties entering into an arrangement in which one party, say X as seller imposes upon another party, say Y as the buyer, an obligation to deal with X, to the exclusion of all competitors to X or to sell a substantial parts of its goods and services solely to X. It could also take the form of a manufacturer who demands that a certain distributor buys from him only to the exclusion of his competitors, or a distributor who agrees with a particular supplier that only that distributor shall be supplied with goods of that supplier, and this, to the exclusion of his competitors. Competition concerns regarding exclusive dealing arrangements include the fact that such arrangements may foreclose competition in a substantial share of the line of commerce affected. The true test of legality of an exclusive arrangement is whether it promotes or suppresses competition.[171]

348. In *Exclusive Dealing in the Kenyan Tobacco Industry,*[172] decided by the Monopolies and Price Commission, R J Reynolds complained that distributors and stockists of the company British American Tobacco (BAT), which at that time controlled over 80% of the cigarette market in Kenya, were not allowed to stock R J Reynolds products. RJ Reynolds pointed out that its marketing materials including billboards and posters were uprooted by BAT representatives and sales agents and that its stockists were threatened by BAT sales agents. RJ Reynolds further averred that BAT had violated section 4 of the RTPMPCA, which defined a restrictive trade practice as acts by persons involved in production or distribution of goods aimed at

171. Crocioni, P., 2007, pp. 493–494, 'Leveraging of Market Power in Emerging Markets: A Review of Cases, Literature and a Suggested Framework', Journal of Competition law and Economics, 4(2), 449; Zenger, H., 2012, p. 759, 'Loyalty Rebates and the Competitive Process', Journal of Competition law and Economics, 8(4), 717.
172. UNCTAD, 1999, 'Competition Cases Involving More Than One County', TD/B/COM.2/CLP/9, June 7.

preventing persons or companies that need certain goods and services from acquiring them. When contacted by the Monopolies and Price Commission, the BAT representatives denied influencing distributors and stockists against selling competing brands. BAT representatives argued that BAT had a 'gentleman agreement' with its distributors to exclusively stock its products. BAT also asserted that it had exclusivity over stands where its products were displayed and sold, and other Kiosk owners and retailers were free to stock products from other companies.

349. Investigations carried out by the Commission established that BAT sales representatives had removed posters and billboards of RJ Reynolds and threatened and cautioned RJ Reynolds distributors stocking competing products. The Commission also found that BAT had exclusive dealing arrangements with its distributors and had actually stopped supplying its cigarettes to those who stocked the Aspen brand of cigarettes, contrary to sections 6.1.a.1 and section 10.1.a of the RTPMPCA. However, before the Commission could invoke section 15 of the Act, which empowers the Commissioner to ask enterprises alleged to have committed restrictive trade practices to comment on the allegations, propose appropriate remedial measures and align their conduct with the RTPMPCA, RJ Reynolds informed the Commission that BAT had ceased its unfair business practices. The case was, therefore, terminated.

C. *Predation*

350. Predatory pricing is a deliberate strategy by a vertically dominant enterprise of setting very low prices for a given period, so its competitors will have no option but to leave that particular market. This is a situation where the dominant entity manipulates a rival's downstream margins by raising either the upstream or downstream margins or both. The affected competitors are, as a result, deterred from entering the critical market due to increase in the price of upstream inputs. Predation is an exclusionary practice that alters the market structure. It is premised on an entity's ability to force or exclude competitors and potential rivals out of the market. Once the predator has successfully excluded existing competitors and deterred initial market entry of new ones, it can raise prices and earn higher profits.[173]

351. Kenya has provisions that deal directly with predatory pricing. However, section 24.2.b of the Competition Act clearly outlines acts of abuse of dominance

173. Bravo, F.L. and Siciliani, P., 2007, pp. 245–246, 'Exclusionary Pricing and Consumers Harm: The European Practice in DSL Market', Journal of Competition law and Economics, 3(2), 243; Obiero, E., 2012, 'Is Regulation of Fuel Price Good for Kenya?', available at: http://ollows.com/index.php/is-regulation-of-fuel-price-good-for-kenya [accessed August 2014]; Akman, P., 2008, 'Exploitative Abuse in Article 82EC: Back to Basics?', available at: www.uea.ac.uk/polopoly_fs/1.105848!wp091_exploitative_abuse_in_article82EC_PA.pdf [accessed August 2014]; Sama, D., 2012, 'The Antitrust Treatment of Loyalty Discounts and Rebates in the EU Competition Law: in Search of an Economic Approach and a Theory of Consumer Harm', Munich Personal RePEc Archive.

that constitute the offence of predation. These include limiting or restricting production, market outlets or market access, investment, distribution, technical development or technological progress through predatory or other abusive practices. Predatory pricing depends on the purchasers' willingness to buy from the predator (or the intended victim) at the predatory price.

352. In Fly 540 Aviation Ltd[174] a suit against Kenya Airways alleging that Kenya Airways through its wholly owned subsidiary Jambo Jet was engaging in predatory pricing contrary to section 24 of the Competition Act. This conduct, it was alleged, could force Fly 540 and other smaller firms out of business to the detriment of consumers. The CAK dismissed the case for lack of evidence. Founded in 1977, Kenya Airways is one of the best and most respected airline companies in Africa. It is not only a strong domestic player in Kenya but has also asserted its dominance across Africa and enjoys a reasonable global presence. The company's largest shareholder is the Kenyan government, with 29.8% shares in the company

1. Proof of an Intention to Eliminate

353. Price lowering of prices is another strategy used by dominant companies to eliminate its competitors, or prevent the entry into the market of new establishments. Illegal predation includes situations where the predator company lowers the price below the average cost of the competitor, forcing the competitor to lower its prices below average. The effect is loss of profits or market share, followed by bankruptcy and total exit from the market. Establishment of prices less than average variable costs (AVC) is viewed as illegal since a dominant undertaking has no interest in applying such prices, except that of eliminating competitors so as to enable it subsequently to raise its prices by taking advantage of its monopolistic position. It follows, therefore, that if the dominant enterprise's prices are set above the AVC, but below Average Total Costs (ATC), unlawful predation may be established based on additional evidence. As predation is not the sole economic rationale for such a pricing policy, competition authorities are required to produce additional elements of proof: prices below AVC 'will be regarded abusive if it can be established that they are solely for eliminating a competitor'.[175] In Kenya, intent to eliminate is an essential element in establishing a case of predation.

---

174. CAK, 2014/2015, 'Fly 540 Aviation Ltd Vs Kenya Airways and Jambojet': https://www.cak.go.ke/arch/sites/default/files/annual-reports/FY%202014-2015%20CAK%20Annual%20Report.pdf [accessed January 2026].
175. Posner, R.A., 1974, 'Exclusionary Practices and the Antitrust Laws', University of Chicago Law School, Chicago Unbound, Journal Articles, Faculty Scholarship; International Competition Network, 2008, 'Report on Predatory Pricing prepared by the Unilateral Conduct Working Group', Presented at the 7th Annual Conference of the ICN Kyoto, April; Rousseva E, 2006, 'The Concept of "Objective Justification" of an Abuse of a Dominant Position: Can It Help to Modernize the Analysis under Article 82 EC?' The Competition Law Review, 2(2), March.

2. Defining Variable and Fixed Costs

354. There are two categories of costs: fixed and variable costs. Fixed costs, also called overheads, are costs that are unaffected by output, i.e., independent of quality of goods and services produced. Fixed costs are time-related costs and generally include salaries, insurance, rent, machinery, buildings, etc. Variable costs change with the amount of output. Variable costs, unlike fixed costs fixed costs are zero when production is zero; as capital and labour increase, variable costs rise with them. Variable costs vary according to services and goods produced and often, wages or materials used in production. Total costs are the sum of fixed and variable costs. In some cases, high fixed costs discourage new competitors from entering a market and/or help eliminate smaller competitors (i.e., fixed costs can be a barrier to entry). This is also the case where a number of companies with different fixed and variable costs are competing in the same market. Typical fixed costs differ widely among industries, and capital-intensive businesses have more long-term fixed costs than other businesses. Businesses that largely depend on labour rather than physical assets do not have as many fixed costs. This is why comparison of fixed costs is generally most meaningful among companies within the same sector.[176]

3. Meeting Competition Defence

355. This defence affords an undertaking a ground to argue that it acted in a particular way (for instance, lowering the price of a particular product or service) to meet competition of other competing firms in the market, or to retain its position in the market. If a dominant company has favoured a particular customer, it may be argued that it did so in order to enable that customer to meet the price offered by a competing company. If established, it lends justification to conduct that under section 24 of the Competition Act would be an abuse of dominance unless exempted under section 25 of the Act. It is for this reason that arguments for objective justification usually involve, for instance, public policy concerns or certain market conditions that force an undertaking to act in a particular way.

356. Competition defences provide a balance between the need to enforce the law against abuse of dominance and the need to provide a suitable environment for legitimate competition in the market. In the absence of such defences, the law on abuse of dominance would end up being too hard on the market players.[177]

176. Petzold, D., 2015, p. 2, 'It Is All Predatory Pricing: Margin Squeeze Abuse and the Concept of Opportunity Costs in EU Competition Law', Journal of European Competition law & Practice; Barazza, S., 2012, p. 467, 'Post Danmark: The CJEU Calls for an Effect: Based Assessment of Pricing Policies', Journal of European Competition law & Practice, 3(5), 466, Spector, D., 2014, p. 494, 'The European Commission's Approach to Long-Term Contracts: An Economist's View', Journal of European Competition Law & Practice, 5(7), 492.

177. OECD Global Forum on Competition, 2001, 'Global Forum on Competition: Contributions from Kenya', CCNM/GF/COMP/WD (2001)2; du Plessis, L. and Blignaut, L., 2009,'Staying Safe – Dominant Firms' Pricing Decisions in Industries Where High Prices Do Not Attract Entry', Third

4. Tying and Bundling

357. Tying and bundling are very similar practices that quite often produce the same results. The practices do however have some differences. Tying occurs when a supplier makes the sale of one product (the tying product) conditional upon the purchase of another distinct product (the tied product) from the supplier or someone designated by the latter. Only the tied product can be bought separately.[178] An illustration where the purchase of product X (the tying product) is conditional on the purchase of product Y (the tied product); X cannot be purchased alone, while Y can. Tying may be evident in a contractual arrangement or take the form of a dominant company refusing to supply a tied product, or when the tied product is integrated in a technical product like software. In a bundling arrangement, a company sell the products in a package of two or more products and charges more for the bundle than for the constituent parts of the bundle. Bundling and tying arrangements have the same effect, and are, so to say, practices that lots of undertakings engage in. The effects of these practices are not necessarily harmful to competition so long as there is no foreclosure or exclusion motive or malevolent plan to maintain market dominance.[179]

358. There are two forms of bundling: pure and mixed. In pure bundling, the components of the package are not available separately. X cannot be purchased without purchasing Y as well. Mixed bundling on the other hand is where the two components can be purchased separately, but it is cheaper to buy them together. Tying and bundling arrangements have both welfare benefits and anticompetitive effects. Efficiency justification of both practices includes the fact that they can lead to significant savings in production and distribution costs, lower product prices and improved product quality. The consumers also benefit because they have information about the products that should be tied together. On the other hand, either of the practices may be considered exclusionary trade practices if any of the following four conditions are established: if the practice:

1. is carried out by an undertaking with pre-existing dominance;
2. if the tied products are distinct, whether two or more;

Annual Competition Commission, Competition Tribunal and Mandela Institute Conference on Competition Law, Economics and Policy in South Africa; OECD, 2011, 'Directorate for Financial and Enterprise Affairs Competition Committee', available at: http://ec.europa.eu/competition/international/multilateral/2011_oct_excessive_prices.pdf [accessed August 2014].

178. Papadopoulos, P., 2006, 'Article 82: Tying and Bundling', Competition Law Insight, June; Bork, R.H., 2010, 'The Antitrust Parado', Nabu Press, September, 378–379; Whish, R. and Bailey, D., 2012, 'Competition Law', Oxford publishing, 7th edition.

179. Crocioni, P., 2007, pp. 474–480, 'Leveraging of Market Power in Emerging Markets: A Review of Cases, Literature and A Suggested Framework', Journal of Competition law and Economics, 4(2), 449; Liebowitz, J.S. and Margolis, E.S., 2008, pp. 1–10, 'Bundles of Joy: The Ubiquity and Efficiency of Bundles in New Technology Markets', Journal of Competition law and Economics, 5(1), 1.

3. the practice is likely to have a foreclosure effect; and
4. there is no objective justification for the practice.[180]

359. For competition purposes, it can be argued that tying and bundling practices fall under section 24.2.d, which prohibits agreements, concerted practices or decisions, which make the conclusion of contracts subject to acceptance by other parties, of supplementary conditions, which by their nature or according to commercial usage have no connection with the subject of the contracts.

D. Refusal to Deal

360. In the interest of protecting a free-market economy, undertakings have the freedom to choose whom to deal with or not to deal with. In stressing this fact, Advocate General Jacobs pointed out in *Oscar Bronner GmbH & Co.*[181] that the 'the rights to choose one's trading partners and to freely dispose of one's property is a recognised right, and that incursions on those rights require careful justification'. In the interest of preserving healthy competition, competition laws in many countries sometimes override this freedom by providing ground rules for governing the manner in which undertakings trade. Refusal to deal may include refusal to supply key input products and services; to provide essential proprietary information; to license intellectual property rights or to grant access to an essential facility or network. Refusal to deal is often considered unlawful or exclusionary under competition laws if it is used as strategy to exclude competitors from a market and as a result enhance monopoly, prevent buyers from obtaining available products, services, or as a tool for diminishing effective competition in a market.

361. Refusal to deal is either a restrictive practice under section 21.3.i Competition Act or an abuse of dominance under sections 24.2.c and d of the Competition Act. The CAK is yet to develop guidelines for dealing with cases where a manufacture puts a cap on distributors of its products or services, or rather refuses to deal. The EAC's expansion has provided businesses in Kenya with the opportunity to expand regionally, and it may be time for the CAK in Kenya to work with competition authorities in other EAC countries to develop EAC-specific guidelines that address this, and many other guideline-lacking matters addressed in this monograph.

E. Margin Squeeze

362. Section 24 of the Competition Act prohibits a dominant undertaking from directly or indirectly imposing unfair purchase or selling prices or other unfair

180. Brennan, T., 2008, pp. 355–363, 'Bundled Rebates as Exclusion Rather than Predation', Journal of Competition law and Economics, 4(2), 335.

181. *Oscar Bronner GmbH & Co. v. Mediaprint Zeitungs-und Zeitschriftenverlag GmbH & Co KG* (1999)4 CMLR 11.

trading conditions. According to the Guidelines on Restrictive Trade Practices,[182] the CAK in determining whether there is price squeeze looks into whether the price of a good or service is excessively high or low. According to these Guidelines, a price is excessive if it bears no reasonable relation to the economic value of a good or service, or if it is higher than the normal economic value. Excessively high prices may take the form of a price or margin squeeze, and occur in three instances where for instance, vertically integrated entity with a dominant position:

a. with more than one production level, not only does it supply itself with an essential product or service in a downstream market but also supplies rivals in the downstream market, which are in competition with its own business downstream;
b. with a dominant position in an upstream market prevents its non-vertically integrated downstream competitors from achieving an economically viable price-cost margin;
c. charges its downstream competitors a higher upstream price than it charges its own downstream business;
d. lowers its downstream price below the costs of production and adequate margin with the intention of eliminating an effective competitor and recouping short-term losses at a later period.

363. The Guidelines consider a price excessive if it is used by a dominant entity as a tool to weaken and eliminate competitors from the market, or to exploit the end beneficiaries of the goods or services. For the price of a good or service to be considered excessive, the levying entity must be in total control of a product or service that is essential to its rivals in a market. The good or service must also have no readily available substitutes. Moreover, a price is low if a dominant enterprise uses it as a predatory strategy to eliminate rivals from the market so it can have room to exploit customers.

364. The CAK will remedy any predatory pricing strategy that may affect competition negatively, or lead to the elimination of significant or efficient competitor by analysing the:

a. prices charged to various customers and suppliers (including affiliated companies);
b. structure of costs of production of goods or services;
c. actual costs of production of goods or services;
d. prices and costs in a competitive market or comparable market; and
e. profitability of the dominant undertaking.

182. CAK, Undated, 'Consolidated Guidelines on the Substantive Assessment of Restrictive Trade Practices', available at: http://www.cak.go.ke [accessed August 2015].

F. Other Forms of Abuse

365. With the advent of technology, hubs of new innovations and inventions have sprung up in Kenya, like in the rest of the world. These innovations and inventions have led to new forms of competition, opened new markets for the creation and delivery of innovative products and services, and increased the importance of IP rights. Whereas IP right holders/undertakings have to protect the valuable IP assets, they must not use their IP rights in inefficient and anticompetitive ways.[183]

366. Sections 24.1 and 2.e of the Competition Act prohibit the abuse of a dominant position in the Kenyan market. The provision deems IP rights as business assets and an abuse thereof, an abuse of a dominant position. These sections extend to transactions outside Kenya as long as the transaction involves a Kenyan, an asset, or IP rights generated or protected in Kenya.

183. Alison J. and Sufrin B., 2011, 'EU Competition Law, Text, Cases and Materials', Oxford University Press, 4th edition; Singer, H., 2006, p. 320, 'The Competitive Effects of Cable Television Operator's Refusal to Carry DSL Advertising', Journal of Competition law and Economics, 2(2), 301; Sidak, J.G., 2006, pp. 386–389, 'A Consumer Welfare Approach to Network Neutrality Regulation of the Internet', Journal of Competition law and Economics, 2(3), 349.

Chapter 3. Concentrations

§1. Introduction

367. The Competition Act does not define the term 'concentrations' with regard to mergers or takeovers. It only deals with 'concentration' in the sense of unwarranted concentration of economic power in Part V. Though the Competition Act deals separately with mergers, the rules in Part V thereof can be applied to mergers. In terms of section 2 of the Competition Act, a merger occurs when one or more firms directly or indirectly acquire or establish direct or indirect control over the whole or part of the business of another undertaking. Concentrations involve a situation in which two or more previously independent companies merge on a permanent basis. It also includes scenarios where one or more natural persons or undertakings acquire by purchase of securities or assets, or by contract or other means, the direct or indirect control of whole or parts of one or more other undertakings. A concentration can also occur when two or more undertakings merge to create a joint venture that performs on a permanent basis the functions of an autonomous economic entity.[184]

§2. Horizontal Mergers

368. Rapid technological advances have increased economies of scale in almost all industries. This has increased competition and forced most companies to merge and combine assets and resources to stay afloat and continue producing new and improved technologies. The mergers are either horizontal, vertical or conglomerate. All these mergers occur in virtually all markets. In Kenya, all merger types generally correspond to international M&A classifications, but are influenced by Kenya's regulatory and commercial environment. Each of these mergers raises different competition concerns and impacts differently on market structure, market efficiency and the overall performance in a market. While horizontal mergers have the effect of enhancing power in a market by eliminating competitors, they can lead to efficiency gains or alter investment decisions. Vertical mergers bring together market buyers. Conglomerate mergers, on the other hand, raise practically no competition issues. Whether a merger is horizontal, vertical or conglomerate, a two-pronged test applies; namely, the definition of the relevant market and the assessment of the merger on that market.[185]

184. Shan, W. and Kinnear, M., 2012, p. 628 'The Legal Protection of Foreign Investment: A Comparative Study', Hart Publishing UK.

185. Wang, W. and Rudanko, M., 2012, 'EU Merger Remedies and Competition, Concerns: An Empirical Assessment', European Law Journal, 18(4), 555, pp. 557–557; Ezrachi, A. and Thanassoulis, J., 2013, pp. 395–396, 'Upstream Horizontal Mergers and the Absence of Retail Effects', Journal of Competition Law and Economics, 9(2), 395.

369. Horizontal mergers can take place between entities operating in the upstream markets of vertically related industries, or may involve two or more entities producing substantially similar goods or services in the same relevant market at the same level of business (e.g., between two manufacturers, two distributors or two retailers). In other words, a merger is a business transaction in which two companies fuse to become a single entity. Mergers legally bring together the ownership of physical and intangible assets formerly subject to separate controls by the merging entities. Mergers are either vertical or horizontal, depending on the competitive relationships between the merging entities. All three types of mergers raise distinct competitive concerns. Horizontal mergers are used by undertakings to sell a type of product in multiple markets. Horizontal mergers can also occur between wholesalers dealing with retailers. Horizontal mergers may either yield valuable outcomes (firms can use them to expand their business, enter new markets, increase revenue or reduce costs) or disadvantage consumers through unilateral, uncoordinated effects in the form of price increase and erosion of product quality.[186]

370. The Guidelines on horizontal, vertical and conglomerate mergers are generally developed; the CAK are applied to a broad range of factual situations on a case-by-case basis.[187] The merger control provisions are dealt with in Part IV of the Competition Act. Sections 41–49 of the Competition Act set forth the criteria for review of the mergers. According to the Act, mergers include takeovers and acquisitions. In 2013–2014, Kenya recorded an increase in merger activities, which rose by 35%. As already stated in Part I, Chapter 3, §5, III of this monograph, in determining mergers, whether horizontal or vertical, the CAK takes into account both the SLC and the PIT.[188]

371. The CAK reviews the Guidelines from time to time in the light of new developments, to reflect any significant changes in the structure of the regulatory market or in national or regional policies. Of importance to note is that though the Guidelines are of relevance in dealing with antitrust concerns, they have no legal force, and cannot be used to determine breaches under the Competition Act.

372. The CAK has recently dealt with and approved two notable mergers in *the Acquisition of Essar Telecom Kenya Limited (ETKL) by Airtel Network Kenya Limited (Airtel).*[189] This merger involved two competitors, ETKL and Airtel, trading at the same level of service delivery in the mobile communication sector. In a bid to

186. Bardong, A., 2012, p. 483, 'Germany: the Bundeskartellamt's New Merger Guidelines', Journal of European Competition Law and Practice, 3(5), 481; Thomas, S., 2013, p. 395, 'Close Competitors in Merger Review', Journal of European Competition Law and Practice, 4(5), 391; Shapiro, C., 2002, 'Competition Policy and Innovation', STI Working Papers, 2002/11, DSTI/DOC(2002) 11, 22 April.

187. CAK, Undated, 'Consolidated Guidelines on the Substantive Assessment of Restrictive Trade Practices', available at: http://www.cak.go.ke [accessed August 2015].

188. CAK of Kenya, 2014, 'Public Interest Test in Merger Determinations', available at: http://www.cak.go.ke [accessed December 2014].

189. CAK, Undated, '*Acquisition of Essar Telecom Kenya Limited (ETKL) by Airtel Network Kenya Limited (Airtel)*', p. 22, available at: http://www.cak.go.ke [accessed August 2015].

divide its business assets between Airtel and another competitor, Safaricom, ETKL sold and transferred its mobile business, subscribers and its global standard for mobiles (GSM) licenses to Airtel. The three companies are in the business of providing mobile telecommunication connectivity services. Airtel provides, in addition, mobile money platform. The CAK, in analysing the downstream (for mobile telecommunication services and finance ancillary services) and upstream (for attraction and retention of mobile subscribers) markets in the telecommunication sector, found that the merger did not raise any competition concerns at all. The merger, the CAK pointed out, salvaged a failing ETKL and saved jobs that would have been lost had ETKL been eased out of the telecommunication market. The CAK noted that, in particular, through the merger, the market shares of Airtel would increase as follows: in the market for subscribers: from 16.5% to 24.5% in the market for voice: from 10.9% to 18.5%; in the market for sms: from 2.7 % to 3.1%; and in the market for mobile data from: 13.7% to 17.6%.

373. In the second merger case, *Acquisition of Essar Telecom Kenya Limited by Safaricom Kenya Limited*, ETKL merged with Safaricom,[190] and sold and transferred its passive infrastructure and frequency license to Safaricom. The purpose of this sale and transfer was to enable the smooth parcelling out of ETKL's business and assets between Safaricom and Bharti Airtel Kenya Ltd. In this merger, the CAK considered the wholesale/upstream (where firm's sale inputs to other firms) and the retail/downstream market (where firms sell services/products to end users) segments. The relevant market in the upstream market was that of the electromagnetic spectrum and telecommunication towers, while the downstream product market was the market for wireless telecommunications services and finance ancillary services. The CAK found an overlap with respect to the national market for electromagnetic spectrum and telecommunication towers of both companies. The CAK concluded that the merger was a strategy likely to spur growth, create jobs, and strengthen telecommunication services. Moreover, because of the merger, Safaricom's shares in the spectrum market would increase to 43% from 27% while its share of the market for telecom tower market would increase to 56% from 49%.

I. Non-coordinated Effects

374. This occurs where any would-be competitive constraints on an enterprise are removed as a result of a merger, i.e., when an entity's resources and total capital are combined. Non-coordinated effects are mostly occasioned by a merger of two competitors. An example thereof is where there are two undertakings, A and B. Before the two merge, an increase in price by enterprise A will lead to a loss of customers to enterprise B. Enterprise A will, therefore, have a reason not to raise its prices. The coordinated effect that ensues from the merger is elimination of competition and increased market power. This is so because, as a result of the merger,

190. *Ibid.*, p. 23.

the market elements that prevent Enterprise A from raising its prices are removed, and the new entity can increase its prices at will without any constraints.[191]

375. Under sections 42.2–3 of the Competition Act, all mergers whether conglomerate, vertical or horizontal must be authorised by the CAK. All unauthorised mergers have no legal effect unless the merger is excluded from the provisions of the Act by the CAK under section 41.1 of the Competition Act. Further, section 46.2.b empowers the CAK in the exercise of its mandate to consider the extent to which the proposed merger would be likely to result in any undertaking, including an undertaking not involved as a party in the proposed merger, acquiring a dominant position in a market or strengthening a dominant position in a market.

A. *Where the Merging Firms Have Large Market Shares*

376. Merger regulations guard against the possibility of a merger endowing unnecessary market power on the merged entity, leading to post-merger increase in prices and other anticompetitive outcomes. According to CAK's Guidelines on Horizontal Mergers (hereinafter 'CAK Horizontal Guidelines'),[192] mergers should not be permitted to create or enhance an entity's market power or enable it to unduly exercise such power.

B. *Where the Merging Firms Are Close Competitors*

377. Mergers between close competitors may raise a number of distinctive competitive concerns, as for example, the elimination of competition depending on the size of the firms and the extent to which the products they are trading in are substitutable, and the creation of substantial market power that enables the merged competitors to unilaterally raise prices of their products. In other words, such mergers may create what is called a Significant Impediment of Effective Competition (SIEC). An indication of whether a merger will cause an SIEC is the level of substitutability between the products of the merging undertakings. The higher the level of substitutability, the higher the competitive problems. Section 46.2 of the Competition Act provides that the CAK may, when analysing a merger, look into any

191. Castendyk, O., Dommering E.J., Scheuer, A. and Böttcher, K., 2008, p. 186, 'European Media Law', Alphen aan den Rijn Kluwer Law; Wang, W. and Rudanko, M., 2012, 'EU Merger Remedies and Competition, Concerns: An Empirical Assessment', European Law Journal, 18(4), pp. 555, 558; Ezrachi, A. and Thanassoulis, J., 2013, pp. 395–397, 'Upstream Horizontal Mergers and the Absence of Retail Effects', Journal of Competition Law and Economics, 9(2), 395; Calvino, N., 2011, pp. 524–525, 'When Do Mergers Raise Concerns? An Analysis of the Assessment Carried out by the European Commission under the New Merger Regulation', Journal of European Competition Law and Practice, 2(6), 521; Proctor, J.A., 2014, pp. 960–961 and 970–972, 'Tacit Collusion Indicators in Merger Control under Varied Focal Points', Journal of Competition Law and Economics, 10(4), 959.

192. CAK, Kenya, 2012, 'Guidelines on Horizontal Mergers', available at: http://www.cak.go.ke 1 [accessed September 2014].

criteria which it considers relevant to the circumstances involved in the proposed merger, including the extent to which the proposed merger would prevent or lessen competition, restrict trade or the provision of any essential service or endanger the continuity of key supplies or services.

C. Where Customers Have Limited Opportunities for Switching Suppliers

378. Two competitive problems arise where suppliers merge, leaving the customers with no possibility of switching suppliers. In such cases, price increase and restricted competition through reduced product choice may become a normal trend in the affected market. A further problem could be that such customers have an alternative, but the cost of switching to the alternative is too prohibitive for them.[193]

D. Where Competitors Are Unlikely to Increase Supply If Prices Increase

379. Where competitors to the merging entities face expansion challenges or capacity limitations, the merging entities may be able to restrict output and may be able to control the prices in a market. Under section 46.2.f of the Competition Act, the CAK in considering a merger application shall consider the extent to which the proposed merger would be likely to affect the ability of small undertakings to gain access to or to be competitive in any market.

E. Where the Merged Entity Is Able to Stifle Expansion by Competitors

380. As explained above, in this case as well, the merged entity may be able to control output and may consequently control prices as well. This exposes consumers to possible price increase.

F. Where a Merger Eliminates an Important Competitive Force

381. A merger that eliminates a competitive force would create a potential monopoly and a real possibility of an unconscionable post-merger increase in prices.

II. Coordinated Effects

382. Coordinated effects arise where a merger changes the nature of competition in a market in such a way that entities that previously were not coordinating

193. Proctor, J.A., 2014, pp. 960–961 and 970–972, ' Tacit Collusion Indicators in Merger Control under Varied Focal Points', Journal of Competition Law and Economics, 10(4), 959.

their behaviour begin to coordinate, and thereby raise prices or otherwise harm effective competition. A merger may also make coordination easier, more stable or more effective for the entities which were coordinating prior to a merger.[194] According to paragraphs 44–47 of the CAK[195] Horizontal Guidelines, coordination may take the form of keeping prices above the competitive level, carving out bidding zones, or allocating markets by geographical area or by customer or product characteristics.

383. Coordination requires market conditions in which:

a. a common understanding on the terms of coordination can be reached;
b. monitoring by the coordinating firms is possible to detect deviation; and
c. deterrence mechanisms are available to 'punish' deviation, and there is lack of outsider reaction from current and future competitors as well as customers that might jeopardise the gains from coordination.

A. *Reaching Terms of Coordination*

384. According to paragraphs 47–52[196] of the CAK Horizontal Guidelines, coordination is more likely to emerge if competitors can easily arrive at a common perception as to how the coordination should work. Paragraph 49 of these Guidelines states that the less complex and the more stable the economic environment, the easier it will be for undertakings to reach a common understanding on the terms of coordination. Coordinating undertakings should therefore have similar views regarding which actions align with specific market behaviour and which ones do not.

385. For instance, it is easier to coordinate among a few players than among many in market where the conditions of demand and supply of products are predictable. Coordinating entities can also agree on a common price for products, especially if they are trading in a market with many differentiated products. In such cases, they can fix terms of the market shares, for customers and territorial restrictions, so long as this is not carried out in an anticompetitive manner. Obtaining key information about rival undertakings and the market may also help outline the terms of coordination.

194. Calvino, N., 2011, pp. 524–525, 'When Do Mergers Raise Concerns? An Analysis of the Assessment Carried Out by the European Commission under the New Merger Regulation', Journal of European Competition Law and Practice, 2(6), 521.
195. CAK, Kenya, 2012, 'Guidelines on Horizontal Mergers', available at: http://www.cak.go.ke 1 [accessed September 2014].
196. *Ibid.*

B. Monitoring Deviations

386. According to paragraph 53[197] of the CAK Horizontal Guidelines, coordinating entities may attempt to increase their share of the market by deviating from the terms of coordination agreed upon by the entities they are coordinating with. Deviation tactics may include, for instance, lowering prices to build own market shares or win contracts, offering rebates or discounts on products or services, increasing product quality or capacity or expanding geographical reach into existing markets with a view of winning new customers.

387. Though retaliation and transparency may help keep undertakings from deviating, the coordinating entities have to be able to monitor the deviations from coordination. Transparency depends on the number of participants in market, and how transactions are carried out in that market, as well as on available information regarding product, market strategies and participants, and how that information is interpreted and put to use.

C. Deterrent Mechanisms

388. According to section 56[198] of the CAK Horizontal Guidelines, coordination is not sustainable unless the consequences of deviation are sufficiently severe to convince coordinating entities that it is in their best interest to adhere to the terms of coordination. Furthermore, coordination cannot work if the deviations are not accompanied by a timely and commensurate punishment. Such punishments may take the form of cancellation of joint ventures or termination of any existing cooperation agreements or disposal of shares in jointly owned companies, etc. The threat of future retaliation certainly serves to sustain any extant policy of coordination.

D. The Reactions of Outsiders

389. Coordination takes place, for instance, if the actions of non-coordinating enterprises, potential competitors and customers are not allowed to hinder the outcomes expected from coordination. Section 61[199] of the CAK Horizontal Guidelines states that if coordination aims at reducing overall capacity in the market, this may only hurt consumers if non-coordinating firms are unable, or have no incentive to respond to this reduction by increasing their own capacity sufficiently to prevent a net decrease in capacity, or at least to render the coordinated capacity decrease unprofitable.

197. *Ibid.*
198. *Ibid.*
199. *Ibid.*

III. Mergers with Potential Competitors

390. According to the CAK Horizontal Guidelines, the merger of an undertaking already active in a relevant market with a potential competitor in the same market can have similar anticompetitive effects as a merger between two undertakings already active in the same relevant market. Both mergers may significantly impede effective competition, in particular through the creation or the strengthening of a dominant position. Paragraph 64 of these Guidelines gives the conditions that must be met for a merger with a potential competitor to have anticompetitive effects: the first is that the potential competitor must already exert a significant constraining influence, and the second is that there must be a significant likelihood that the potential competitor could grow into an effective competitive force. Evidence that a potential competitor has plans to enter a market in a significant way could help the CAK in reaching such a conclusion. Second, there must not be a sufficient number of other potential competitors, which could maintain sufficient competitive pressure after the merger.[200]

IV. Mergers Creating or Strengthening Buyer Power in Upstream Markets

391. Paragraph 65[201] of the CAK Horizontal Guidelines mandates the CAK to analyse to what extent a merged entity will increase its buyer power in upstream markets. The CAK takes cognizant of the fact that a merger that strengthens the market power of a buyer may significantly impede effective competition, mostly by creating or strengthening a dominant position. Because of the market power, the merged entity may be in a position to obtain lower prices by reducing its purchase of inputs. This according to the CAK may also cause the merged enterprise to lower its level of output in the final product market, and thus harm consumer welfare.

392. Competition in the downstream markets is also adversely affected if, in particular, the merged entity uses its buyer power against its suppliers to foreclose its rivals. As per paragraph 66 of these Guidelines, increased buyer power may be beneficial for competition. If increased buyer power lowers input costs without restricting downstream competition or total output, then a proportion of these cost reductions is likely to be passed onto consumers in the form of lower prices. All possible competitive conditions in upstream markets must be analysed and evaluated in order to determine if a merger could completely eliminate effective competition and hinder expansion of competitors.

---

200. *Ibid.* Slaughter and May 2012, 'The European Union Merger Regulation; An Overview of the European Merger Control Rules', March 2012, available at: https://www.lexology.com/library/detail.aspx?g=d75de26b-8c27-4991-9c27-3a550827c1b7 [accessed January 2026]: Karanja-Ng'ang'a, J and Muthang'ato, W., 2013, 'Kenya', The Mergers and Acquisitions Law Review, 7th Edition, Law Business Research Limited, available at: www.TheLawReviews.co.uk [Accessed March 2015].

201. CAK, Kenya, 2012, 'Guidelines on Horizontal Mergers', available at: http://www.cak.go.ke 1 [accessed September 2014].

V. Defences

A. *Countervailing Buyer Power*

393. Paragraph 38[202] of the CAK Horizontal Guidelines defines countervailing buyer power as the ability of large buyers in concentrated downstream markets to extract price concessions from suppliers. Countervailing buyer power is the force that buyers apply to prevent the exercise of suppliers' increased market power. According to paragraph 39 of these Guidelines, though in some markets, buyers may have sufficient bargaining power to prevent the exercise of suppliers' market power, this does not necessarily mean that there is countervailing buyer power in the market. Factors that will influence the ability of buyers to constrain exercise of supplier power include:

a. a small number of large and informed buyers;
b. the buyer's ability to find credible alternative suppliers;
c. the ease with which buyers can switch suppliers, i.e., switching costs relative to product prices; and
d. the ability of the buyers to produce the goods or services themselves or sponsor new entry.

394. The CAK Horizontal Guidelines further point out that while buyer power can offset the market power of suppliers, the customers do not necessarily enjoy the benefits from the exercise of buyer power in lowering suppliers' prices. Such a result is highly dependent on how effective competition is between the various buyers in the market that they supply. The Competition Act was recently amended to introduce section 24A and D. Section 24A prohibits any conduct that amounts to abuse of buyer power in a market in Kenya, or a substantial part of Kenya, is prohibited. Section 24D states buyer power as 'the influence exerted by an undertaking or group of undertakings in the position of a purchaser of a product or service to obtain from a supplier more favourable terms, or to impose a long term opportunity cost including harm or withheld benefit which, if carried out, would be significantly disproportionate to any resulting long term cost to the undertaking or group of undertakings'. Under sections 36.d, 42.6 and 47.3, the CAK has the mandate to impose on any undertaking contravening the new provisions a penalty of up to 10% of the undertaking's preceding year's gross annual turnover in Kenya.

202. *Ibid.*; Budzinski, O. and Wacker, K., 2007, p. 286, 'The Prohibition of the Proposed Springer PROSIEBENSAT.1 Merger: How Much Economics in German Merger Control?', Journal of Competition Law and Economics, 3(2), 281: Bardong, A., 2012, p. 483, 'Germany: The Bundeskartellamt's New Merger Guidelines', Journal of European Competition Law and Practice, 3(5), 481: Thomas, S., 2013, p. 395, 'Close Competitors in Merger Review', Journal of European Competition Law and Practice, 4(5), 391.

B. Entry

395. In paragraphs 60–62 and 187–189[203] of the CAK Horizontal Guidelines, the CAK does consider the possibility of entry of new competitors into a market as a factor that may curtail the exercise of market power. The exercise of market power is unlikely when entry is 'likely', 'timely,' and 'sufficient.' For the analysis of conditions of entry, the CAK takes into account the behaviour that a hypothetical entity that wishes to enter into the market must adopt. In this step, it is not necessary to identify an entity with a real intention of entering the market. However, the CAK assumes that a hypothetical entity is not similar to potential entrants. Examples of the new entities entering the market in the last five years may be used as evidence for conditions of entry.

C. Efficiencies

396. Efficiencies are not easy to evaluate. Paragraph 70[204] of the CAK Horizontal Guidelines provides that the CAK considers efficiencies whose magnitude and possibility of occurrence can be verified by reasonable means, and for which the causes and the moment at which they will be obtained are reasonably specified. Strict proof of the efficiencies is necessary. Paragraph 71 lists efficiencies related to horizontal mergers. These include economies of scale and scope obtained from combining production, distribution and marketing activities to greater innovation yields that are a result of combining investment in R&D and reduced transaction costs.

D. Failing Firm Defence

397. In the competitive world in which we live, weaker and smaller entities facing financial hardships will try to merge with stronger and larger ones in order to survive in the marketplace. Some of these entities may plead the Failing Firm Defence (FFD) if their impending merger raises competition concerns. As such, it is the duty of the CAK to scrutinise each merger, more so if the rescue of the entity experiencing financial difficulties is the reason for merger. In such a case, the CAK bears the responsibility of laying down the conditions required for a successful application of the FFD.[205]

203. CAK, Kenya, 2012, 'Guidelines on Horizontal Mergers', available at: https://cak.go.ke/sites/default/files/downloads/2024-08/ConsolidatedMergerGuidelines.pdf1 [accessed September 2014].
204. *Ibid.*
205. OECD, 2010, 'Roundtable on Failing Firm Defence', DAF/COMP(2009)38, 10 August; Kokkoris, I and Olivares-Caminal, R., 2009, 'Antitrust Law Amidst Financial Crisis', Cambridge University Press.

§3. VERTICAL MERGERS(VM(S))

I. Introduction

398. The two types of non-horizontal mergers, namely, vertical and conglomerate mergers, are discussed in the next paragraphs. VMs are mergers between entities that have potential or actual supplier or customer relationship (i.e., producer and retailer). The implications of VMs are different from horizontal and conglomerate mergers.[206]

399. VMs are defined in the Guidelines on VMs released by the CAK of Kenya. Paragraph 2 of the VM Guidelines states that VMs occur, for instance, when undertakings (manufacturer and supplier) operating at different levels within a sector's supply chain, and producing different goods and services, merge their operations. In most cases, the goal of such companies is to decrease reliance, make production process more efficient and increase profitability. An example of vertical merger is where a manufacturer of a certain product merges with one of its distributors. In such a merger, the downstream undertaking purchases: (a) either the output from the upstream undertaking and uses it as an input in its own production, which it then sells on to its customers, or (b) finished products from the upstream undertaking for sale to its customers.

400. VMs hardly raise competition concerns except where the merged entity gains significant degree of market power in at least one of the markets concerned. Thus, the extent to which the proposed merger may hinder competition largely depends on the degree of market dominance and power enjoyed by the merged entities.

II. Non-coordinated Effects: Foreclosure

401. There are two key ways in which market power created by a vertical merger may result in foreclosure through non-coordinated effects. The first is where the merger increases the costs of downstream rivals by restricting their access to an essential input. The second is where the merger forecloses upstream rivals by restricting their access to a sufficient customer base. The term 'foreclosure' describes any instance where actual or potential rivals' access to supplies or markets is hampered or eliminated, thereby reducing these companies' ability and/or incentive to compete. The resulting foreclosure gives the merging companies and some of their competitors the opportunity to increase consumer prices, thereby impeding competition.

206. Thomas, S., 2013, p. 395, 'Close Competitors in Merger Review', Journal of European Competition Law and Practice, 4(5), 391.

A. Input Foreclosure

402. According to paragraph 36 of the VM Guidelines, input foreclosure arises in cases whereby the newly merged entity limits access to the products or services that it would have otherwise supplied in the absence of the merger, and consequently raises its downstream rivals' costs. This in turn makes it harder for the foreclosed rivals to obtain supplies of the input under similar prices and conditions before the merger, and gives the merged entity an opportunity to harm consumers through increased prices.

403. For input foreclosure to bring about an anticompetitive harm, merged entities' rivals need not be forced to exit the market. CAK's main consideration is whether the increased input costs would lead to higher prices for consumers. In assessing the probability of an anticompetitive input foreclosure, the CAK applies a three-fold test, which consists of three closely intertwined factors. These include the ability of the merged entity: (a) to foreclose competitors' access to inputs; (b) its incentive to foreclose; and (c) the overall likely impact of the foreclosure on effective competition.[207]

404. A good example of input foreclosure is a South African case, *Senmin International (Pty) Ltd.*[208] In November 2012, the Competition Tribunal of South Africa conditionally approved the intermediate merger of Senmin International, a subsidiary of AECI Limited, with Cellulose Derivatives. This merger was a vertical integration by Senmin with its upstream supplier of Carboxymethylcellulose (CMC). Senmin supplies and distributes mining chemicals, which are used in the extraction and recovery of precious metals. Cellulose Derivatives manufacturers' CMC is a cellulose product derived from wood pulp that is used in various industrial applications, including the recovery of platinum as part of the flotation process. Senmin sources all of its technical grade CMC requirements from Cellulose Derivatives, which is also the only local manufacturer of CMC in South Africa. The Commission prohibited the merger because it was concerned that Senmin's competitors that purchase technical grade CMC from Cellulose Derivatives for use in mining applications would after the merger, be foreclosed by Senmin from accessing the locally produced technical grade CMC. The merging entities appealed to the Tribunal to reconsider the Commission's decision. Following a hearing, the Tribunal reversed the Commission's prohibition and approved the merger subject to Senmin's guarantee that, after the merger, and to avoid any anticompetitive vertical effects, it

207. Bundeskartellamt, 2013, 'Vertical Restraints in the Internet Economy Meeting of the Working Group on Competition Law' 10 October: Adenas, M. and Hutchings, M., 2005, pp. 221–237, 'Vertical Mergers', Current Competition Law, Vol. III, British Institute of International Comparative Law: CAK, Undated, 'Consolidated Guidelines on the Substantive Assessment of Mergers under the Competition Act', available at: https://cak.go.ke/sites/default/files/downloads/2024-08/ConsolidatedMergerGuidelines.pdf [accessed January 2026].

208. South African Competition Tribunal, 2012, '*Senmin International (Pty) Ltd and Cellulose Derivatives (Pty) Ltd*', Case No: 14/AM/Feb12, available at: http://www.comptrib.co.za [accessed March 2015].

would continue to supply technical grade CMC to its downstream competitors on the same terms that such competitors got from Cellulose Derivatives.

B. Customer Foreclosure

405. Paragraph 58 of the VM Guidelines deals with customer foreclosure, which is said to occur when a supplier merges with an important customer in the downstream market. Because of this downstream presence, the merged entity may foreclose access to a customer base to its actual or potential rivals in the upstream market (the input market) and, as a result, reduce their ability or incentive to compete. Downstream rivals may, therefore, find it harder to supply input supplies in the downstream market.[209] In assessing the likelihood of an anticompetitive customer foreclosure scenario, the CAK follows a three-step analysis similar to that for input foreclosure described above.

III. Other Non-coordinated Effects

A. Disclosure of Sensitive Information

406. Paragraph 74 of the VM[210] Guidelines gives situations where merged entities may exchange sensitive information. This includes situations in which the merged entity, by vertically integrating, gains access to commercially sensitive information regarding the upstream or downstream activities of rivals. For example, by becoming the supplier of a downstream competitor, an entity may obtain critical information, which allows it to price less aggressively in the downstream market to the detriment of consumers. It may also put competitors at a competitive disadvantage, thereby dissuading them from entering the market.

407. Kenya lacks comprehensive data protection laws. Nevertheless, section 31 of the Constitution of Kenya guarantees the right to privacy of communication. The Data Protection Bill 2014, which is supposed to implement sections 31, 34 and 35 of the Constitution and improve transparency of both private and public bodies, has been drafted but has yet to be adopted by the Parliament. Until the Data Protection becomes law, section 20 of the Competition Act provides that parties to a transaction falling under the Act may not disclose business secrets, know-how, commercial information, or any other information of a confidential or proprietary nature relating to matters to which the Act may be applied. Under the said section, the CAK may declare information confidential if it determines that information is commercially sensitive or if its disclosure may adversely affect the competitive position of any

209. Cuts CCIER, 2015 'Vertical Restraints', available at: https://www.yumpu.com/en/document/view/39355922/types-of-vertical-restraints-cuts-ccier [accessed January 2026].

210. CAK, Kenya, 2012, 'Guidelines on Vertical Mergers', available at: http://www.cak.go.ke [accessed September 2014]: Wilson, R. et al., 2012, 'South Africa: Tribunal Reverses Commission Prohibition of a Vertical Merger', available at: http://www.mondaq.com [accessed September 2014].

person or business. The CAK can also, under the same section, allow the disclosure of information if the law permits such disclosure.

IV. Coordinated Effects

A. *Introduction*

408. The description of coordinated effects under vertical type of mergers is similar to that given under horizontal mergers in section 3.B.II above.

B. *Explicit Coordination*

409. Explicit Coordination is not defined in the Competition Act or in the VM Guidelines, but refers to a situation where a merger makes it significantly easier for entities in a given sector to coordinate. In such cases, the merging entities agree on how they will compete or refrain from competing even though they know that this conduct may violate competition law.

1. Reaching Terms of Coordination

410. Paragraphs 78–80 of the VM Guidelines state that a vertical merger may make it easier for the entities in the upstream or downstream market to reach an agreement regarding the terms of coordination. Indeed, when a vertical merger leads to foreclosure, it results in a reduction in the number of effective competitors in the market, making it easier to coordinate among the remaining market players. Further, a merger may involve the elimination of a maverick in a market. A maverick is defined as a supplier that for its own reasons is unwilling to accept the coordinated outcome and thus maintains aggressive competition. The vertical integration of the disruptive supplier/maverick may alter its incentives to such an extent that coordination will no longer be prevented.

2. Monitoring Participants

411. In paragraph 81 of the VM Guidelines, it is pointed out that vertical integration may facilitate coordination by increasing the level of market transparency between entities through access to sensitive information on rivals or by making it easier to monitor pricing. Such concerns may arise when, for example, the level of price transparency is higher downstream than upstream. This could be the case when prices to final consumers are made public, while transactions at the intermediate market are reached privately. Vertical integration may give upstream producers control over final prices and thus help them monitor deviations more effectively. Moreover, a vertical merger may cause a reduction in the number of effective competitors in a market when it causes foreclosure. This in turns makes it easier to monitor each other's actions in the market.[211]

3. Deterrent Mechanisms

412. According to paragraph 81 of the VM Guidelines, VMs do enhance coordinating of the entities' incentives to adhere to the terms of coordination. The reason for this may be that a vertically integrated firm may be in a position to more effectively punish rival undertakings when they choose to deviate from the terms of coordination, because it is either a crucial customer or supplier to them.

4. Reactions of Outsiders

413. VMs may limit the chances available for outsiders to destabilise the coordination by increasing barriers to enter the market or otherwise limiting the ability to compete on the part of non-participants in the coordination. Per paragraph 85 of the VM Guidelines, a vertical merger may also involve the elimination of a disruptive buyer in a market. If upstream entities view sales to a particular buyer as sufficiently important, they may be tempted to deviate from the terms of coordination in an effort to secure their business. Likewise, a large buyer may be able to tempt the coordinating entity to deviate from agreed terms by concentrating a large amount of its requirements on one supplier, or by offering long-term contracts. The acquisition of such a buyer would certainly heighten the risk of coordination in a market.

5. Tacit Coordination

414. Just like explicit coordination, this term is not directly referred to in the Competition Act or the VM Guidelines. It refers to a situation in which a merger results in a market structure that causes entities to reach an agreement on price and output rather than to compete – in other words, to coordinate their competitive behaviour with a view to influencing competitors' expectations and reducing competition. In a tacit coordination, enterprises set their prices higher than those of their competitors, thereby earning more profits than they would in a competitive environment. Tacit coordination can occur without explicit contracts. Tacit coordination requires the coordinating entities to monitor through intensive communication

211. CAK, Kenya, 2012, 'Guidelines on Vertical Mergers', available at: http://www.cak.go.ke [accessed September 2014].

adherence to agreed coordination terms, put in place some form of a deterrent mechanism to be applied in case of deviations, and to ensure that the reaction of the outsiders does not jeopardise the outcomes expected from the coordination.[212]

C. *Market/Product Extension Mergers*

415. The VM Guidelines are silent on the market/product extension mergers. Such mergers are briefly discussed in the context of conglomerate mergers below.

§4. Conglomerate Mergers

416. These are fully covered under the CAK's Guidelines on Conglomerate Mergers (hereinafter 'GCM'). Conglomerate mergers involve entity that operates in different product markets or closely related markets. Such mergers are neither vertical nor horizontal; they may be pure conglomerate mergers or market or product extension mergers. Market/ product extension mergers are mergers between undertakings that produce different but related products. Entities that expect efficiencies more often than not prefer conglomerate mergers. Such mergers rarely lead to competition concerns solely because of their conglomerate effects except in exceptional circumstances, such as where the products acquired are complementary to the acquirer's own products, thus giving rise to 'portfolio power'.

417. When assessing conglomerate mergers, the CAK considers, among other factors, the possible effects of the merger on competition, i.e., whether such mergers can harm competition by giving the merged businesses market power or lessen competition in a market. The CAK also considers the substantiated efficiencies benefiting consumers, effects of the merger on employment and on a particular industrial sector or region. The CAK further looks into how the merger may endanger the continuity of supplies or services and the ability of national industries to compete in international markets.

418. In analysing conglomerate mergers, the CAK looks into the definition of the relevant market, the market participants, market concentration, market power and other possible public benefits of the merger. According to the GCM, conglomerate mergers can also hinder competition through non-coordinated effects and coordinated effects. Paragraph 23 of the GCM states that non-coordinated effects may principally arise when a conglomerate merger gives rise to foreclosure, thereby reducing these companies' ability and/or incentive to compete. Because of such anticompetitive foreclosure, the merging companies – and, possibly, some of their

212. Proctor, J.A., 2014, pp. 960–961 and 970–972, ' Tacit Collusion Indicators in Merger Control under Varied Focal Points', Journal of Competition Law and Economics, 10(4), 959.

competitors as well – may be able to profitably increase the price charged to consumers, or to provide their customers with better products, engage in tying and bundling. Like other exclusionary practices, tying and bundling may eliminate rivals in a given market and/or altogether reduce the ability and the incentive to compete.

419. According to paragraphs 50–52 of the GCM,[213] in certain circumstances, conglomerate mergers may facilitate anticompetitive coordination in markets, even in the absence of an agreement or a concerted practice. In particular, coordination is more likely to emerge in markets where it is easy to identify the terms of coordination and where such coordination is sustainable. Conglomerate mergers may influence the likelihood of coordinated outcomes in a given market by reducing the number of effective competitors to such an extent that tacit coordination becomes a real possibility. As a result, vulnerable rivals excluded from the market may choose not to contest the situation of coordination, but may prefer instead to live under the shelter of the increased price level. Besides, a conglomerate merger may increase the extent and importance of multimarket competition, and therewith increase the competitive interaction on several markets. Other than the provisions of the Competition Act or the respective laws governing or applicable to a merger, whether horizontal, vertical or conglomerate, merging entities with regional operations are expected to consider the implications of the COMESA Regulations, 2025 and the 2025 Rules,[214] The CAK continues to work with the authorities in other EAC and COMESA regions to ensure that a harmonised framework for regulation of national, regional and COMESA competition issues is in place and working to bring about national and regional economic benefits to the countries and entities involved in mergers. So far, only Kenya and Tanzania have national competition laws and merger Guidelines. In Rwanda, Uganda and Burundi, respective trade ministries are responsible for the approval of merger processes. The Amendment Act introduces several updates relating to various types of mergers in order to strengthen the enforcement of competition law. According to a Memorandum of Understanding between the CCCC and the EACCA signed in June 2025, the two agencies agreed to cooperate in order to strengthen regional enforcement of competition law, exchange information, jointly review mergers and void duplication of tasks. This cooperation is intended to help create fair markets, enhance cross-border competition, enable joint investigations, and improve consumer protection across both eastern and southern Africa.[215]

213. CAK, Kenya, 2012, 'Guidelines on Conglomerate Mergers', available at: http://www.cak.go.ke [accessed September 2014]: Church, J., 2005, pp. 797–801, 'The Church Report's Analysis of Vertical and Conglomerate Mergers: A Reply to Cooper, Froeb, O'brien and Vita', Journal of Competition Law and Economics, 1(4), 797.

214. COMESA Competition Commission, 2025, 'COMESA Competition and Consumer Protection Regulations 2025', available at: https://comesacompetition.org/resources/regulations/comesa-competition-and-consumer-protection-regulations-2025/ [accessed January 2026]; COMESA Competition Commission, 2025, 'COMESA Competition and Consumer Protection Rules 2025', available at: https://comesacompetition.org/resources/rules/comesa-competition-and-consumer-protection-rules-2025/ [accessed January 2026].

215. EAC, 2025, 'EAC, COMESA Sign MoU to Strengthen Cooperation in Competition and Consumer Protection'; available at: https://www.eac.int/press-releases/157-trade/3389-eac,-comesa-sign-mou-to-strengthen-cooperation-in-competition-and-consumer-protection [accessed January 2026].

§5. Joint Ventures

420. This has already been discussed in Part I, Chapter 4, §8 and Part I, Chapter 3, §3 of this monograph.

Part III. Administrative Procedure

Chapter 1. Administrative Investigations Before the Antitrust Authority

§1. Initiative

421. The functional responsibilities of the CAK are described in detail in section 9 of the Competition Act, which gives the CAK the mandate, among other things, to promote and enforce compliance with the Act. The CAK has power to deal with complaints received from legal, natural persons and consumer bodies regarding competition issues, and to provide such persons or bodies with information, guidelines and remedies. CAK has the mandate to exercise the powers conferred to it under the Competition Act either on its own motion or after a complaint has been made to it by any person, entity, Government agent or Ministry as provided under section 31 of the Act. Under section 15 of the Act, the CAK can delegate a number of its functions to any of its members except:

a. duties to make decision under the Act;
b. power of delegation itself;
c. the powers to revoke or vary delegation.

422. Delegated power must be exercised according to the instructions and limitations given by the CAK, and may be revoked or varied by the CAK at will.

I. General Sector Inquiries

423. Section 9.1.g of the Competition Act gives the CAK the power to carry out inquiries, studies and research into matters relating to competition and the protection of the interests of consumers. Moreover, under section 18 of the Competition Act, CAK may also conduct inquiries and sectoral studies into matters affecting competition that fall within its jurisdiction, and send an appropriate report to the Minister for Finance. The report must outline sectors in which unwarranted concentrations of economic power subsist, and in the report give advice regarding measures which may ameliorate such situations. Before conducting inquiries and sectoral studies, the CAK gives notice of an intended inquiry or sectoral study by publishing a notice in the Gazette and in at least one daily newspaper of national circulation. The notice informs the public about the subject matter of the intended inquiry and invites submissions on the subject from members of the public to be made within a specified period.

424. Additionally, the CAK may, where it considers it necessary or desirable for the purpose of carrying out its functions, carry out an inquiry into any kind of matter touching on competition or consumer welfare either on its own motion or at the request of a regulatory body and publish a report on the inquiry. Before carrying out an inquiry or sectoral study, the CAK has to give notice under section 18 of the Act of the intended inquiry or sectoral study by:

(1) (a) publishing a notice in the Gazette and in at least one daily newspaper of national circulation specifying:
   (a) the subject matter of the intended inquiry;
   (b) inviting submissions on the subject from members of the public within a specified period;
   (c) in the case of an inquiry conducted at the direction of the Minister, the terms of reference issued by the Minister.
(2) sending written notice of the inquiry to:
   (a) undertakings whose interests the CAK considers likely to be affected by the outcome of the inquiry;
   (b) industry and consumer organisations which the CAK considers may have an interest in the matter;
   (c) the Minister.

425. In the matter of *Lafarge and East African Portland Cement Company (EAPC)*,[216] the CAK conducted an inquiry pursuant to section 50 of the Competition Act across six East and Southern African countries; namely, Kenya, Tanzania, Zambia, South Africa, Botswana and Namibia with the goal of determining if there was unwarranted concentrations of economic power in the cement industry. Section 50 sanctions such inquiries if their purpose is to investigate sectors where concentration of economic power is suspected. The CAK had received a complaint against Lafarge regarding possible price-fixing owing to its cross-directorship in EAPCC and Bamburi Cement, and to a 41.7% stake in EAPCC and a 58.9% stake in rival Bamburi. The CAK pointed out that this kind of cross-shareholding was anticompetitive and could lessen and dampen competition in the production, supply and distribution of cement in Kenya. The CAK found that Lafarge's sizeable shareholding in Kenya's leading cement makers, Bamburi and the EAPCC, gave it a monumental control of more than half of Kenya's cement market and amounted to monopolistic behaviour and unwarranted concentration of economic power.

216. *Lafarge and East African Portland Cement Company (EAPC)*,in CAK of Kenya, 2012/2013, 'Annual Report', p. 21, available at: http:// https://www.cak.go.ke/arch/sites/default/files/annual-reports/FY%202012-2013%20CAK%20Annual%20Report.pdf [accessed January 2026].].

426. In 2012, CAK carried out another sectoral study in the sugar industry with the objective of gaining a deeper understanding of the competition issues this industry faces. The inquiry not only investigated market structure and concentration, determinants of sugar prices at various levels in the value chain, geographic markets, entry barriers and vertical arrangements in the industry but also compared ex-factory sugar prices across different countries, i.e., Kenya, South Africa, Zambia and Tanzania. The inquiry found that the ex-factory prices in Kenya were the highest because of factors like high overhead costs, raw materials and issues on operational efficiency.[217]

II. Ex Officio Investigations

427. These kinds of investigations can be done by the CAK on its own initiative, where there has been no formal complaint filed. This is pursuant to the powers provided to the CAK under section 9 as read with sections 18 and 31 of the Competition Act. Section 9.1.i grants the CAK the power to investigate impediments to competition, including entry into and exit from markets, in the economy as a whole or in particular sectors and publicises the results of such investigations. Further, under section 9.1.j the CAK has power to investigate policies, procedures and programs of regulatory authorities to assess their effects on competition and consumer welfare and publicise the results of such studies.

III. Complaints

428. Under section 9.1.b of the Competition Act, the CAK can receive and investigate complaints from legal natural persons and consumer bodies. After receiving such complaints, the CAK investigates the reported allegations. If the CAK decides not to conduct an investigation after receiving a complaint, it is required to inform that person in writing of the reasons for its decision. Among the cases, the CAK include the *Acquisition of Synovate* by IPSOS. Synovate had a strong presence in Kenya, Tanzania, Uganda and Zambia before acquisition by IPSOS. With the acquisition, IPSOS bought the entire stock of Synovate, and created the world's third-largest global market research company, with the Kenyan unit continuing to dominate research covering politics, consumer markets and corporate intelligence. Upon investigations, the CAK established that IPSOS had merged with Synovate and started trading in Kenya without notifying or obtaining the approval CAK of the acquisition/ merger as required by section 42.2 of the Competition Act. The failure to obtain approval carries under section 42.5 of the Competition Act, an imprisonment term not exceeding five years or a fine not exceeding KES 10 million or both. The CAK concluded that this was a criminal case and requested the Director of Prosecutions and the Inspector General of Police to deal with the matter. In

217. CAK of Kenya, 2012/2013, 'Annual Report', pp. 21and 26, available at: http:// https://www.cak.go.ke/arch/sites/default/files/annual-reports/FY%202012-2013%20CAK%20Annual%20Report.pdf [accessed January 2026].

addition, the CAK also decided that it would review the merger provisions in the Competition Act to provide for administrative sanctions in lieu of criminal provisions for mergers concluded without its approval.[218]

§2. Powers

429. Before making any decision, the CAK has to collect and assess information. There are two ways through which the CAK can obtain the required information, which are through requests for information or dawn raids.

I. Request for Information

430. In case the CAK decides to investigate a matter, under section 31.4. of the Competition Act, it may, by notice in writing served on any person, require that person to:

a. furnish to the CAK by writing signed by that person or, in the case of a body corporate, by a director or member or other competent officer, employee or agent of the body corporate, within the time and in the manner specified in the notice, any information pertaining to any matter specified in the notice which the CAK considers relevant to the investigation;
b. produce to the CAK, or to a person specified in the notice to act on the CAK's behalf, any document or article specified in the notice which relates to any matter which the CAK considers relevant to the investigation;
c. appear before the CAK at a time and place specified in the notice to give evidence or to produce any document or article specified in the notice; or
d. if he possesses any records considered relevant to the investigation, to give copies of those records to the CAK or alternatively to submit the record to the CAK for copying within the time and in the manner specified in the notice.

431. In accordance with section 9.1.b of the Act, information may be received from legal or natural persons or from consumer bodies. Section 20 of the Act serves to protect the information disclosed to the CAK, and which it has declared is of confidential nature. Under this provision, a claim of information confidentiality can be raised in respect of the entire or part of any information given or disclosed to the CAK by the person. The reasons for the claim of confidentiality must be provided by the person claiming confidentiality to enable the CAK to decide whether the material is of confidential nature. Under section 20.8.b, the CAK grants confidentiality for material disclosed if it is of the view that its disclosure could adversely affect the competitive position of any person, or if the information disclosed is commercially sensitive. Confidentiality claim forms are available on the CAK's website for anyone wishing to make such a claim.

218. *Ibid.*, p. 20.

II. Investigating and Search Powers

432. Section 32 of the Competition Act provides for situations whereby the CAK may obtain information through dawn raids on undertakings to collect implication information. This happens when the CAK it is necessary to use of this kind of investigation technique, instead of the friendlier request for information. A person authorised by the CAK in writing may enter any premises in the occupation or under the control of a trader, manufacturer, producer, commission agent, clearing and forwarding agent, transporter, or other person believed to be in possession of relevant information and documents and inspect the premises and any goods, documents and records situated thereon.

433. Section 33 of the Competition Act confers upon the CAK a further power to receive in evidence any statement, document, information or matter that may assist in dealing effectively with an investigation it conducts. The receipt of any statement, document, information or matter is subject to the rules under the Evidence Act, Chapter 80 of the laws of Kenya. In the exercise of this power, the CAK may take evidence on oath or affirmation from any person attending before it. The CAK may permit any person appearing as a witness before it to give evidence by tendering or verifying by oath or affirmation a written statement. A person attending before the CAK is entitled to the same immunities and privileges as a witness before the High Court.

III. Cooperation with Other State Institutions

434. The Competition Act applies by virtue of section 6 not just to Kenyans carrying on business in the country but also to persons outside Kenya who have shares or have acquired assets of an undertaking doing business in Kenya. This section, therefore, indirectly empowers the CAK to cooperate with foreign state institutions inside and outside Kenya to ensure that unwarranted competition concerns do not hinder the exchange of goods and services. Section 9.1.m and n requires the CAK to cooperate with the Government, regulatory and public bodies in all matters relating to competition, consumer protection and welfare. Moreover, during the carrying out of investigations, the CAK may seek the assistance of law enforcement agencies. The Kenya Police Department is very useful at this. With their investigation skills and general law enforcement knowledge, they are able to support the CAK, especially when it encounters resistance. The CAK also mentions a number of institutions as its partners on its website. These include the National Treasury, the Capital Markets CAK, the State Law Office, Kenya Bureau of Standards, Kenya Intellectual Property Institution, Ministry of Trade, International Competition Network (ICN), and African Competition Forum, among others.

435. Kenya has also been cooperating with competition authorities in COMESA and EAC countries, and has been instrumental in drafting EAC and COMESA competition laws. In its annual reports, the CAK acknowledges that though section 5.2

of the Competition Act gives it jurisdiction over all competition and consumer protection matters, there are some overlapping roles with some sector regulators in and outside Kenya. As such, while implementing the Competition Act in Kenya, it endeavours to cooperate with these sectors to identify and establish the procedures for dealing with the overlap in mandates, for providing information and protecting any confidential information.[219]

§3. Right to Defence

I. Content and Notice of Opening Notifications

436. Under section 34 of the Competition Act, once the CAK has concluded an investigation and made a decision to the effect that an undertaking is guilty of a practice that is prohibited by the Act, it gives written notice of the proposed decision to the affected undertaking. The notice given contains the reasons for the proposed decision and the details of the possible reliefs that the CAK may or is intending to impose. The CAK then request the affected undertaking to submit written representations to the CAK within the time specified in the notice and to indicate whether it wants to make oral representations to the CAK. This administrative procedure serves the purpose of ensuring that the affected undertaking is duly informed about the decisions that the CAK is likely to make in relation to the prohibited practice that it is accused of. It also provides an opportunity to the Undertaking concerned to prepare its defence.

II. The Proceedings: Hearings, Access to File, Briefs

437. A hearing conference is convened under section 35 of the Competition Act when an undertaking expresses the wish to be heard or to defend itself before the CAK. The conference is held as per the terms determined by CAK, which also decides on the place, time and date of the hearing. The undertaking involved is promptly informed about the impending hearing in writing. Any legal or natural person who has lodged a complaint with the CAK concerning the conduct, which was the subject matter of the CAK's investigation, whose presence at the hearing the CAK considers crucial, is also informed by the CAK about the hearing. Persons notified of the hearing have the right to be accompanied by an advocate or any person who may offer assistance at the conference. This measure is to ensure that the affected persons understand the proceedings and the information that is expected from them.

438. The proceedings at a conference are carried out in as informal a manner and depend on the scope of subject matter. The CAK is required by section 35(4) of the

219. *Ibid.*, pp. 32–33; Kariuki,W.F., 2014, 'Informal Cooperation Among Competition Agencies 14th IGE July; 2014', available at: http://unctad.org/meetings/en/Presentation/CCPB_IGE2014_PRESRTInfCoop_Kenya_en.pdf [accessed March 2015].

Competition Act to keep a record of the conference and document everything said at the hearing. The conference is terminated when the CAK is satisfied that a reasonable opportunity has been given for the expression of the views of participating person or undertaking.

III. Statement of Objections

439. The Competition Act does not have any provisions for the CAK to issue a statement of objections. In other jurisdictions, a statement of objections is issued by a competition authority, and sets out all the objections to an undertaking's defence that the authority intends to rely on in making a case against the undertaking. In Kenya, the CAK simply issues a decision under section 36 of the Competition Act after the hearing has ended. No objections are raised before the hearing.

IV. Final Hearing and Decision

440. Section 36 of the Competition Act sets out the actions the CAK may take after concluding an investigation or a hearing and after considering any written representations and any matters raised at a conference. The CAK may take the following measures:

a. declare the conduct which is the subject matter of the CAK's investigation, to constitute an infringement of the prohibitions contained in the Act;
b. restrain the undertaking or undertakings from engaging in that conduct;
c. direct any action to be taken by the undertaking or undertakings concerned to remedy or reverse the infringement or the effects thereof;
d. impose a financial penalty;
e. grant any other appropriate relief.

441. Interim relief can be provided by the CAK, for instance, when the CAK has reason to believe that an undertaking has engaged, is engaging, or is intending to engage, in conduct that constitutes or may constitute an infringement of the prohibitions contained in the Competition Act, and that it is necessary for the CAK to act as a matter of urgency to:

a. prevent serious, irreparable damage to any person or category of persons; or to
b. protect the public interest.

442. The CAK may direct the undertaking concerned to stop and desist from engaging in such conduct until the ongoing investigation is concluded. This direction is made in writing. Alternatively, an agreement of settlement may be entered into by the CAK with the undertaking involved in an investigation. This settlement may be entered at any time, whether during or after the investigation. The agreement may be that either a monetary penalty or damages are awarded to the complainant. Section 39 requires the decision of the CAK touching on interim reliefs granted or a settlement to be published in the Kenya Gazette. A number of cases dealt with by the CAK shed light on kinds of decisions or interim measures it makes and takes.[220]

§4. Appeals to the Competition Appeals Tribunal

443. Section 70 of the Competition Act establishes the Competition Tribunal, which is an appellate body. Any person aggrieved by the decisions of the CAK can appeal to the Tribunal in writing as provided under section 40 of the Act. Section 72 of the Act states that the appellant can appear before the Tribunal either in person or by an advocate on the day and at the time fixed for the hearing of the appeal. However, the Tribunal may postpone the hearing on an appeal where it is satisfied that the appellant is prevented from attending a hearing because of sickness or is absence from Kenya.

444. The Tribunal has the discretion to determine who will bear the costs of such a postponement of a hearing. Section 73 of the Act lists the persons who may file an appeal to the Tribunal. These include persons who are:

a. directed to discontinue or not to repeat any trade practice;
b. issued with a stop and desist order or any other interim order;
c. permitted to continue or repeat a trade practice subject to conditions prescribed by the order;
d. directed to take certain steps to assist existing or potential suppliers or customers adversely affected by any prohibited trade practices;
e. ordered to pay a pecuniary penalty or fine; or
f. aggrieved by a stop and desist order or any other interim order of the CAK.

445. In addition, persons who, by an order of the CAK in respect to a merger or acquisition barred from proceeding with an impending merger, or are authorised to proceed with a merger subject to conditions given by the CAK in a merger order, are also entitled to appeal to the Tribunal. Section 74 of the Competition Act states that hearings before the Tribunal shall be conducted in camera. In-camera hearings are conducted after the CAK has considered the interests of the parties involved vis-à-vis public interest. The publication of the names and description of parties to appeals before is possible; however, reports or descriptions of the proceedings (whether heard in public or in private) or of any part of the proceedings in any appeal before the Tribunal cannot be published.

446. Under section 74 of the Act, the Tribunal may confirm, modify, or reverse the order appealed against, or any part of that order. Additionally, the Tribunal may refer appeals back to the CAK for reconsideration. Under section 75 of the Act, the

---

220. CAK of Kenya, 2014, 'Safaricom, Airtel sign Sh10.5bn Deal to Acquire YU Mobile Assets' and 'Safaricom and Airtel to absorb 175 YU Mobile Staff', available at: http://www.cak.go.ke [accessed March 2015].

Tribunal may ask the reconsideration to be done in respect to a general or a specified matter. Reasons and directions are to be given to the CAK when a reference for reconsideration is made.

447. Where an appeal against a determination of the CAK concerns a merger, the merger to which the appeal relates may not be finalised pending the determination of the appeal. As provided under section 48 of the Competition Act, applications for review of mergers should be made to the Tribunal within thirty days of the notice given by the CAK on the determination of a proposed merger. The Tribunal then gives notice within thirty days of receipt of the application and invites any person to make representations on the matter. The Tribunal is required by section 48.3 to render its decision within four months of making an application for review. The CAK has, in accordance with section 77 of the Competition Act, the right to appeal to the High Court of Kenya against any order of the Tribunal that it is not satisfied with. The appeal to the High Court must be made within thirty days after the date on which a notice of that decision has been served. The decision rendered by the High Court is final.

I. Interim Relief

448. Section 76 provides that where an appeal is brought against a determination by the CAK regarding restrictive trade practices, consumer welfare matters or abuse of dominant positions, any stop and desist order or any other interim order or conditions made by the CAK must be observed and implemented, unless the Tribunal otherwise orders, pending the determination of a pending appeal.

Chapter 2. Voluntary Notifications and Clearance Decisions: Merger Control

§1. Pre-merger Filing Obligations

I. Introduction

449. Before effecting a merger, the undertakings involved are required to give notice to the CAK as provided under section 43 of the Act. Without such notice and approval of the merger by CAK, section 42.3 stipulates that the merger shall not have any legal effect, and neither will any obligation imposed upon the parties by the merger agreement be enforceable.

450. Section 43 requires that all merger notices be given to the CAK in writing or in a prescribed form, i.e., by using a merger notification form. These forms are available on the CAK's website for download or can be obtained from the CAK's offices. According to section 3 of the Guidelines for the Exclusion of Proposed Mergers from Provisions of Part IV of the Competition Act, No. 12 of 2010 (hereinafter 'Exclusion Guidelines'), effective from 1 August 2013, the following documents must be attached to the merger notification form before it is forwarded to the CAK:

a. a signed copy of the sale and purchase Agreement of the undertaking;
b. the audited financial statements for the last three years;
c. Board resolutions;
d. latest annual reports;
e. list of employees;
f. plans showing means to achieve savings on costs;
g. plans showing investment evaluations; and
h. other documents related to the merger.

451. These requirements vary according to the nature of the merger. This means that if necessary, the CAK may ask for further documents or information from the merging enterprises to help it better determine the merger.[221] As per section 42, an undertaking may apply to be excluded from the requirements of the section. In such a case, fewer requirements are needed as compared to those undertakings whose thresholds are within or above those which can be excluded from the application of the Act. Under section 20 of the Act, the merging enterprises can move the CAK to declare information submitted to it confidential.

221. CAK of Kenya, 2014, 'Guidelines on Exclusion of Proposed Mergers from Provisions of Part IV of the Competition Act, no. 12 of 2010', available at: http://www.cak.go.ke [accessed December 2014].

II. Criteria and Thresholds

452. The CAK has power under section 42.1 of the Competition Act to make rules exempting undertakings from the operation of Part IV of the Act. To implement this section, the CAK has formulated Exclusion Guidelines, which lay out sectoral thresholds that form the basis of exclusion of specific undertakings from the operation of the Competition Act. Paragraphs 4 and 5 of the Exclusion Guidelines set out the thresholds that undertakings exempted from the operation of Part IV of the Act are supposed to meet. According to paragraph 4 of the Exclusion Guidelines, an undertaking with a minimum combined threshold or turnover of KES 1 billion merging with an undertaking whose turnover is more than KES 100 million cannot be considered for exclusion under section 42.1 of the Act by the CAK.

453. In the health sector, if an undertaking has a combined threshold of minimum of five hundred (KES 500) million that merges with one whose turnover is more than KES 50 million, both entities will not be entitled to an exemption under the Competition Act. Also not exempted are undertakings in the mineral, carbon-based sector that have minimum combined turnover of KES 4 billion that include the value of the reserves and the associated exploration assets of the combined undertakings. For the oil sector, the threshold may be below KES 4 billion as long as the merger involves pipelines and pipeline systems, which receive oil and gas from processing fields belonging to, and passing through the meters of the undertaking.

454. In paragraph 5 of the Exclusion Guidelines, the CAK sets out the thresholds for those mergers that can be exempt from the provisions of the Competition Act. These include ordinary merging entities whose combined threshold is between KES 100 million and KES 1 billion. In the health sector, the combined turnover of the merging parties must be between KES 50 million and KES 500 million for such parties to be considered for exclusion. Merging mineral carbon-based sector is exempted if the value of the reserves, the rights and the associated exploration assets to be held because of the merger is below KES 4 billion. According to the CAK, exemption of merging entities from the provisions of the Competition Act may promote consumer welfare by enabling smaller firms to collaborate in improving the quality of products or services in the relevant market through standardisation and specialisation efforts. Exemption may also enable upcoming entities to participate in innovation through a collaborative effort.[222]

III. Turnover Calculation

A. *Turnover*

455. According to section 3 of the Exclusion Guidelines, the term 'turnover' means 'the value of the annual sales turnover for the merging parties within Kenya,

222. *Ibid.*

based on the audited accounts of the holding company, the subsidiaries and other related companies for the preceding year'. Thus, to determine the turnover of the merging companies, the CAK considers and relies on the audited accounts, and not the provisional and management accounts of such entities.

B. Associated Undertakings

456. An associated undertaking is an undertaking which is not a subsidiary, but one over which another entity exercises substantive influence and has a participating interest. The Exclusion Guidelines are silent on how turnover of associated undertakings is calculated.

C. Joint Ventures and Intra-Group Turnover

457. Because joint ventures retain their own identities when they venture into a commercial deal with other undertakings, the turnovers of each of the undertakings in the joint venture are calculated separately. However, the extent of control of the other undertakings in the joint venture is taken into account. If a joint venture does not have autonomy, its turnovers may be included in the calculation of turnover of the merging undertaking. In determining autonomy, the control of the day-to-day operations is reviewed alongside the provision of finance, assets and staff for the running of the venture. Like with associated undertakings, the Exclusion Guidelines are silent on how turnover of joint ventures and intra-groups is to be determined.

D. Financial and Credit Institutions

458. The CAK does not provide Guidelines as to how the turnover of financial and credit institutions is to be calculated. The SCA and Companies Act under which most of these institutions are registered are also silent on how the turnover should be determined.

IV. Market Share Calculation

459. In order to determine the criteria for market share calculation, it is first important to define the term 'relevant market'. The Guidelines on Relevant Market Definition (hereinafter 'Market Guidelines')[223] show how the CAK applies the concept of relevant market in its enforcement of the Competition Act. The CAK underscores in paragraphs 1–6 of its Market Guidelines the importance of the definition of relevant market. Market definition is important because it sets the stage on which competition takes place, by helping assess not only the strength of existing

223. CAK, 2014, 'Guidelines on Relevant Market Definition', available at: http://www.cak.go.ke [accessed July 2013].

competition and the potential for a new entry, but also the market reaction across both early and later mergers. Through the definition of relevant market, the CAK is also able to size up actual competitors in a market, gauge their compliance with the competition rules and the obligation, identify the market boundaries and calculate market share. Information regarding the market share held by an undertaking may influence the decision of the CAK on whether a proposed merger should be allowed with or without conditions.[224] The concept of relevant market has been defined in Part I, Chapter 4, §2 of this monograph. The CAK applies the Small but Significant Non-transitory Increase in Price (SSNIP) test and Herfindahl-Hirschman Index (HHI) to determine the market shares held by undertakings proposing to merge. The CAK's interpretation of relevant market is without prejudice to the interpretation that may be given by a court of competent jurisdiction.

460. The Competition Act lays down some of the factors to be considered when determining mergers. These factors are crucial in gauging the impact of such mergers on the market share. Section 46.2 states that these shall include the extent to which the proposed merger, acquisition or takeover would be likely to:

a. prevent or lessen competition or to restrict trade or the provision of any service or to endanger the continuity of supplies or services;
b. result in any undertaking, including an undertaking not involved as a party in the proposed merger, acquiring a dominant position in a market or strengthening a dominant position in a market;
c. result in a benefit to the public which would outweigh any detriment which would be likely to result from any undertaking, including an undertaking not involved as a party in the proposed merger, acquiring a dominant position in a market or strengthening a dominant position in a market; and
d. affect a particular industrial sector or region, employment, ability of small undertakings to gain access to or to be competitive in any market or the ability of national industries to compete in international markets.

461. In calculating the market share, the CAK also takes into account any benefits to be derived from the proposed merger, as for instance, those relating to R&D, technical efficiency, increased production, efficient distribution of goods or provision of services and access to markets.

462. Two cases dealt with by the CAK are illustrative of the essential role market definition plays in determining the market share. The first is the *Acquisition of CFAO by Toyota Tshusho*,[225] a global merger involving Toyota Tshusho Corporation (TTC), which, through its subsidiary in Kenya, Toyota Kenya Limited, supplies cars to the Kenyan Market and CFAO. At the time of the merger, DT Dobie

224. CAK of Kenya, 2014, 'Guidelines for Market Definition', available at: http://www.cak.go.ke [accessed December 2014].
225. CAK of Kenya, 2012/2013, 'Annual Report', p. 20, available at: https://www.cak.go.ke/arch/sites/default/files/annual-reports/FY%202012-2013%20CAK%20Annual%20Report.pdf [accessed January 2026].

was a fully owned subsidiary of CFAO, and was involved in the sale of spare parts, maintenance and repair of several brands of cars that it distributed via three dealerships based in Nairobi, Nakuru and Mombasa. It was established that the relevant product markets for this merger were the markets for the supply of personal saloon vehicles (below and above 1800 cc), and the market for supply of personal passenger cars, commercial vehicles, motorbikes and spare parts. The CAK concluded that the market that seemed to be dominant after market analysis was the market for the supply of saloon cars (below and above 1800 cc). Through Toyota Kenya Limited, TTC had a market share of 44.5% while DT Dobie had one of 8.6%. The CAK established that after merger, the total market share would be 53.1%, a dominant market share. The CAK allowed the merger, but subject to the condition that the conduct of both undertakings in the market would not infringe the provisions of the Competition Act.

463. The second case the CAK dealt with involved the *Brookside/Buzeki*[226] *dairies merger*. The acquisition of Buzeki Diaries by Brookside Dairies, worth Sh 1.2 billion, raised the latter's shares in the milk Industry by about 44%, extended its regional reach into South Sudan, and cemented its market position in the milk industry. In determining whether to approve the takeover, the CAK gave weight to formal and informal channels of milk supply by the merging parties and other competitors in the same industry, and took into account the location of the merging parties and transport costs for raw milk in defining the geographical market. The CAK approved the merger, concluding that the informal players in the milk industry still account for 80% of the milk market, and Brookside's 44% market share gained after the merger did not place it in monopolistic position in the dairy sector, or give it the leverage that enables it to dictate market price for milk products.

V. Other Relevant Notions

§2. Structure of Proceedings

I. Preliminary Assessment and Full Investigations

A. *Pre-notification*

464. As mentioned earlier, section 43 of the Competition Act requires that the CAK be notified of any proposed merger. According to the Exclusion Guidelines, this notification must be accompanied by documents, including the sales and purchase agreement and the audited financial statements. Where the CAK is not satisfied with the information that has been provided, it may request further information from one or more of the involved undertakings. This should be done in writing within thirty days of receipt of the unsatisfactory information.

---

226. CAK of Kenya, 2013, '*Brookside Finalises Buy-Out*', available at: https://www.cak.go.ke/arch/sites/default/files/annual-reports/FY%202013-2014%20CAK%20Annual%20Report.pdf [accessed January 2026].

B. *Time Frame*

465. Section 44 of the Act lays down the time frame in which the CAK is required to determine applications from undertakings intending to merge. Once the CAK has received all the relevant information from the relevant undertaking together with the merger notification form, it has a period of sixty days to make a determination. The period of sixty days runs from the date on which the CAK receives the notification of merger. If further information had been requested, the sixty days will run as from the date on which the information was received by the CAK. In the alternative, the CAK may decide to hold a hearing conference to aid in its making of a determination. If this is done, the CAK should make a determination within thirty days after the conclusion of the conference.

466. However, the CAK has the discretion to extend the periods set out in section 44 for a further sixty days where it opines that the period already set out is not sufficient to make a determination. This is particularly the case where the CAK finds that a proposed merger encompasses a myriad of complex issues. This extension should be notified to the affected undertakings, in writing, before the time frame set out in the Competition Act expires. An extension of only sixty more days is allowed under the Act.

II. Right of Defence

A. *The Right to Be Heard*

467. The CAK may consider, in some circumstances, holding a hearing conference in relation to a proposed merger. This only happens where the CAK considers it appropriate and necessary to have such a conference. When it so decides, it is required to give notice to the merging undertakings in writing within the time frames set out in section 44 of the Competition Act.

B. *Access to File*

468. Under the same section, the notice to be sent out to the merging entities must set out the time, date and venues for the conference and the issues to be addressed. During the hearing conference, the undertakings can make representations regarding their merger for consideration by the CAK. Under sections 50.2. and 3 of the Competition Act, in order to control monopolies and concentration of economic power, the CAK may order any participant in the affected sector to grant it or any person authorised in writing by it access to records relating to patterns of ownership, market structure and percentages of sales. In addition, the CAK may require any person possessing the previously mentioned records to provide it with copies of the records.

§3. Clearance and Conditional Clearance

469. After the CAK has considered all the information obtained, it goes ahead to make a decision on the proposed merger. In section 46 of the Competition Act, the CAK may allow mergers, subject to a number of conditions, decline to give approval of a merger or give approval subject to specified conditions. The CAK applies the criteria set forth in section 46.2 of the Act, already in Part III, Chapter 3, §2, section IV of this monograph, to arrive at its decisions. Further, section 46.6.b requires the CAK to give reasons when it allows or prohibits a merger conditionally. This helps the merging undertakings to know what actions to take once the CAK has reached a decision.

I. Conditions and Undertakings

A. *Content*

1. Specific Types of Remedies

470. Remedies are generally essential to address the competition concerns raised by mergers. The CAK is yet to clarify its approach to merger remedies. Though the Competition Act makes no mention of merger remedies, it offers various ways of dealing with anticompetitive mergers and preventing the merged company alone or in coordination with others from unilaterally wielding market power gained as result of the merger. If the CAK establishes that the merger was based on materially incorrect or misleading information, or if a condition attached to the approval of the merger is not fully complied with by any of the parties to the merger, the CAK may under section 47.1.b revoke the merger. In such a case, it is under an obligation to notify entities intending to merge and any affected third parties of its decision.[227]

§4. Relations with Other Merger Control Authorities

I. Other Authorities Within the Local Jurisdiction

471. The Capital Markets (Takeovers and Mergers) Regulations 2002,[228] published by the Capital Markets Authority, apply to mergers of listed companies in Kenya. Section 4.1.d of the Act requires the notification of the then Commissioner of Monopolies and Prices (now CAK of Kenya) if the offerees and offeror in the proposed merger engage in the same business. The Capital Markets Authority must thus inform the CAK of any proposed merger or takeover. However, under section 8. D of the Regulations, the Capital Markets Authority can only inform the CAK of

227. Hewitt, G., 2005, pp. 76–79, 'Merger Remedies', OECD Journal of Competition Law and Policy, 7(2).

228. KLR, 1989, 'Capital Markets Merger Regulations' Chapter 485A of the Laws of Kenya', available at: http://www.kenyalaw.org [accessed March 2015].

a proposed merger where the companies involved are in the same business. Under section 17 of the Regulations, the Capital Markets CAK may withdraw the merger approval if the requisite approvals have not been obtained from the CAK or any other relevant approval authority. Section 34 of the Regulations also provides that the Commissioner of Monopolies and Prices/CAK are to sit in sub-committee meetings that discuss matters of mergers and takeovers.

472. In addition to cooperating with the Capital Markets Authority, the CAK also cooperates in merger cases with the Kenya Bureau of Standards. The duties of the Kenya Bureau of Standards under section 4 of the Standard Act[229] include, *inter alia*, the promotion of standardisation in industry and commerce, and the provision for cooperation with the Government, the representatives of any industry or with any local authority or other public body or any other relevant persons.

II. Regional and International Coordination

473. Regionally, the CAK has been working closely with the EAC and Common Market for Eastern and Southern Africa (hereinafter 'COMESA'). Like its counterparts in other EAC countries, the CAK recognises that the existence of fully functional CAK is essential for effective competition within the EAC. Article 75 1.i of the Treaty Establishing the East African Community[230] requires EAC members to develop a protocol regarding competition. Article 33 of the Protocol on the Establishment of East African Community Common Market (the Common Market Protocol) prohibits practices that may adversely affect trade and distort competition in EAC countries. It is on the strength of the EAC Treaty and the Common Market Protocol that in 2004, amended in 2009 to create a single market with four freedoms: free movement of goods, labour, services and capital, that the EAC Council of Ministers adopted Competitions Policy for EAC countries to help deter unconscionable practices that may hinder free trade and hamper competition within the EAC.[231]

474. The East African Competitions Act proscribes anticompetitive practices, including price collusion, collusive tendering and market allocation, and quantitative restraints on investment or sales. It also establishes an EAC Competition Committee, composed of one representative from each of the EAC Member States, which has the power to investigate and to compel evidence, hold hearings, and impose sanctions and remedies.[232]

---

229. KLR, 1974, 'Standards Act Chapter 496 of the Laws of Kenya', available at: https://new.kenyalaw.org/legislation/ [accessed January 2026].
230. EAC, 1999, 'The Treaty for the Establishment of the East African Community', available at: https://www.eacj.org/?page_id=33 [accessed January 2026].
231. EAC, 2010, 'The Protocol on the Establishment of the East African Community (EAC) Common Market', available at: http://www.eac.int [accessed May 2014].
232. The EAC Secretariat, 2006, 'Thc East African Community Trade Report 2006', available at: http://www.eac.int [accessed March 2015].

475. The national competition laws and institutions remain in effect in respective EAC countries, while the EAC Competition law once operational will take care of the intra-regional trade. Unfortunately, because the East African Competitions Act is not operational, it does not apply to activities within EAC and has no cross-border effects. This coupled with the fact that only Kenya and Tanzania have national competition authorities, while in Rwanda, Uganda and Burundi, trade ministries deal with competition issues, has made cross-border cooperation in respect to competition matters, including mergers between the EAC countries, very difficult.

476. Another example of cooperation is that between Kenya and COMESA, to which Kenya is a party. In 2004, the COMESA Competition Regulations and Competition Rules (hereinafter 'COMESA Regulations') were adopted with the goal of regulating mergers and business conduct in cross-border cases, and ensuring consumer protection in countries parties to COMESA. Sections 6 and 12 of the COMESA Regulations establish the CCC and Board of Commissioners. CCC is responsible for monitoring anticompetitive practices and reviewing merger control filings and cooperating with competition authorities in COMESA Member States. The Board of Commissioners has powers to adjudicate on matters touching on the COMESA Regulations, make appropriate rulings, impose remedies and hear appeals against decisions of the CCC. The COMESA Regulations have some implications on cross-border mergers where the undertakings involved are not exclusively from Kenya. Where an undertaking carries on business in one or more Member States, section 24 of the Regulation requires that the CCC be informed of an intended merger. According to the COMESA Regulations on the Determination of Merger Notification Threshold, COMESA applies zero turnover thresholds under this regime. Under sections 24 and 25, within thirty days of the decision to merge, undertakings are required to submit relevant documents to the CCC, after which the CCC will have 120 days to make a determination.[233]

477. Until recently, there was very little coordination between the CCC and CAK. This made the enforcement of the COMESA Competition Regulations and Competition Rules in Kenya very difficult. In its annual report of 2012/2013, the CAK noted the challenge of borderless markets, and in particular that of implementing the COMESA Regulations. These challenges include the process of domesticating the regulations at national level, undefined merger thresholds, very high merger filing fees and the issues relating to uneven development of competition law in the COMESA region. A strengthening of cross-border relations in respect to mergers, effective laws in the Member States and enhanced coordination are possible solutions to this problem. The CAK has recently entered into a cooperation agreement with the CCC in which both bodies agreed to cooperate where they are

233. COMESA, 2025, 'COMESA Competition and Consumer Protection Regulations', 2025, available at: https://comesacompetition.org/resources/regulations/comesa-competition-and-consumer-protection-regulations-2025/ [accessed January 2025]: COMESA, 2012, 'Rules on the Determination of Merger Notification Threshold', available at: http://www.comesa.int/competition/wp-content/uploads/2014/06/2012_Gazette_Vol_17_Annex_15-Determination-of-Merger-Notification-Threshold.pdf [accessed May 2014].

investigating related matters and to share relevant information to ensure effective enforcement of their respective competition laws.

478. The CAK also recognises that because of expansion of international commerce, entities in various countries including Kenya operate largely on markets outside their home zones. This means that competition issues occurring around the globe are, in some cases, similar and competition authorities across the globe have to apply the same methods to address the problems that have more and more in common. The need for cooperation whether at bilateral, regional or multinational level with other international bodies has become not just necessary, but advantageous. Examples of international cooperation between CAK and other bodies include cooperation ICN, the United Nations on Trade and Development (UNCTAD), the Organisation for Economic Co-operation and Development (OECD) and the WTO. Some of the benchmarking activities aimed at promoting and enhancing the CAK capacity to deal with completion issues include CAK's cooperation with ICN in setting merger thresholds and developing various guidelines. Another quite beneficial cooperation is that between the CAK and the Anti-Monopoly Bureau of the Chinese Ministry of Commerce. Following this meeting, the CAK signed an agreement with the Anti-monopoly Bureau under which the two Authorities will exchange ideas on drafting complementary regulations on competition regulation.[234]

234. CAK of Kenya, 2012/2013, 'Annual Report', pp. 27–28, available at: https://www.cak.go.ke/arch/sites/default/files/annual-reports/FY%202012-2013%20CAK%20Annual%20Report.pdf [accessed January 2026]: Ndimi, F., 2014, 'Regional Cooperation: Current and Anticipated', the Sixth Annual African Dialogue Consumer Protection Conference, Lilongwe Malawi, September: CAK of Kenya, 2014, 'The CAK Signs M.O.U with the Anti-Monopoly Bureau of the Ministry of Commerce of the Peoples Republic of China', available at: http://www.cak.go.ke/index.php/latest-news/172-press-release.html [accessed January 2015].

Chapter 3. Challenging the Administrative Decision

§1. Competent Courts

I. Administrative Appeals

479. All administrative decisions of the CAK can be appealed to the Competition Tribunal by any aggrieved undertaking or person. A number of provisions in the Competition Act provide instances in which appeals can be made to either the Tribunal or the High Court of Kenya. For instance, if the CAK denies a person or an undertaking its request for confidential treatment of information, such a person or undertaking may appeal to the Tribunal under section 21.9. Section 40 allows appeals to the Tribunal by an undertaking or a person aggrieved by any decision of the CAK reached after investigations into prohibited practices stipulated in Part III.E of the Competition Act.

480. Under section 48 of the Competition Act, entities whose merger application has been rejected by the CAK can make an application to the Tribunal for the decision made to be reviewed. After receipt of this application, the Tribunal is required to notify interested parties, by notice in the Gazette, of the applications for review. In this notice, the Tribunal also invites the parties to make submissions on the matter in question. A number of decisions can be reached on such appeals. The Tribunal can, for example, overturn the CAK's decision, amend it, confirm it or refer it to the CAK for reconsideration. Section 72 contains general provisions on appeal to the Tribunal. The section lays out the procedures for hearing and determining appeals to the Tribunal. As per the section, the appellant should appear before the Tribunal either in person or by an advocate on the day and at the time fixed for the hearing of the appeal. However, if it is proved to the satisfaction of the Tribunal that, owing to absence of the appellant from Kenya, or due to sickness, or other reasonable cause, an appellant is prevented from attending at the hearing of the appeal, the Tribunal may postpone the hearing of the appeal, as it deems necessary. In such cases, the Tribunal has the discretion to determine who shall bear the costs of an appeal. All the appeals against the decisions of the Tribunal lie with the High Court of Kenya.

II. Criminal Cases

481. Fines and imprisonment provided for under the Competition Act are penalties that are criminal in nature. As per section 92 of the Act, any magistrate's court has the power to impose any penalty provided for in the Competition Act. Therefore, where a fine has been imposed on an undertaking, in the first instance, by, say, a District Magistrate's Court, an appeal can be lodged to the next magistrate's court, which is the Resident Magistrate's Court, and thereafter to the higher court in hierarchy and so on. The monetary limits of jurisdiction of district and resident of the magistrate's courts as laid down in the Magistrates' Courts Act, Cap 10, are to be taken into consideration when imposing fines on individuals or undertakings.

III. Civil Damages Claims

482. Section 16 of the Competition Act states that bona fide actions taken by the CAK in the course of discharging its functions, powers or duties pursuant to the Competition Act shall not subject the CAK to any action, claim or demand whatsoever. Under the same section 16, the CAK is liable to pay compensation or damages to any person for any injury to him, his property or any of his interests caused by the exercise by the CAK of any power conferred by the Competition Act.

483. Otherwise, all damage claims are dealt with by the magistrate's courts as stipulated in section 92 of the Competition Act. A magistrate's court can award civil damages upon proof by the party claiming such damages. Appeals against the decision of the magistrate's court in civil cases are heard by the next highest court in the hierarchy.

§2. Time Limits

484. Section 40 of the Act provides that any person or entity aggrieved by a decision of the CAK in respect to restrictive agreements, practices and decisions, or abuse of dominant position or exemption of certain restrictive practices may appeal to the Competition Tribunal against such decision. If aggrieved by the decision of the Tribunal, such person or entity may, within thirty days, after the date on which a notice of that decision has been served on them, appeal against the decision in the High Court whose decision on matters brought before it from the Tribunal is final. The same procedure (*see* sections 49, 53 and 64 of the Competition Act) applies to those aggrieved about approval of a merger by the CAK or Tribunal, or the Tribunal decisions regarding the control of unwarranted concentrations *of* economic power or injuries/loss suffered because of defective goods.

485. The Tribunal is then to notify the undertakings concerned within thirty days of receipt of the application, when they should make representations before it. Within four months, the Tribunal should render its decision. If an aggrieved party appeals to magistrate's courts, the timelines set forth under Order 42 of the Civil Procedure Rules made under the Civil Procedure Act 2010 apply.

§3. Scope of Judicial Review

I. Judicial Review: Meaning

486. Judicial review is one of the fundamental principles of administrative law concerned with the decision-making of administrative agencies, quasi-judicial agencies or tribunals. Through judicial review, courts are granted powers to declare acts of the government al authorities unconstitutional, and therefore, unenforceable.[235] Court decisions reflecting this definition are plenty. In *Republic v. Commissioner of Customs Services,*[236] the court held that 'judicial review is a constitutional supervision of public authorities involving a challenge to the legal validity of the decision'. And in *Republic v. Permanent Secretary/Secretary to the Cabinet,*[237] it was held that a judicial review enables the judicial branch of the government to reassess and remedy, where necessary, the decisions and actions of the executive and legislative bodies that:

a. are not made in good faith;
b. exceed the powers conferred onto them;
c. do not conform to the Constitution or the applicable law; or that are
d. contrary public interest.

487. Judicial review is not just about protecting the rule of law, i.e., voiding the unconstitutional acts of the legislative and the executive decisions or actions, but also declaring them intra vires.[238] According to Mr Justice Nyamu, in *Mureithi,*[239] judicial review is also about protecting the rule of law and constitutionalism. The ultra vires doctrine, which is primary to judicial review, literally means 'beyond its powers', and entails a situation where a public body acts beyond its statutory powers. The concept of ultra vires helps the courts, through reviews, to clip the powers of the executive bodies that do not comply with principles of natural justice, and thereby accord an aggrieved individual the appropriate judicial remedy. The nature of judicial review varies from country to country.

235. Hertogh, M. and Halliday, S., 2004, pp. 15–19, 'Judicial Review and Bureaucratic Impact: International and Interdisciplinary Perspectives (Cambridge Studies in Law and Society', Cambridge University Press: Mbote, P.K. and Akech, M., 2011, 'A Review of AfriMAP and the Open Society Initiative of Eastern Africa', Published by the *Open Society Initiative of East Africa: Republic v. City Council of Nairobi and four others*, Judicial Review 277 of 2012.

236. *Republic v. Commissioner of Customs Services ex parte Imperial Bank Limited*, HCCC Miscellaneous Application No. 123 of 2014.

237. *Republic v. Permanent Secretary/Secretary to the Cabinet and Head Of Public Service Office of the President & 2 Others ex-parte Stanley Kamanga Nganga* [2006] *eKLR: Republic v. Kenya National Examinations Councilex parte Geoffrey Gathenji and 9 Others* Civil Appeal No. 266 of 1996 *Republic v. Kenya Association of Music Producers (KAMP) and 3 Others*, Judicial Review Case No. 335 of 2013; *Republic v. Judicial Service Commission*, Misc. Civil Application No. 1025 of 2003.

238. Wade, W. and Forsyth, C., 2009, 'Administrative Law', 10th Edition, Oxford University Press: Visram, A., 2010, 'Review of Administrative Decisions of Government by Administrative Courts and Tribunals', 10th Congress of the International Association of Supreme Administrative Jurisdictions (Sydney – March 2010), available at https://www.aihja.org/wp-content/uploads/2022/12/IASAJ_General-report-2010.pdf [accessed January 2026]: Craig, P., 1998, pp. 63–90, 'Ultra Vires and the Foundations of Judicial Review', The Cambridge Law Journal, 57: *Commissioner of Lands v. Kunste Hotel Ltd*, Civil Appeal No. 234 of 1995, [1997] eKLR.

239. *Mureithi and Two Others v. Attorney General and Four Others*, Misc. Civil App. No. 158 of 2005 Cane, P., 2004, p. 16, 'Understanding Judicial Review and Its Impact' in Hertogh, M. and Halliday, S., 'Judicial Review and Bureaucratic Impact: International and Interdisciplinary Perspectives', Cambridge University Press UK.

488. In Kenya, the inappropriateness of the decisions of governmental authorities is reviewed via two types of remedies: private law remedies of lawsuit and judicial review through notice of motions. Judicial review comes into play in Kenya in matters relating to selection of candidates for appointment to governmental positions and promotion of Government employees. For instance, in the *Center for Rights Education*,[240] in which the applicants challenged the President's power to appoint Commissioners, the High Court of Kenya ruled that the President had no power under the Constitution of Kenya to appoint or deploy county Commissioners.

489. Section 89.10 of the Constitution states that any person may apply to the High Court for review of the decision of the Independent Electoral and Boundaries Commission (IEBC). This was further confirmed in case of *Ex-Chef Peter Odoyo Ogada*,[241] in which the Supreme Court of Kenya underscored the power of the High Court of Kenya to review IEBC's decisions.

II. Judicial Review and the Constitution of Kenya

490. Before the enactment of the Constitution of Kenya, 2010, sections 8 and 9 of the Law Reform Act[242] constituted the substantive basis for judicial review of administrative actions, whereas Order 53 of the Civil Procedure Rules (hereinafter 'Order 53') was the procedural basis for judicial review of administrative actions.[243] The new Constitution of Kenya expressly sets forth the grounds for judicial review, lists the actions that may lead to review and sets the judicial review jurisdiction.

491. Judicial review ensures that executive acts are performed in accordance with the constitution and all applicable laws, or rather that the rule of law is enforced. Thus, the legitimacy of judicial review is, therefore, based on the rule of law.[244] The Constitution of Kenya empowers the courts, the CAK, to share the powers of administrative bodies that act in excess of their legal authority. The Preamble to the Constitution of Kenya echoes the promotion of the rule of law by emphasising the right to a government, based on essential values of human rights, equality, freedom, democracy, social justice and the rule of law.

---

240. *Center for Rights Education and Awareness and 8 Others v. Attorney General*, eKLR 2012.

241. *Ex-Chef Peter Odoyo Ogada & Others v. Independent Electoral and Boundaries Commission & 14 Others*, Court of Appeal at Nairobi, Civil Appeal No. 307 of 2012 [2013]eKLR.

242. KLR, 1960, 'Law Reform Act, Chapter 26 of the Laws of Kenya', available at: v https://new.kenyalaw.org/akn/ke/act/1956/48/eng@1966-07-12 [accessed January 2026].

243. *Republic v. Public Procurement Administrative Review Board & 2 Others, ex-parte Selex Sistemi Integrati*, Misc Civil Appli 1260 of 2007 [2008] eKLR.

244. In the Marbury case, CJ Marshall established and justified the power of judicial review by declaring that 'it is emphatically the province and duty of the judicial department to say what the law is'. *Marbury v. Madison*, 5 U.S., 1 Cranch, 137, 2L. Ed. 60 *Republic v. City Council of Nairobi and four others*, Judicial Review 277 of 2012.

492. According to section 2 of the Constitution, the Constitution is the supreme law of the land and binds all persons and all State organs at both levels of government, and any act, omission or law, including customary law, that is inconsistent with the Constitution is void to the extent of the inconsistency. In *Nancy Makokha Baraza*,[245] the High Court of Kenya reiterated that the 'new Constitution gives the court wide and unrestricted powers which are inclusive rather than exclusive, and therefore, allows the court to make appropriate orders and grant remedies as the situation demands and as the need arise'.

493. Section 10 of the Constitution indirectly underscores the rule of law by categorically stating that national values and principles of governance set forth in the Constitution bind all State organs, State officers, public officers and all persons whenever they:

a. apply or interpret the Constitution;
b. enact, apply or interpret any law; or
c. make or implement public policy decisions.

494. Section 22 of the Constitution gives any person whose fundamental rights have been violated, infringed or threatened the right to institute court proceedings.[246] Persons acting in their own interest, or on behalf of another person who cannot act in their own name, as well as persons acting as a member of, or in the interest of, a group or class of persons, or persons acting in public interest, may also institute proceedings to enforce the infringed rights. The public interest aspect of judicial review was captured in the *Republic v. Kenya Cricket Association ex parte Maurice Odumbe*[247] case. In this case, the High Court of Kenya refused to grant leave to the applicant Maurice Odumbe, who had file an application seeking judicial review of a decision banning him from playing cricket for five years. The court held it could only grant leave to file an application for judicial review if the body issuing the decision is exercising public law functions or if the exercise of by that body of its functions has public law consequences.

495. Sections 23.1 and 2 of the Constitution confers on the High Court of Kenya the jurisdiction to hear and determine applications for redress of a denial, violation or infringement of, or a threat to any of the fundamental rights ensconced in the Constitution. These include judicial review applications. In addition, the Parliament is mandated to promulgate legislation (s) that gives original jurisdiction as and when necessary to subordinate courts to hear and determine applications for redress of grievances in respect to constitutional rights.

---

245. *Nancy Makokha Baraza v. The Judicial Service Commission and Nine Others*, Constitution and Human Rights Division Petition No. 23 of 2012: *Republic v. Judicial Service Commission & Another, Exparte Joyce Manyasi* [2012] eKLR, Judicial Review 299 of 2012.

246. *See also Mike J C Mills and another v. the Post and Telecommunications*, Nairobi HCMA No. 1013 of 1996.

247. *Republic v. Kenya Cricket Association ex parte Maurice Odumbe*, HCCC Miscellaneous Application No. 1723 of 2004.

496. Moreover, section 47 of the Constitution accords everyone the right to an administrative action that is lawful, quick, efficient, reasonable and procedurally fair. In cases where the fundamental rights guaranteed under the Constitution are to be adversely affected by an administrative action, the affected persons have to be given the reasons for action. Under this section, the Parliament is charged with the duty of enacting legislations that:

a. provide for the review of administrative action by a court or, if appropriate, an independent and impartial tribunal; and
b. promote efficient administration.

497. A further section of the Constitution that deals with judicial review is section 165. It establishes and vests in the High Court of Kenya an unlimited original jurisdiction in criminal and civil matters. The latter includes judicial review. The section further gives the High Court supervisory jurisdiction over the subordinate courts and over any person, body or authority exercising a judicial or quasi-judicial function. Administrative and governmental authorities definitely fall under this section.

III. Administrative Procedure

A. Fair Administrative Action Act

498. Recently, the Fair Administrative Action Act,[248] 2015 (hereinafter 'Fair Administrative Act'), was promulgated, among other things, to give effect to Article 47 of the Constitution and for 'connected purposes'. Section 2 of the Act defines administrative action subject to judicial review to include:

a. the powers, functions and duties exercised by authorities or quasi-judicial tribunals; or
b. any act, omission or decision of any person, body or authority that affects the legal rights or interests of any person to whom such action relates.

499. The procedure for judicial review is set forth in sections 9 and 10 of the Fair Administrative Act. The provisions stipulate that persons aggrieved by an administrative action may pursuant to section 22.3 of the Constitution apply either to the High Court or to a subordinate court with original jurisdiction for the review of the action. Section 10 of the Act provides that an application for judicial review once accepted by the High Court is heard and determined without undue regard to any associated procedural technicalities. Any person aggrieved by an order of the High Court regarding judicial review jurisdiction may appeal to the Court of Appeal. Section 10 of the Act further empowers the Chief Justice to make rules of

248. KLR, 2015, 'Fair Administrative Act, No. 4 of 2015', available at: http://www.kenyalaw.org [accessed July 2016].

practice for regulating the procedure and practice in matters relating to judicial review of administrative action. Applications for the review of an administrative action or an appeal must according to section 8 of the Act be determined within ninety days of filing the application.

B. Order 53 of the Civil Procedure Rules

500. As already indicated in section 3.II of this chapter, the regimes that governed judicial review of administrative actions in Kenya before the promulgation of the Constitution were Order 53 and sections 8 and 9 of the Law Reform Act. Despite the enactment of the Fair Administrative Act, Order 53, which also spells out the procedure for judicial review, is still in force, and it is unclear which of the two statutes applies to judicial review of administrative actions.

Nevertheless, it may be presumed that section 14 of the Fair Administrative Act overrules the application of other legislations (including Order) to matters regarding judicial review. The provision states that:

> in all proceedings pending, whether preparatory or incidental to, or consequential upon any proceedings in court at the time of the coming into force of this Act, the provisions of this Act shall apply, but without prejudice to the validity of anything previously done.

501. As such, the procedure for judicial review under Order 53 is not discussed in this monograph.

IV. Grounds for Judicial Review

502. According to section 7.2 of the Fair Administrative Act, a tribunal or court may review an administrative action or decision if:

a. the person who made the decision:
   - was not authorised to do so by empowering provisions;
   - acted in excess of jurisdiction or power conferred under any written law;
   - acted pursuant to delegated power in contravention of any law prohibiting such delegation;
   - was biased or was suspected of bias; or
   - denied the person to whom the administrative action or decision relates a reasonable opportunity to be heard.
b. a mandatory and material procedure or condition prescribed by an empowering provision was complied with;
c. the administrative action or decision complained of was taken:
   - with an ulterior motive or purpose calculated to prejudice the legal rights of the applicant; or if such an action or decision was:
     - not proportionate to the interests or rights affected;

- procedurally unfair, and not connected to the purpose for which it was taken;
- materially influenced by an error of law, in bad faith or unreasonable so far instance is affected by corruption, bribery, dishonesty or similar malpractice;
- violated the legitimate expectations of the person to whom it relates; or
- made in abuse of power, i.e., is ultra vires its jurisdiction;

d. the administrator acted on the direction of a person or body not authorised or empowered by any written law to give such directions;
e. there was an abuse of discretion, unreasonable delay or failure to act in discharge of a duty imposed under any written law.

503. Similar grounds as the ones set forth in section 7.2 of the Fair Administrative Act were laid down in *Pastoli v. Kabale District Local Government Council.*[249] Under section 9.2 of the Fair Administrative Act, judicial review is only possible if the applicant has exhausted all internal mechanisms for appeal or review and all remedies available under any other written law.

V. Fine Procedures

504. In cases where the fundamental rights enshrined in the Constitution have been threatened, denied, violated or infringed, section 23.3 stipulates that any of the following reliefs may be granted:

a. a declaration of rights;
b. an injunction;
c. a conservatory order;
d. a declaration of invalidity of any law that denies, violates, infringes, or threatens a right or fundamental freedom in the Bill of Rights and is not justified under Article 24 (i.e., where a fundamental right is limited by the law);
e. an order for compensation; and
f. an order of judicial review.

505. Under section 9.2 of the Fair Administrative Act, in proceedings for judicial review, the following orders may be granted. An order:

a. declaring the rights of the parties in respect of any matter to which the administrative action relates;
b. restraining the administrator from acting or continuing to act in breach of duty imposed upon the administrator under any written law or from acting, or continuing to act in any manner that is prejudicial to the legal rights of an applicant;

249. *Pastoli v. Kabale District Local Government Council and Others* [2008] 2 EA 300.

c. directing the administrator to give reasons for the administrative action or decision taken by the administrator;
d. prohibiting the administrator from acting in a particular manner;
e. setting aside the administrative action or decision and remitting the matter for reconsideration by the administrator, with or without directions;
f. compelling the performance by an administrator of a public duty owed in law and in respect of which the applicant has a legally enforceable right;
g. granting a temporary interdict or a temporary relief;
h. for the award of costs or other pecuniary compensation in appropriate cases.

506. In proceedings for judicial review relating to failure to take an administrative action, the court may grant any order that is just and equitable, including an order:

a. directing the taking of the decision;
b. declaring the rights of the parties in relation to the taking of the decision;
c. directing any of the parties to do or to refrain from doing, any act or thing the doing, or the refraining from the doing, of which the court or tribunal considers necessary to do justice between the parties; or
d. as to costs and other monetary compensation.

507. In conclusion, the law relating to judicial review is still evolving. Indeed, the Court of Appeal of Kenya recognised this fact in *Republic v. Attorney General and Registrar of Societies,*[250] in which it held that the rule that the law relating to judicial review has not yet reached the furthest or the last frontier, and accordingly encouraged courts in Kenya to expand the grounds of intervention depending on the circumstances before them.

250. *Republic v. Attorney General and Registrar of Societies Miscellaneous*, Application 769 of 2004.

Selected Bibliography

Articles

Atieno, Y., 2009, 'Corporate Governance Problems Facing Kenyan Parastatals: A Case Study of the Sugar Industry', available at: https://www.semanticscholar.org/paper/Corporate-Governance-Problems-facing-Kenyan-%3A-A-of-Atieno/8513d123efb7ab69525ca0fa6b395e95b9108a8d.

Barazza, S., 2012, 'Post Danmark: The CJEU Calls for an Effect: Based Assessment of Pricing Policies', Journal of European Competition law & Practice, 3(5), 466.

Bardong, A., 2012, 'Germany: the Bundeskartellamt's New Merger Guidelines', Journal of European Competition Law and Practice, 3(5), 481.

Beamish, W.P. and Nathaniel C. Lupto, C.N., 2009, 'Managing Joint Ventures', Academy of Management Perspectives, available at: http://aom.org/.

Bork, R.H, 2010, 'The Antitrust Parado', Nabu Press, September, 378–379.

Borill, J.R., Jimenez, J.L, and Garcia, C., 2013, 'Evaluating Antitrust Leniency Programs', Journal of Competition Law and Economics 10(1), 107.

Brennan, T., 2008, 'Bundled Rebates as Exclusion rather than Predation', Journal of Competition law and Economics, 4(2), 335.

Bravo, F.L and Siciliani, P, 2007, 'Exclusionary Pricing and Consumers Harm: The European Practice in DSL Market', Journal of Competition law and Economics, 3(2), 243.

Budzinski, O and Wacker, K., 2007, 'The Prohibition of the Proposed Springer PROSIEBENSAT.1 Merger: How Much Economics in German Merger Control?', Journal of Competition Law and Economics, 3(2), 281.

Bulmash, H., 2012, 'An Empirical Analysis of Secondary Price Discriminations and Motivations', Journal of Competition Law and Economics, 8(2), 361.

Buttigieg, E. 2010, 'Lingering Uncertainty over the Antitrust Approach to Resale Price Maintenance', Journal of European Competition Law and Practice, 1(5), 397.

CAK, 2009, 'Guidelines for Market Definition', available at: https://cak.go.ke/arch/sites/default/files/Guidelines%20on%20Relevant%20Market%20Definition%20(1).pdf.

CAK, Undated, 'Consolidated Guidelines on the Substantive Assessment of Mergers under the Competition Act', available at: https://cak.go.ke/sites/default/files/downloads/2024-08/ConsolidatedMergerGuidelines.pdf [accessed January 2026].

Selected Bibliography

CAK, Undated, 'Consolidated Guidelines on the Substantive Assessment of Restrictive Trade Practices under the Competition Act', available at: http://www.cak.go.ke [accessed August 2016].

CCK, 2025, 'Fourth Quarter Sectors Statistics Report for the Financial Year 2024/2025' (1 April–30 June 2025), available at https://www.ca.go.ke/sites/default/files/2025-09/Sector%20Statistics%20Report%20Q4%202024-2025_1.pdf.

Calvino, N., 2011, 'When Do Mergers Raise Concerns? An Analysis of the Assessment Carried out by the European Commission under the New Merger Regulation', Journal of European Competition Law and Practice, 2(6), 521.

Cytonn, 'The Kenya National Social Security Fund, March 2025', available at: https://cytonn.com/topicals/the-kenyan-national-3 [accessed May 2025].

CGD Bills Digest, 2005, 'The National Social Security Pensions Trust Bill: The Making of a Better NSSF', Issue 03/05 August.

Chitere, P. and Kibua, T., 2004, 'Efforts to Improve Road Safety in Kenya: Achievements and Limitations in the Matatu Industry', Institute of Policy Analysis and Research, available at: https://www.ssatp.org/.

Choi, Y.S., 2011, 'The Per Se Rule on Minimum Resale Price Maintenance in Korea: A Time to Change', International Review of Intellectual Property and Competition Law.

Church, J., 2005, 'The Church Report's Analysis of Vertical and Conglomerate Mergers: a Reply to Cooper, Froeb, O'brien and Vita', Journal of Competition Law and Economics, 1(4), 797.

Competition Bureau Canada, 2012, 'Abuse of Dominance: A Serious Competitive Offence', available at: https://competition-bureau.canada.ca/en/how-we-foster-competition/education-and-outreach/abuse-dominance-enforcement-guidelines.

Cotran, E., 1983, 'The Development and Reform of the Law in Kenya', Journal of African Law, 27(1).

Craig, P., 1998, 'Ultra Vires and the Foundations of Judicial Review', The Cambridge Law Journal.

Crocioni, P., 2007, 'Leveraging of Market Power in Emerging Markets: A Review of Cases, Literature and A Suggested Framework', Journal of Competition law and Economics, 4(2), 449.

David, M., 1981, 'The Transition in Smallholder Banking in Kenya: Evidence from Rural Branch Bank Loans', The Journal of Developing Areas, 16(1).

Devlin, A. and Jacobs, M., 2011, 'Joint Venture Analysis after American Needle', Journal of Competition Law and Economics, 7(3), 543.

Dutoit, B., 1989, 'Joint Ventures and Intellectual Property', International Review of Intellectual Property, 4.

Ewald, C., 2012, 'The Economics of Resale Price Maintenance- Why Europe is Right not to Follow the USA on the Slippery Slope of Leegin', Journal of European Competition Law and Practice, 3(3), 300.

Ezrachi, A., 2012, 'Buying Alliances and Input Price Fixing', Journal of Competition Law and Economics, 8(1), 47.

Ezrachi, A. and Thanassoulis, J., 2013, 'Upstream Horizontal Mergers and the Absence of Retail Effects', Journal of Competition Law and Economics, 9(2), 395.

Faella, G., 2008, 'The Antitrust Assessment of Loyalty Discounts and Rebates', Journal of Competition law and Economics, 4(2), 375.

Friedrich-Ebert-Stiftung, 2012, 'Regional Disparities and Marginalisation in Kenya', available at: http://www.fes-kenya.org.

Gachino, G., 2009, 'Industrial Policy, Institutions and Foreign Direct Investment: The Kenyan Context', African Journal of Marketing Management, 1(6).

Geradin, D. and Petit, N., 2006, 'Price Discrimination under EC Competition Law: Another Antitrust Doctrine in Search of Limiting Principles', Journal of Competition law and Economics, 2(3), 479.

Heimler, A., 2012, 'Cartels in Public Procurement', Journal of Competition Law and Economics, 8(4).

Hewitt, G., 2004, 'Substantive Criteria Used for Assessment of Mergers: Background Note', OECD Journal of Competition Law and Policy, 6(3).

Hewitt, G., 2005, 'Merger Remedies', OECD Journal of Competition Law and Policy, 7(2).

Hojnik, J., 2013, 'De Minimis Rule Within the EU Internal Market Freedoms: Towards a More Mature and Legitimate Market?', European Journal of Legal Studies, 6 (1), 25.

IMF Survey Online, 2012, 'Truly Integrated Market Would Bring Benefits to East Africa', 15 March.

IRA, 2024, 'Insurance Industry Report for the Period Janaury–December 2023', Fourth Quater Release, February 2024, available at: https://www.ira.go.ke/assets/file/Q4_2023_Industry_Release.pdf.

Kaplow, L., 2011, 'On the Meaning of Horizontal Agreements in Competition Law', available at: http://ssrn.com/.

Karanja-Ng'ang'a, J. and Muthang'ato, W., 2013, 'Kenya', The Mergers and Acquisitions Law Review, 7th Edition, Law Business Research Limited, available at: www.TheLawReviews.co.uk.

Kato, M., 2009, 'Transitoriness of Market Power and Antitrust Activity', Journal of Competition Law and Economics, 6(2), 393.

Kauper, E.T., 1996, 'The Problem of Market Definition', Fordham International Law Journal, 20(5), 1682, available at: http://ir.lawnet.fordham.edu/cgi/viewcontent.cgi?article=1804&context=ilj.

KCB, Undated, 'KCB Group History', available at: https://kcbgroup.com/our-history/.

Kinoro, A.J., 2013, 'Factors Affecting New Vehicle Sale in the Kenya Motor Industry: A Case of General Motors (East Africa) Limited', International Journal of Social Sciences and Entrepreneurship, 1(2), 664.

Lapsset Corridor Development Authority, Status Report, September 2017, available at: https://aid.nepad.org/m_assets/uploads/document/15054818871514304844.pdf [accessed May 2025].

Lianos, I., 2007, 'Commercial Agency Agreements, Vertical Restraints and the Limits of Article 81.1 EC: Between Hierarchies and Networks', Journal of Competition law and Economics, 3(4), 625.

Liebowitz, J. S and Margolis, E. S., 2008, 'Bundles of Joy: The Ubiquity and Efficiency of Bundles in New Technology Markets', Journal of Competition law and Economics, 5(1), 1.

Selected Bibliography

KPMG, 2014, 'East Africa's Changing Auto Industry', 23 June.

Maina, C.P. and Kijo-Bisimba, H., 2007, 'Law and Justice in Tanzania: Quarter Century of the Court of Appeal', A publication for Legal and Human Rights Centre, Mkuki na Nyota Publishers, Dar-es-Salaam, Tanzania.

Makoloo, O.M. and Ghai, Y., 2005, 'Kenya: Minorities, Indigenous Peoples and Ethnic Diversity'.

Mapenzi Bahati, E., 2009, 'The Influence of Marketing Strategies on Popularity of Toyota and Nissan Brands in Kenya', available at: https://erepository.uonbi.ac.ke /bitstream/handle/11295/22970/MAPENZI_BAHATI_E._MBA_2009.pdf.

Marth W. R., 2009, 'Antitrust Treatment of Joint Ventures: Analyzing Competitor Collaborations', available at: https://www.robinskaplan.com/newsroom/insights/ antitrust-treatment-of-joint-ventures-analyzing-competitor-collaborations.Miriri, D., 2013, 'UPDATE 2-Rebound in Key Sectors Seen Driving Kenya Economy in 2013', Reuters, 23 May.

Mullen, Tom, 2007, 'Reflections on Jackson v Attorney General: Questioning Sovereignty', Legal Studies, 27(1).

Mwaura, K., 2007, 'The Failure of Corporate Governance in State Owned Enterprises and the Need for Restructured Governance in Fully and Partially Privatized Enterprises: The Case of Kenya', Fordham International Law Journal 31(1).

Njehu, K.F., 2010, 'Competition Law in Kenya: A Snapshot', Centre for Competition, Investment & Economic Regulation, available at: http://www.cuts-international.org.

Njenga, N.G., 2010, 'A Synopsis of the History of Kenya Before Colonisation', available at: https://www.studocu.com/row/document/umma-university/bachelor-of-education-arts/a-synopsis-of-kenyas-pre-colonial-history-insights-and-analysis/129567646.

Obala, R., 2013, 'President Uhuru Kenyatta Unveils Team to Restructure Parastatals', Standard Digital, Kenya, July 24.

Okundi, B., 2013, 'There's a Need to Breath New Life into State Corporations Through Reforms', Daily Nation, Kenya, 25 September.

Ole Turana, J., 2013, 'Kenya's Economy May Expand at Fastest Rate in Six Years in 2013', Bloomberg, May.

Ombok, E., 2010, 'Kenya National Social Security Fund's Assets Fall 9.2% in Year to June '09', Bloomberg, June 29.

Ombok, E., 2013, 'Kenya Second-Quarter Tea Output Seen Rising 22% on Improved Rain', Bloomberg, 18 April.

Owino, K., 2006, 'Kenya', in Mehta, P., 2006 'Competition Regimes in the World: A Civil Society Report', CUTS International.

Omondi, G., 2013, 'Agriculture's Strong Growth Spurs Kenya Economy to 4.6pc', Business Daily, Kenya, May.

Papadopoulos, P., 2006, 'Article 82: Tying and bundling', Competition Law Insight, 6 June.

Park, S., 2009, 'Market Power in Competition for the Market', Journal of Competition Law and Economics, 5(3), 571.

Patel, P., 2001, 'Multi-Party Politics in Kenya', Revista Ciencia Política, XXI(1).

Petzold, D., 2015, 'It Is All Predatory Pricing: Margin Squeeze Abuse and the Concept of Opportunity Costs in EU Competition Law', Journal of European Competition law & Practice.

Posner, R.A, 1974, 'Exclusionary Practices and the Antitrust Laws', University of Chicago Law School, Chicago Unbound, Journal Articles, Faculty Scholarship.

Presse Release, Central Bank of Kenya, 8 April 2025 available at: https://www.centralbank.go.ke/uploads/mpc_press_release/2072351219_MPC%20Press%20Release%20-%20Meeting%20of%20April%208%202025.pdf.

Proctor, J.A., 2014, ' Tacit Collusion Indicators in Merger Control under Varied Focal Points', Journal of Competition Law and Economics, 10(4), 959.

Rousseva, E., 2006, 'The Concept of "Objective Justification" of an Abuse of a Dominant Position: Can It Help to Modernize the Analysis under Article 82 EC?' The Competition Law Review, 2(2), March.

Safaricom, 2025, Annual Report, 2025, available at: https://www.safaricom.co.ke/images/Downloads/Annual-2025-Reporrt.pdf.

Sama, D., 2012, 'The Antitrust Treatment of Loyalty Discounts and Rebates in the EU Competition Law: In Search of an Economic Approach and a Theory of Consumer Harm', Munich Personal RePEc Archive.

Schrer Katja, 'Lamu Port in Kenia: Meilenstein oder Millionengrab?', available at: https://wirtschaftinafrika.de/lamu-port-in-kenia// [accessed May 2025].

Shapiro, C., 2002, 'Competition Policy and Innovation', STI Working Papers, 2002/11, DSTI/DOC(2002) 11, 22 April.

Sidak, J.G, 2006, 'A Consumer Welfare Approach to Network Neutrality Regulation of the Internet', Journal of Competition law and Economics, 2(3), 349.

Singer, H.G, 2006, 'The Competitive Effects of Cable Television Operator's Refusal to Carry DSL Advertising', Journal of Competition law and Economics, 2(2), 301.

Sixth Development Strategy 201/22-2025/26, available at: https://faolex.fao.org/docs/pdf/mul214454.pdf [accessed May 2025].

Slaughter and May, 2012, 'The European Union Merger Regulation; an Overview of the European Merger Control Rules', March 2012, available at: https://www.lexology.com/library/detail.aspx?g=d75de26b-8c27-4991-9c27-3a550827c1b7.Spector, D., 2014, 'The European Commission's Approach to Long-Term Contracts: an Economist's View', Journal of European Competition law & Practice, 5(7), 492.

Syekei, J., Coulson, P. and Märzheuser-Wood, B., 2014, 'Kenya', Franchise Law Review, 1st Edition, p. 360.

Ten Kate, A., and Niels, G., 2009, 'The Relevant Market: a Concept Still in Search of Definition', Journal of Competition Law and Economics, 5(2).

CAK Kenya, 2010, 'The Competition Act no. 12 of 2010', available at: https://new.kenyalaw.org/akn/ke/act/2001/3/eng@2022-12-31.

Thomas, S., 2013, 'Close Competitors in Merger Review', Journal of European Competition Law and Practice, 4(5), 391.

UK Trade and Investment, 2013, 'Automotive Sector in Kenya', February.

Waema Mwololo, T., 2007, 'Kenya. Telecommunications Sector Performance Review: A Supply Side Analysis of Policy Outcomes', School of Computing and Informatics, University of Nairobi, Kenya.

Wang, W. and Rudanko, M., 2012, 'EU Merger Remedies and Competition, Concerns: An Empirical Assessment', European Law Journal,18(4), 555.

Waithaka, J., 2012, 'The Kenya Wildlife Service in the 21st Century: Protecting Globally Significant Areas and Resources', The George Wright Forum, 29(1).

Warner, K.A., 1990, 'Judicial Reasoning and Precedent: Negligently Inflicted Psychological Injuries', Legal Studies, 10(1), 63.

Were, E. and Ligami, C., 2011, 'Nairobi, Africa's New HQ for Multinational Firms', The East African, 24 July.

Wilson, R., Van Der Meulen, S., Lloyd, K., and Konstant, A., 2012, 'South Africa: Tribunal Reverses Commission Prohibition of a Vertical Merger', available at: http://www.mondaq.com.

Zenger, H., 2012, 'Loyalty Rebates and the Competitive Process', Journal of Competition law and Economics, 8(4), 717.

Zhang, H.A., 2013, 'Toward an Economic Approach to Agency Agreements', Journal of Competition Law and Economics, 9(3), 553.

Books

Alison, J. and Sufrin, B., 2011, 'EU Competition Law, Text, Cases and Materials', Oxford University Press, 4th edition.

Broberg, C., 2002, 'Kenya in Pictures (Visual Geography (Twenty-First Century))', Lerner Publications, Rev Exp edition.

Bundeskartellamt, 2013, 'Vertical Restraints in the Internet Economy Meeting of the Working Group on Competition Law' 10 October.

Cane, P., 2004, 'Understanding Judicial Review and Its Impact' in Hertogh, M and Halliday, S., 2004, 'Judicial Review and Bureaucratic Impact: International and Interdisciplinary Perspectives', Cambridge University Press UK.

Castendyk, O., Dommering, E.J., Scheuer, A. and Böttcher, K., 2008, 'European Media Law', Alphen aan den Rijn Kluwer Law.

Cotran, E., 1970, 'Kenya', Annual Survey of African Law, in Rubin, N. and Cotran, E., 1970, Frank Cass and Company Limited, London.

Geiger, R., 2010, 'The Development of World Economy and Competition Law' in Zäch, R, Heinemann, A and Kellerhals, A., 2010, 'The Development of Competition Law: Global Perspectives', Edward Elgar Publishers.

Goyders, J. and Albors Llorens, A., 2009, 'EC Competition Law', 5th Edition, Oxford University Press.

Jephcott, M., 2005, 'Horizontal Agreements and EU Competition Law', Anthony Rowe Ltd.

Jones, A. and Sufrin, B., 2010, 'Texts Cases and Materials', 2010, 'EU Competition Law: Text, Cases & Materials', 4th Edition, Oxford University Press.

Kokkoris, I and Olivares-Caminal, R., 2009, 'Anti-trust Law Amidst Financial Crisis', Cambridge University Press.

Mbote, P.K. and Akech, M., 2011, 'A Review of AfriMAP and the Open Society Initiative of Eastern Africa', Published by the Open Society Initiative of East Africa.

Melischek, A.C., 2013, 'The Relevant Market in Economic Law: A Comparative Antitrust and GATT Analysis', Cambridge University Press.

Mey, B., 2013, 'The Legal Duel: The TRIPS Agreement and Drug Access Issues: Is the Agreement Actually the Cunning Manoeuvre It Has Been Dubbed?', Peter Lang GmbH, Internationaler Verlag der Wissenschaften; New edition edition (16 August 2013).

Muigai, G., 1992, 'The Judiciary in Kenya and the Search for a Philosophy of the Law: The Case of Constitutional Adjudication', in Kibwana, K., 1992, 'Law and Administration of Justice in Kenya, International Commission of Jurists (Kenya Section)', General Printers Ltd, Nairobi, Kenya.

Murungi, M., 2011, 'Cyber Law in Kenya', Wolters Kluwer, Kluwer Law International, the Netherlands.

Mwangi, S.K., Mbaku, M.J. and Mwaniki, N., 2003, 'Restarting and Sustaining Economic Growth and Development in Africa: The Case of Kenya (Contemporary Perspectives on Developing Societies)', Ashgate Pub Ltd, England, USA.

Ntarangwi, M. & Ingham, K., 'The History of Kenya', November 2024 available at: https://www.britannica.com/topic/history-of-Kenya.

OECD, 2002, 'Competition and Co-operation in Innovation in OECD Science, Technology and Industry Outlook 2002', OECD Publishing.

Ogot, B., 1995, 'Transition from Single-Party to Multiparty Political System 1989–83', in Ogot, B. and Ochieng, W., 1995, 'Decolonization & Independence in Kenya, 1940–93', East African Education Publishers, Nairobi, Kenya and Ohio University Press, USA.

Rubini, L. 2009, 'The Definition of Subsidy and State Aid: WTO and EC Law in Comparative Perspective', Oxford University Press.

Shan, W and Kinnear, M., 2012, 'The Legal Protection of Foreign Investment: A Comparative Study', Hart Publishing UK.

Wade, W and Forsyth, C., 2009, 'Administrative Law', 10th Ed, Oxford University Press.

Shantayanan, D. Dollar, D. and Holmgren, T., 2001, 'Aid and Reform in Africa: Lessons from Ten Case Studies', World Bank Publications, Washington, D.C.

Sidak, J.G., 2006, ' A Consumer Welfare Approach to Network Neutrality Regulation of the Internet', Journal of Competition law and Economics, 2(3), 349.

Singer, H., 2006, 'The Competitive Effects of Cable Television Operator's Refusal to Carry DSL Advertising', Journal of Competition law and Economics, 2(2), 301.

Taylor, Martin, 2006, 'International Competition Law: A New Dimension for the WTO', Cambridge University Press.

Trebilcock, J.M. and Daniels, J.R., 2008, 'Rule of Law Reform and Development: Charting the Fragile Path of Progress', Edward Elgar Publishing Ltd, UK, USA.

Tudor, J., 1986, 'The Law of Kenya', Kenya Literature Bureau; 3rd edition, Nairobi, Kenya.

Whish, R., 2003, 'Competition Law', Lexis Nexis, Butterworths.

Whish, R. and Bailey, D., 2012, 'Competition Law', 7th ed. Oxford University Press.

Documents

African Antitrust Competition Law, 2019, Styles Industries (Darling) Kenya, available at: https://africanantitrust.com/category/distribution/.

Selected Bibliography

African Development Bank, 2011, 'African Economic Outlook 2012: Promoting Youth Employment-Kenya', available at: http://www.afdb.org.

African Economic Outlook, 2012, 'Kenya', available at: http://www.afdb.org.

Aidan, E. and Gitau, J.M., 2007, 'Economic Policy and Performance in East Africa: A Survey of Tanzania, Kenya, Uganda and Rwanda', in East African Scenarios Project Research Compendium, a publication of the Society for International Development (SID).

Bird, N., and Kirira, N., 2009, 'Government Institutions, Public Expenditure and the Role of Development Partners: Meeting Kenya's Environmental Challenges', an Overseas Development Institute Report produced on behalf of the Danish Embassy – Nairobi.

Blanchard, P.L., 2013, 'U.S.-Kenya Relations: Current Political and Security Issues', 23 September, CRS Report for Congress Prepared for Members and Committees of Congress, R42967.

Bonge, M.G., 2010, 'Towards EAC Competitions Law and Policy', East African Business Council, Issue 5, 2010, August, available at: http://eabc.info.

CAK, 2012/2013, 'Annual Report', pp. 21, 48–50, available at: http://www.cak.go.ke.

CAK, 2014, 'Guidelines on Relevant Market Definition', available at: http://www.cak.go.ke.

CAK, 2012, 'Exemption Guidelines', available at: http://www.cak.go.ke.

CAK, 2012, 'Exemption Guidelines for Horizontal Practices, 2012', available at: http://www.cak.go.ke.

CAK, 2012, 'Guidelines on Conglomerate Mergers', available at: http://www.cak.go.ke.

CAK, 2012, 'Guidelines on Horizontal Mergers', available at: https://cak.go.ke/sites/default/files/downloads/2024-08/ConsolidatedMergerGuidelines.pdf.

CAK, 2012, 'Guidelines on Vertical Mergers', available at: http://www.cak.go.ke.

CAK, 2013, 'Brookside Finalises Buy-out', available at: http://www.cak.go.ke.

CAK, 2013, 'Proposed Merger Thresholds', available at: http://www.cak.go.ke.

CAK, 2013/2014, 'The Annual Report 2013/2014', available at: http://www.cak.go.ke.

CAK, 2014, 'Guidelines on Exclusion of Proposed Mergers from Provisions of Part IV of the Competition Act, no. 12 of 2010', available at: http://www.cak.go.ke.

CAK, 2014, 'Public Interest Test in Merger Determinations', available at: http://www.cak.go.ke.

CAK, 2014, 'Safaricom, Airtel sign Sh10.5bn Deal to Acquire YU Mobile Assets' and 'Safaricom and Airtel to absorb 175 YU Mobile Staff', available at: http://www.cak.go.ke.

CAK, 2014, 'Guidelines on Engaging with Other Consumer Organisations', available at: http://www.cak.go.ke.

CAK, 2014, 'The CAK Signs M.O.U with the Anti-Monopoly Bureau of the Ministry of Commerce of the Peoples Republic of China', available at: http://www.cak.go.ke.

CAK, Undated, 'Consolidated Guidelines on the Substantive Assessment of Restrictive Trade Practices', available at: http://www.cak.go.ke.

CAK, 2023, 'Consolidated Guidelines on Restrictive Trade Practices', available at: https://cak.go.ke/arch/sites/default/files/Consolidated%20Guidelines%20on%20 Restrictive%20Trade%20Practices%20.pdf.

Center for Governance and Development, 2005, 'A Decade of Parastatal Waste–A Study of the Audited Accounts of State Corporations Over the Period from 1993–2002', available at: https://books.google.de/books/about/A_Decade_of_ Parastatal_Waste.html?id=3_y7AAAAIAAJ&redir_esc=yf.

Colonial Reports Annual, 1929, 'Colony and Protectorate of Kenya: Report for 1929', No. 1510, available at: http://libsysdigi.library.illinois.edu/.

COMESA, 2013, 'Draft Merger Assessment Guideline under the COMESA Competition Regulations (2004)', 'Draft Market Definition Guidelines', 'Guidelines on the Application of Public Interest Criteria', 'Draft Guidelines on the Application of Articles 16 and 19 of the COMESA Competition Regulations (2004) to Horizontal and Vertical Business Practices', and 'Draft Guidelines on the Application of Article 18 of the COMESA Competition Regulations (2004) Prohibiting Abuses of a Dominant Position', available at: http://www.comesacompetiti on.org.

Communications Commission of Kenya, 2012–2013, ' Annual Report 2012 – 2013', available at: https://www.cak.go.ke/arch/sites/default/files/annual-reports/ FY%202012-2013%20CAK%20Annual%20Report.pdfCuts CCIER, 2015 'Vertical Restraints', available at: https://www.yumpu.com/en/document/read/393559 22/types-of-vertical-restraints-cuts-ccierCuts International, 2008, 'Services Trade and Domestic Regulation in Kenya', Briefing Paper No. 5, available at: http:// www.cuts-citee.org/pdf/Briefing_Paper08-Services_Trade_and_Domestic_Regul ation_in_Kenya.pdf.

du Plessis, L. and Blignaut, L., 2009, 'Staying Safe: Dominant Firms' Pricing Decisions in Industries Where High Prices do not Attract Entry', Third Annual Competition Commission, Competition Tribunal and Mandela Institute Conference on Competition Law, Economics and Policy in South Africa.

EAC, 2001–2005, 'The Second EAC Development Strategy', available at: http:// www.eac.int.

EAC, 2025, 'EAC, COMESA Sign MoU to Strengthen Cooperation in Competition and Consumer Protection'; available at: https://www.eac.int/press-releases/157-trade/3389-eac,-comesa-sign-mou-to-strengthen-cooperation-in-competition-and -consumer-protection.

GATS, 1994, 'KENYA: Schedule of Specific Commitments', GATS/SC/47, 15 April.

Gakunga, M., 'Tripartite Framework Win Accolades at the AU Mid-Year Summit', available at: https://www.comesa.int/tripartite-framework-win-accolades-at-the-au-summit/.European Commision, 2023,'Guidelines on the applicability of Article 101 of the Treaty on the Functioning of the European Union to Horizontal Co-operation Agreements'; available at: https://competition-policy.ec.euro pa.eu/system/files/2023-07/2023_revised_horizontal_guidelines_en.pdf.

Government of Kenya, 1986, 'Sessional Paper no. 1 of 1986 on Economic Management for Renewed Growth', Government Printer, Nairobi, Kenya.

Selected Bibliography

Government of Kenya, 2008, 'Vision 2030: A Globally Compeproptitive and Prosperous Kenya', available at: https://repository.kippra.or.ke/server/api/core/bitstreams/0755280f-2564-4e5a-b457-4a490a4ca520/content.

Hammond, D.S., 2004, 'Cornerstone of an Effective Leniency Program', ICN Workshop on Leniency Programs, Sydney, Australia, 22–23 November.

International Competition Network, 2008, 'Report on Predatory Pricing Prepared by the Unilateral Conduct Working Group', Presented at the 7th Annual Conference of the ICN Kyoto, April.

Karanja, J. and Maina, R., 2014, 'Issues and Challenges in Competition: Kenya Overview', Global Competition Review, World Edition, available at: http://globalcompetitionreview.com.

Kariuki, W.F., 2014, 'Informal Cooperation Among Competition Agencies 14th IGE July 2014', available at: http://unctad.org/meetings/en.

Kenya National Bureau of Stastistics, '2023 Statistical Abstract'- https://www.knbs.or.ke/wp-content/uploads/2024/07/Statistical-Abstract-2023.pdf.

Kenya High Commission UK, 2010, 'Economic Survey 2010', available at: http://www.kenyahighcommission.net/khccontent/economy.html.

Migai-Akech, J.M., 2006, 'Development Partners and Governance of Public Procurement in Kenya: Enhancing Democracy in the Administration of Aid', IILJ Working Paper 2006/3; Global Administrative Law Series, available at: https://iilj.org/wp-content/uploads/2016/08/Akech-Development-Partners-and-Governance-of-Public-Procurement-in-Kenya-2006-2.pdf.

Ministry of Education, 2014, 'Approved List of School Textbooks and Other Instructional Materials for ECDE, Primary Schools and Teachers Training Colleges', Revised 13th Edition Vol. 1, January.

Ministry of Education, 2014b, 'Approved List of School Textbooks and other Instructional Materials for Secondary Schools', Revised 13th Edition Vol. 2, January.

Ministry of Finance Kenya, 1998, 'Policy Paper on Public Enterprise Reform and Privatisation', available at: http://www.pc.go.ke.

Ministry of Finance Kenya, 2012, 'State Corporations Annual Budget for 201/2014 Financial Year', DGIPE/A/1/10.

Ministry of Tourism and Wildlife, 2024, 'Annual Tourism Sector Performance Report 2024' available at https://tri.go.ke/wp-content/uploads/2025/02/TRI-Tourism-Sector-Performance-Report-2024.pdf [accessed May 2025].

Moshi, L., 2006, 'The Globalized World Languages: The Case of Kiswahili', Selected Proceedings of the 36th Annual Conference on African Linguistics: Shifting the Center of Africanism in Language Politics and Economic Globalization, Cascadilla Proceedings Project, Somerville, MA.

Nairobi Securities Exchange, 'NSE', available at: https://www.nse.co.ke/about-nse/ [accessed November 2024].

National Council of Population Development, 'The State of Kenya Population-2020', p. 3,available at: https://kenya.unfpa.org/sites/default/files/pub-pdf/state_of_kenya_population_report_2020.pdf.

Ndimi, F., 2014, 'Regional Cooperation: Current and Anticipated', the Sixth Annual African Dialogue Consumer Protection Conference, Lilongwe Malawi, September.

Njiru, E., 2008, 'The Role of State Corporations in a Developmental State: The Kenyan Experience', 30th AAPAM Annual Roundtable Conference, Accra Ghana, 6th –10th October 2008.

Odongo, M., 2011, 'Towards an East African Community Common Market: Challenges and Opportunities', The Institute of Economic Affairs, Kenya, Trade Notes, Issue 33, January.

OECD, 1993, 'Recommendation of the Council Concerning Effective Action Against Hard Core Cartels', C(98)35/FINAL.

OECD, 2008, 'Resale Price Maintenance: Series Roundtables on Competition Policy, available at: https://www.oecd.org/content/dam/oecd/en/publications/reports/2009/09/resale-price-maintenance_bd8c934a/126ecbc8-en.pdf.

OECD, 2001, 'Global Forum on Competition: Contributions from Kenya', CCNM/GF/COMP/WD (2001)2.

OECD Global Forum on Competition, 2004, 'Challenges/Obstacles Faced by Competition Authorities in Achieving Greater Economic Development Through the Promotion of Competition'; Contribution from Kenya – Session II –; CCNM/GF/COMP/WD(2004)8.

OECD, 2010, 'Collusion and Corruption in Public Procurement', Policy Roundtables, DAF/COMP/GF(2010)6.

OECD, 2010, 'Information Exchanges Between Competitors under Competition Law', DAF/COMP(2010)37.

OECD, 2010, 'Roundtable on Failing Firm Defence', DAF/COMP(2009) 38, 10 August.

OECD, 2012, 'Recommendation of the Council on Fighting Bid Rigging in Public Procurement', available at: http://www.oecd.org.

OECD, 2013, 'Competition and Poverty Reduction: Contribution from Kenya', Session I, DAF/COMP/GF/WD(2013)36.

Office of the President, 2013, 'Report of the Presidential Taskforce on Parastatal Reforms', available at: http://www.cofek.co.ke.

Office of Fair Trading UK, 2004, 'Assessment of Market Power', available at: https://www.gov.uk.

Office of Fair Trading UK, 2004, 'Trade Associations, Professions and Self-Regulating Bodies: Understanding Competition Law', available at: https://www.gov.uk.

Official Journal of the European Union, 2024, Communication from the Commission, 'Commission Notice on the Definition of the Relevant Market for the Purposes of Union Competition Law' (C/2024/1645), avaiable at: https://eur-lex.europa.eu/legal-content/EN/TXT/PDF/?uri=OJ:C_202401645.

Oloo, A., 2010, 'Elections, Representations and the New Constitution', Constitution Working Paper No. 7, Society for International Development (SID).

Sihanya, B., 2010, 'The Presidency and Public Authority in Kenya's New Constitutional Order', Constitution Working Paper No. 2, Society for International Development (SID).

Stein, P., 2010, 'The Economics of Burundi, Kenya, Rwanda, Tanzania and Uganda', A Report prepared for Swedfund International AB.

The EAC Secretariat, 2006, 'The East African Community Trade Report 2006', available at: http://www.eac.int.

Selected Bibliography

The World Bank, 2010, 'Kenya's Tourism: Polishing the Jewel', Finance and Private Sector Development, African Region, World Bank, Washington DC.

The World Bank, 2012, 'Kenya Economic Update', Edition 7, December.

The World Bank, 2012, 'Kenya Economic Update: Walking on a Tightrope. Rebalancing Kenya's Economy with a Special Focus on Regional Integration', Edition No. 6, June.

The World Bank, 2013, 'Kenya Overview', available at: http://www.worldbank.org/en/country/kenya/overview.

The World Bank Group, 'Desk Review on Livelihoods and Self-Reliance for Refugees and Host Communities in Kenya', March 2019, available at: https://documents1.worldbank.org/curated/en/685581553241680189/pdf/135485-WP-P169281-PUBLIC-Livelihoods.pdf.

United Nations, 2004, 'Model Law on Competition, UNCTAD Series on Issues in Competition Law and Policy'.

UNCTAD, 1999, 'Competition Cases Involving more than One County', TD/B/COM.2/CLP/9, 7 June.

UNCTAD,2005, 'Voluntary Peer Review Report on Competition Policy: Kenya', UNCTAD/DITC/CLP/2005/.

UNCTAD, 2008, 'Services and Development: Implications for the Telecommunications, Banking and Tourism Services Sectors in Kenya', UNCTAD/DITC/TNCD/2007/2.

UNCTAD, 2013, 'The Impact of Cartels on the Poor', TD/B/C.I/CLP/24/Rev.1.

United Nations, 2005, 'Review of Recent Experiences in the Formulation and Implementation of Competition Law and Policy in Selected Developing Countries: Thailand, Lao, Kenya, Zambia, Zimbabwe', available at: http://archive.unctad.org/Templates/Page.asp?intItemID=4150&lang=1.

United Nations Economic Commission for Africa, 2012, 'Progress Towards Sustainable Development in Africa: Summary Report'.

USAID 'Economic Growth and Trade-Kenya', 2019 available at: https://de.scribd.com/document/744418970/Kenya-Economic-Growth-February-2020 accessed January 2026].

Visram, A., 2010, 'Review of Administrative Decisions of Government by Administrative Courts and Tribunals', 10th Congress of the International Association of Supreme Administrative Jurisdictions (Sydney – March 2010), available at: https://www.aihja.org/wp-content/uploads/2022/12/IASAJ_General-report-2010.pdf.

Wanyama, L., 2013, 'The Economic Diplomacy of Kenya's Regional Interests', South African Foreign Policy and African Drivers Programme, Occasional Paper No. 137.

Wambua, J. et al., 2005, 'A Decade of Parastatal Waste: A Study of the Audited Accounts of State Corporations over the Period from 1993 to 2002'. A publication of Centre for Governance and Development/USAID, available at: https://books.google.de/books/about/A_Decade_of_Parastatal_Waste.html?id=3_y7AAAAIAAJ&redir_esc=y.

Watkins, D.C., 1993, 'Kenya: Overseas Business Report', OBR9301, USDOC, International Trade Administration.

WIPO, 2015, 'Linking Universities and R&D Institutions to the Public and Private Sector for Management and Promotion and Commercialization of IP Assets', available at: http://www.wipo.int.

World Population Review, 'Literacy Rate by Country -2024', available at: https://worldpopulationreview.com/country-rankings/literacy-rate-by-country.

Statutory Instruments

EAC, 2010, 'EAC Competition Regulation', 2010, available at: http://www.eac.int.

EAC, 2024, 'EAC Competition (Amendment) Act, 2023', Legal notice no. 33 of 31 December 2024.

COMESA, 1993, 'Treaty Establishing a Common Market for Eastern and Southern Africa (COMESA)-COMESA Treaty', available at: https://www.wipo.int/wipolex/en/treaties/details/218.

COMESA Competition Commission, 2025, 'COMESA Competition and Consumer Protection Regulations 2025, available at: https://comesacompetition.org/resources/regulations/comesa-competition-and-consumer-protection-regulations-2025/.

COMESA Competition Commission, 2025, COMESA Competition and Consumer Protection Rules 2025, available at: https://comesacompetition.org/resources/rules/comesa-competition-and-consumer-protection-rules-2025/.

EAC,1999, 'The Treaty for the Establishment of the East African Community', available at: https://www.eacj.org/?page_id=33.

EAC, 2006, 'EAC Competition Act, 2006', Legal notice no. 2/2007, vol. AT; L-003.

EAC, 2010, 'The Protocol on the Establishment of the East African Community (EAC) Common Market', available at: http://www.eac.int.

Finance Bill, 2014, Kenya Gazette Supplement No. 87 (National Assembly Bills No. 25), 12 June.

GATS, 1995, 'The General Agreement on Trade in Services (GATS)',available at: http://www.wto.org/english/tratop_e/serv_e/serv_e.htm.

KLR, 1924, 'Civil Procedure Act, Chapter 21 of the Laws of Kenya', available at: https://new.kenyalaw.org/legislation/.

KLR, 1930, 'The Penal Code, Chapter 63 of the Laws of Kenya', available at: https://new.kenyalaw.org/akn/ke/act/1930/10/eng@2023-12-11.

KLR, 1931, 'Sale of Goods Act, Chapter 31 of the Laws of Kenya', available at: https://new.kenyalaw.org/akn/ke/act/1930/33/eng@1964-11-03.

KLR, 1934, 'The Partnership Act Chapter 29 of the Laws of Kenya', available at: https://new.kenyalaw.org/legislation/.

KLR, 1934, 'Telegraphic Press Messages Act', Chapter 512, available at: https://new.kenyalaw.org/legislation/.

GATT, 1947/1994, 'General Agreement on Tariffs and Trade', available at: http://www.wto.org/english/docs_e/legal_e/gatt47_e.pdf.

KLR, 1956, 'Interpretation and General Provisions Act', Chapter 2 of the Laws of Kenya, available at: https://new.kenyalaw.org/akn/ke/act/1956/38/eng@2022-12-31.

KLR, 1957, 'Trademarks Act, Chapter 506 of the Laws of Kenya', available at: https://new.kenyalaw.org/akn/ke/act/1955/51/eng@2022-12-31.

KLR, 1960, 'Law Reform Act, Chapter 26 of the Laws of Kenya', available at: https://new.kenyalaw.org/akn/ke/act/1956/48/eng@1966-07-12.

KLR, 1961, 'Law of Contract Act, Chapter 23 of the Laws of Kenya', available at: https://new.kenyalaw.org/akn/ke/act/1960/43/eng@2022-12-31.

KLR, 1962, 'Companies Act, Chapter 486 of the Laws of Kenya', https://new.kenyalaw.org/akn/ke/act/2015/17/eng@2024-12-27.

KLR, 1963, 'Evidence Act Chapter 80 of the laws of Kenya', available at: https://new.kenyalaw.org/legislation/ org.

KLR, 1967, 'Judicature Act, Chapter 8 of the Laws of Kenya', available at: https://kenyalaw.org/kl/fileadmin/pdfdownloads/Acts/JudicatureAct_Cap8.pdf.

KLR, 1967, KLR, 1967, 'Kadhis' Courts Act, Chapter 11 of the Laws of Kenya', available at: https://new.kenyalaw.org/akn/ke/act/1967/14/eng@2022-12-31KLR, 1977, 'Kenya Posts and Telecommunications Act of 1977', repealed.

KLR, 1974, 'Standards Act' Chapter 496 of the Laws of Kenya, available at:https://new.kenyalaw.org/legislation/.

KLR, 1986, 'State Corporations Act, 1986, Chapter 446 of the Laws of Kenya', available at: https://kenyalaw.org/kl/fileadmin/pdfdownloads/Acts/StateCorporationsActCap446.pdf.

KLR, 1985, 'Insurance Act Chapter 487 of the Laws of Kenya', available at: https://new.kenyalaw.org/akn/ke/act/1985/1/eng@2023-12-11.

KLR, 1988, 'Restrictive Trade Practices, Monopolies and Price Control Act' (Repealed).

KLR, 1989, 'Capital Markets Merger Regulations' Chapter 485A of the Laws of Kenya', available at: https://new.kenyalaw.org/legislation/.

KLR, 1989, 'Banking Act Chapter 488 of the Laws of Kenya', available at: https://new.kenyalaw.org/legislation/.

KLR, 1997, 'Electric Power Act, 1997, No. 11 of 1997 of the Laws of Kenya' (Repealed by the Energy Act, 2006, Act No. 12 of 2006).

KLR, 1998, Kenya Information and Communications Act , available at: https://new.kenyalaw.org/akn/ke/act/1998/2/eng@2022-12-31.

KLR, 1999, 'Postal Corporation Act, 1999, Chapter 411', available at: https://new.kenyalaw.org/legislation/.

KLR, 2001, 'Industrial Property Act', No. 3 of 2001, available at: https://new.kenyalaw.org/akn/ke/act/2001/3/eng@2022-12-31 [accessed Janauary 2026].

KLR, 2005, 'The Public Procurement and Disposal Act 2005, Chapter 412A of the Laws of Kenya', available at: https://new.kenyalaw.org/legislation/ KLR, 2009, 'Anti-Counterfeit Act Cap 130A the Laws of Kenya', available at: https://new.kenyalaw.org/legislation/?page=2.

KLR, 2009, 'Kenya Communication (Amendment Act) No. 1 of 2009', available at: https://new.kenyalaw.org/legislation/?page=2.

KLR, 2009, 'Value Added Tax Act, No. 35 of 2013', available at: https://new.kenyalaw.org/legislation/.

KLR, 2010, 'Competition Act, 2010, No. 12 of 2010', available at: https://new.kenyalaw.org/akn/ke/act/2010/12/eng@2022-12-31. KLR, 2010, 'Constitution of Kenya', 2010, available at: https://new.kenyalaw.org/legislation/.

KLR, 2010, 'Privatisation Act, Chapter 485 of the Laws of Kenya', available at: https://new.kenyalaw.org/legislation/.

KLR, 2010, 'Public Audit Act, Chapter 412b, Act No. 12 of 2003, Act No. 7 of 2007', available at: https://new.kenyalaw.org/akn/ke/act/2015/34/eng@2022-12-31.

KLR, 2010, 'The Kenya Broadcasting Corporation Act, Chapter 221 of the Laws of Kenya', available at: https://new.kenyalaw.org/legislation/.

KLR, 2010, 'The Kenya Tourist Development Corporation Act, 2010, Chapter 382 of the Laws of Kenya', available at: https://new.kenyalaw.org/legislation/.

KLR, 2011, 'Price Control (Essential Goods Act), No. 26 of 2011', available at: https://new.kenyalaw.org/legislation/.

KLR, 2013, 'Consumer Protection Act, No. 46 of 2013', available at: https://new.kenyalaw.org/akn/ke/act/2012/46/eng@2022-12-31KLR, 2013, 'National Social Security Fund Act, Chapter 258 of the Laws Kenya', available at: https://new.kenyalaw.org/legislation/.

KLR, 2013, 'The Wildlife Conservation and Management Act, No. 47 of 2013', available at: https://www.kenyalaw.org/kl/fileadmin/pdfdownloads/Acts/WildlifeConservationandManagementActCap376_2_.pdf.

KLR, 2015, 'Fair Administrative Act, No. 4 of 2015', available at: http://www.kenyalaw.org.

KLR, 2015, 'Science Technology and Innovation Act', available at: https://new.kenyalaw.org/akn/ke/act/2013/28/eng@2022-12-31.

KLR, 2019, 'Energy Act, 2019, Act No. 1 of 2019', available at: http://www.kenyalaw.org.

Paris Convention, 1883, 'Paris Convention for the Protection of Industrial Property', available at: https://www.wipo.int/wipolex/en/text/288514.

TRIPS, 1994, 'The Trade Related Aspects of Intellectual Property Rights', available at: https://www.wipo.int/wipolex/en/treaties/details/231.

Selected Bibliography

Table of Cases

Airtel Kenya Limited v. Safaricom Limited CAK/EC/05/34/A, 18 July 2014, Competition and Consumer Protection Law Digets, 1st,Edition August 2011-June 2022, available at: https://cak.go.ke/sites/default/files/2024-02/CAK_COMPETITION_AND_CONSUMER_PROTECTION_LAW_DIGEST.pdf., 152

Acquisition of CFAO by Toyota Tshusho, In CAK of Kenya, 2012/2013, 'Annual Report', p. 20, available at: https://www.cak.go.ke/arch/sites/default/files/annual-reports/FY%202012-2013%20CAK%20Annual%20Report.pdf., 462

CAK v. Crown Beverages Ltd, 2014/20, In CAK of Kenya, 2014/2015, 'Annual Report', p. 104, available at: https://www.cak.go.ke/arch/sites/default/files/annual-reports/FY%202013-2014%20CAK%20Annual%20Report.pdf., 288

CAK v. Kenya Private Health Care Providers (PHP) Consortium, In CAK of Kenya, 2012/2013, 'Annual Report', pp. 23 and 50, available at: https://www.cak.go.ke/arch/sites/default/files/annual-reports/FY%202012-2013%20CAK%20Annual%20Report.pdf., 335

Center for Rights Education and Awareness and 8 Others v. Attorney General, eKLR 2013, 488

Commissioner of Lands v. Kunste Hotel Ltd, Civil Appeal No. 234 of 1995, [1997] eKLR, 487

Competition Authority of Kenya v. Crown Paints, PLC and 3 others', CAK/EC/05/166/A 17 June 2019, pp. 6–8, available at: https://cak.go.ke/sites/default/files/2024-02/CAK_COMPETITION_AND_CONSUMER_PROTECTION_LAW_DIGEST.pdf., 244

Consumer Federation of Kenya (COFEK) v. Nakumatt Holdings Ltd, Atul Shah, Kenya Bureau of Standards, Competition Authority of Kenya & Attorney General, Constitutional Petition Number 239/2015, 216

Directline Assurance Company v. Attorney General of the Republic of Kenya and the Ministry for Transport, HCCC, Petition No. 103 of 2010, 238

Dodhia v. National Grindlays Bank, Journal of African Law, 14(1), 34, 79

East African Tea Trade Association v. Competition Authority of Kenya, CT/001 of 2017, *available at:* https://cak.go.ke/sites/default/files/2024-02/CAK_COMPETITION_AND_CONSUMER_PROTECTION_LAW_DIGEST.pdf., 233

Ex-Chef Peter Odoyo Ogada & Others v. Independent Electoral and Boundaries Commission & 14 Others, Court of Appeal at Nairobi, Civil Appeal No. 307 of 2012 [2013]eKLR, 489

Table of Cases

Fly 540 Aviation Ltd v. Kenya Airways and Jambo Jet, Case No. 11, 2014, CAK, 2014/2015, p. 105, 'The Annual Report 2014/2015', available at: https://www.cak.go.ke/arch/sites/default/files/annual-reports/FY%202014-2015%20CAK%20Annual%20Report.pdf [accessed January 2026] *Inter Tropical Timber Trading Ltd v. Top Range Ventures and 5 Others'*, CAK/EC/05/188/A, available at: https://cak.go.ke/sites/default/files/2024-02/CAK_COMPETITION_AND_CONSUMER_PROTECTION_LAW_DIGEST.pdf [accessed June 2025], 352

In the matter of Cooper K- Brands Limited CAK/EC/05/136/A, available at: https://cak.go.ke/sites/default/files/2024-02/CAK_COMPETITION_AND_CONSUMER_PROTECTION_LAW_DIGEST.pdf., 282

Jamii Telkom v. Runda Association, In CAK of Kenya, 2012/2013, 'Annual Report', p. 49, available at: https://www.cak.go.ke/arch/sites/default/files/annual-reports/FY%202012-2013%20CAK%20Annual%20Report.pdf., 248

Judicial Service Commission v. Speaker of the National Assembly and the Attorney General, HCCC 518 of 2013, 227

KTDA Management Services v. Competition Authority of Kenya & the Attorney General, Kericho High Court Miscellaneous Application No. 3/2015, 215

Lafarge and East African Portland Cement Company, In CAK of Kenya, 2012/2013, 'Annual Report', p. 21, available at: https://www.cak.go.ke/arch/sites/default/files/annual-reports/FY%202012-2013%20CAK%20Annual%20Report.pdf., 425

Marbury v. Madison, 5 U.S., 1 Cranch, 137, 2L. Ed. 60, 491

MEA v. CAK and Another, Mea Limited v. Competition Authority of Kenya & another [2016] eKLR, 181

Mike J C Mills and another v. the Post and Telecommunications, Nairobi HCMA No. 1013 of 1996, 494

Mureithi and Two Others v. Attorney General and Four Others, Misc. Civil App. No 158 of 2005, 487

Nancy Makokha Baraza v. The Judicial Service Commission and Nine Others, Constitution and Human Rights Division Petition No. 23 of 2012, 492

National Intelligence Service (NIS) against the Association v. of Kenya Reinsurers (AKR), In CAK of Kenya, 2014/2015, available at: https://www.cak.go.ke/arch/sites/default/files/annual-reports/FY%202014-2015%20CAK%20Annual%20Report.pdf., 244

NSSF shares in East African Portland Cement Company Ltd (EAPCC), In CAK of Kenya, 2012/2013, 'Annual Report', p. 21, available at: https://www.cak.go.ke/arch/sites/default/files/annual-reports/FY%202012-2013%20CAK%20Annual%20Report.pdf., 330

Nyali v. Attorney General [1956] 1 QB 7, 18, 74

Oscar Bronner GmbH & Co. v. Mediaprint Zeitungs-und Zeitschriftenverlag GmbH & Co KG, (1999)4 CMLR112, 360

Pastoli v. KabaleDistrict Local Government Council and Others [2008] 2 EA 300, 503

Republic. v. Kenya Association of Music Producers (KAMP) and 3 Others, Judicial Review Case No. 335 of 2013, 486

Republic v. Attorney General and Registrar of Societies, Miscellaneous Application 769 of 2004, 507

Index

The numbers here refer to paragraph numbers.

Index

www.ingramcontent.com/pod-product-compliance
Lightning Source LLC
Chambersburg PA
CBHW071444230926
51846CB00001B/331
9789403562100